D0776841

THINK
FOR
YOURSELF

THINK
FOR
YOURSELF

Restoring
Common Sense *in*
an Age *of* Experts
and
Artificial Intelligence

VIKRAM MANSHARAMANI

Harvard Business Review Press
Boston, MA

The web addresses referenced in this book were live and correct at the time of the book's publication but may be subject to change.

Library of Congress Cataloging-in-Publication Data

Names: Mansharamani, Vikram, author.
Title: Think for yourself : restoring common sense in an age of experts & artificial intelligence / Vikram Mansharamani.
Description: Boston, MA : Harvard Business Review Press, [2020] | Includes index. |
Identifiers: LCCN 2019057414 (print) | LCCN 2019057415 (ebook) | ISBN 9781633699212 (hardcover) | ISBN 9781633699229 (ebook)
Subjects: LCSH: Common sense. | Critical thinking. | Self-reliance. | Computers and civilization. | Artificial intelligence.
Classification: LCC B105.C457 M367 2020 (print) | LCC B105.C457 (ebook) | DDC 153.4—dc23
LC record available at https://lccn.loc.gov/2019057414
LC ebook record available at https://lccn.loc.gov/2019057415

The paper used in this publication meets the requirements of the American National Standard for Permanence of Paper for Publications and Documents in Libraries and Archives Z39.48-1992.

ISBN: 978-1-63369-921-2
eISBN: 978-1-63369-922-9

To Kai and Tori,
May you always think for yourselves.

CONTENTS

PART FOUR
A Path Forward

Finding My Mind

The origin of this book is a piece I wrote for *Harvard Business Review* called "All Hail the Generalist."[1] The short article struck a nerve and spurred thousands of readers to post comments. Some were angry, some grateful; all, however, were engaged.

The essence of my message was that our love affair with deep expertise has gone too far. Specialization and the siloization of society has produced acute tunnel vision in almost all walks of life. The future, I suggested in the article, might belong to those who are skilled not only at generating the proverbial dots of specialized information but also at connecting them. Those who see the big picture and tap into appropriate expertise when needed, I noted, would likely rule the future.

In an age when expert knowledge seems to be the source of higher income, greater prestige, and a fast track to an all-around better life, what I said was provocative. But as Walter Gretzky, father and early coach to hockey great Wayne Gretzky, said: the key to success is to "skate to where the puck is going, not to where it has been."[2] My main point, one that I've expanded in numerous other pieces, is that the source of competitive advantage in the past may not prove to be as effective in the future.

Or perhaps I am, as a tried-and-true generalist, merely hoping for this to be the case?

After all, my whole life has been a resistance to those who nudged me to specialize. As an undergraduate, I pursued two multidisciplinary degrees—one in East Asian studies and another in ethics, politics, and economics. In the early 1990s, most of those interested in East Asian studies were focused on Japan, the rising economic superpower. I chose to study China. And when I arrived in graduate school after six years of working in business and finance, I ended up earning a master's degree in international security studies before going on to get a PhD, studying technological innovation and entrepreneurship in the gaming industry. Armed with a PhD and the possibility of tenure at a prestigious business school, I opted to return to the world of investing, becoming a global equity analyst and spending enough time on planes that a major airline awarded me elite status for life.

My years of combatting professional pressures to specialize has also bled into my teaching career, leading to a nomadic wandering among departments and schools. I've taught in business administration, political science, engineering, and social science groups as well as in multidisciplinary and nondisciplinary programs. I've taught classes on financial bubbles, business ethics, economic inequality, and systems thinking applied to social problems. My faculty peers have been political scientists, business academics, journalists, scientists, and engineers. Throughout, I've only taught classes that I've designed.

So you might say I have a vested interest in the rise of generalists. That's a valid point.

But my argument about the siloization of knowledge and the rising power of generalists incorporates a related and more practical subject in which I have been increasingly interested—the management of experts. Friends, family, and colleagues have often poked fun at me for asking so many questions before taking advice, and while observers may have found it annoying, I take pride in thinking for myself. I refuse to let others control my fate. And as a generalist, I am comfortable asking what may appear to be naïve questions.

Over several years, I have learned to retake control from experts through a process that begins with awareness of the problem. And in almost every instance, once I've realized the problem, I've adopted a three-step process to reclaim my autonomy. First, I part ways with the expert. Second, I think about what (if anything) I really need from an advisor. Finally, I mindfully and proactively rehire expert help, free and clear of the baggage that accompanies historical relationships, and with an explicitly generalist perspective. In some cases, I've found it useful to return to my prior advisor, and when I've done so, I found the relationship improved. In others, I realized I didn't need help and so went forward on my own. My approach has worked for me, but as you'll read later in the book, the key is for you to have a process that works for you. Context matters, and cookie-cutter recommendations will probably fail.

I've used my approach of fire, aim, and (maybe) rehire in various walks of life. I've done it with my accountant, my financial advisor, my lawyer, my doctor, my mechanic, and many others. In fact, this book you're holding is the result of me taking my own medicine. In the years since I first began working on this project, I've parted ways with various publishing experts as I repeatedly stepped back and clarified my own priorities. (In one humorous incident, an editor suggested to me that he was "an expert," and so I needed to leave behind my own ideas and just follow his advice. I chuckled, asked him if he had read my proposal, and shortly thereafter was working with someone else.)

I hope this book helps you understand and avoid many of the troubles I've encountered when experts and technologies hijacked my thinking. It is filled with strategies and guidance to help you reclaim control. One prescription is to question the advice you are being offered, and (ironically) that's equally true for this book. Whether you agree with my thinking or not, I hope this book helps you think for yourself.

Autonomy Lost

You may not realize it, but you've lost your mind. We all have. In fact, we lose our minds all the time, often several times a day. We do this when we blindly outsource our thinking to technologies, experts, and rules.

The domains in which this occurs vary from everyday decisions such as what we buy (recommendations related to our prior purchases) to the life-or-death choices we make about our health (advice given by medical professionals). Stop and think about the last few decisions you made: Why did you make them? Is it possible that you were influenced by technologies, experts, or rules?

Perhaps your doctor notes your high cholesterol levels suggest you should begin taking a statin. She highlights almost every cardiologist she knows is taking a statin, as its effectiveness has been repeatedly demonstrated in lots of research. She's younger than you are and shares that she herself recently started taking a statin. Do you begin taking the medication?

What about when you're driving to a new destination? Your navigation app suggests you take a route that, on first glance, seems counterintuitive. Even though schools were closed due to an overnight snowstorm, the electronic map shows lots of traffic near the elementary school and your app suggests a longer, more circuitous course which it claims will be faster. Do you follow its recommended path?

Or what about when you log in to your retirement savings account and it asks you a handful of questions before recommending you update your asset allocation? It notes that your risk profile (as determined by your answers to a few questions) indicates you should have a higher allocation to equities. But the markets have recently run up a fair amount, and financial market commentators have been highlighting the risk of a correction. Do you change your investment strategy?

In each of these situations, you're being asked to defer to the advice of an expert or a technology. In some cases it's overt. In others, it's less obvious and subtle. To a certain extent in all of these cases, however, you're outsourcing your thinking. You're letting someone or something else guide you.

This is understandable. The uncertainty and complexity of life in the twenty-first century can be overwhelming. The explosion of data and choices has left many of us with a constant sense of anxiety. For almost every situation, we expect there to be an optimal decision, a best choice, a correct answer. Our engrained desire for optimization—a belief akin to fear of missing out (FOMO), that the optimal decision is out there but might be missed—sends us headlong into the arms of experts and technologies. And while this is, by itself, not a problem, our thinking abilities, as a result of automatically and frequently outsourcing decisions, have atrophied.

As I plan to show throughout this book, managing the influence of experts and technologies on our thinking is one of the most important and vexing challenges of our time. Navigating the complexity of modern life is daunting. But we have been increasingly conditioned to defer our decision making to experts, technology, and rules.

Again, this is understandable. After all, the costs of understanding everything ourselves is high, and why shouldn't we trust those who know more about a specific domain than we do? Deference to expertise—embodied in people, systems, and protocols—is logical and generally makes sense from a cost-benefit perspective.

Experts and technologies are useful—indeed essential—but it is the *mindless and blind* outsourcing to them that must be guarded against, that generates unnecessary risks to our well-being, and that limits opportunities to realize our true potential. This happens, in part, because of the narrow specialization that often accompanies expertise. A tight focus and siloed thinking are increasingly problematic (for both us and the experts we rely upon) as we face complex problems.

Think about the familiar parable of six blind men encountering an elephant. Each of them has a unique focus, yet no one is able to understand the whole. Each observer is focused on what they feel, be it the leg, trunk, tail, or torso: it feels like a tree trunk, must be a tree; it is long, slender and curvy, must be a snake; it is hard, smooth, and pointy, obviously a spear. Not one of the six blind men suspects they have encountered an elephant.

As complexity has increased, and we have increasingly relied on specialization in our response to it, this parable has only become more relevant. Time and time again, experts and specialists have failed to understand complex, interconnected phenomena. History is littered with reputation-destroying predictions of misapplied expertise. Recall Irving Fisher's 1929 statement that the stock market had achieved a "permanently high plateau,"[1] a level that for subsequent decades looked more like a summit. Or what about Stanford biologist Paul Ehrlich, who noted in *The Population Bomb* that "the battle to feed all of humanity is over. In the 1970s and 1980s, hundreds of millions of people will starve to death."[2] Lastly, consider Gordon Chang's *The Coming Collapse of China*, a book that persuasively argued that the Middle Kingdom was destined to fall apart. The book was published in 2001; in the decade that followed, China boomed. There are many more such examples.

Just as overly focused thinking misled the blind men studying the elephant, so too did a narrow focus lead these experts to miss developments taking place outside of their domain. Professor Fisher's economic logic failed to fully grasp how policy might exacerbate market conditions. Professor Ehrlich underappreciated the impact of the green revolution that dramatically increased agricultural productivity. And Chang didn't fully incorporate the impact of China's urbanization, modernization, and globalization efforts that helped the country lift millions from poverty.

None of this is intended to suggest that experts are not valuable. They are. Nor is it meant to suggest that these predictions weren't useful. In provoking thought, they played a valuable role. In certain scientific domains, there are enormous returns to specialization and focus. For anyone needing brain surgery, seeking an experienced expert is preferable to a general surgeon. Likewise, when considering a covert military operation involving Special Forces in treacherous terrain, it's best to seek the input of experienced military specialists and commanders who deeply understand how things can and do go wrong.

I am not arguing that we should be suspicious or cynical about expertise or technology or preset rules in and of themselves. But today's interconnected problems demand *integrated* thinking. And context matters, something that is structurally outside of the focus of those with deep expertise. *What we need is contextualized expertise that complements depth with breadth.*

Yet the primary institution for generating the cultural fabric upon which these norms lie—the higher education system—remains focused on developing specialized experts. Siloed department structures are perpetuating a culture that promotes narrowly focused specialists. As admissions officers at elite colleges remain smitten with "spikey" applicants, yesterday's class of well-rounded individuals has given way to a well-rounded class made up of superstars. The result: tiger moms relentlessly push their children to be amazing at something. Those seeking an elite education today must be first chair in their city's youth symphony orchestra or the state champion in the one hundred-meter hurdles *and* the shot put.

It has created a dynamic where some young people today volunteer not to help victims or society but to impress admissions officers. Yesterday's renaissance women have been transformed into William Deresiewicz's "excellent sheep," methodically collecting accomplishments but not understanding why.[3] Meaning and purpose have been sidelined by focus and accolades. Entire cohorts of our most likely future leaders have not only been overdirected, they've been misdirected.

To employ an appropriate metaphor, we have created generations of individuals studying bark. There are many who have deeply studied its nooks, grooves, coloration, and texture. Few have developed the understanding that the bark is merely the outermost layer of a tree. Fewer still understand the tree is in a forest.

Approximately 2,700 years ago, the Greek poet Archilochus introduced another apt metaphor. He wrote that "The fox knows many things, but the hedgehog knows one big thing."[4] Isaiah Berlin's 1953 essay "The Hedgehog and the Fox" contrasts hedgehogs that "relate everything to a single central vision" with foxes who "pursue many ends connected . . . if at all, only in some *de facto* way."[5] It's really a story of specialists with a single focus versus generalists who pursue many ends.

In the decades since Berlin's essay was published, hedgehogs have come to dominate academia, medicine, finance, law, and many other professional domains. Specialists with deep expertise have ruled the roost, climbing to ever higher positions. To advance in one's career, it has been efficient to specialize. And all of us have come to respect the highly paid expert specialist.

But as said by baseball philosopher Yogi Berra, "the future ain't what it used to be."[6] Our world is increasingly interconnected; seemingly unrelated developments now rapidly and profoundly affect each other. Meddling with interest rates can rapidly affect house prices that drive local school funding, which in turn can impact inequality not only of income and wealth but also of opportunity. Or perhaps a local renewable fuel standard impacts global agricultural prices, generating social unrest in food-vulnerable Africa. Uncertainty and fuzziness plague our existence, which demands daily decisions on everything from the painfully simple to the grossly complex. And in a world in which technology is progressing at breakneck speed, the advantages of a narrow focus and formulaic solutions are rapidly waning.

Deep expertise must be complemented with broad perspective. Not doing so often results in intellectual acrobatics to justify one's perspective in the face of conflicting data. Think about Alan Greenspan's public admission

of finding "a flaw" in his worldview.[7] Academics and serious economists were dogmatically dedicated to the efficient market hypothesis—
contributing to the inflation of an unprecedented credit bubble between
2001 and 2007. Yet the global financial crisis demonstrated that while
markets may be efficient most of the time, they can and do become mas-
sively inefficient as well.

There is also robust research suggesting that generalists are better at
navigating uncertainty. Philip Tetlock, a professor at the University of
Pennsylvania, has found experts are less accurate predictors than nonexperts in their areas of expertise. His conclusion: when seeking accuracy
of predictions, it is better to turn to those like "Berlin's prototypical fox,
those who know many little things, draw from an eclectic array of tradi-
tions, and accept ambiguity and contradictions."[8] Ideological reliance on
a single perspective appears detrimental to one's ability to successfully
navigate the vague situations that are more prevalent today than ever
before.

The future has always been uncertain, but our ability to navigate it
has been impaired by an increasingly narrow focus. The closer you are to
the material, the more likely you are to believe it. In psychology jargon,
you anchor on your own beliefs and insufficiently adjust from them. In
more straightforward language, a man with a hammer is more likely to
see nails. Expertise means being closer to the bark and being less likely
to see ways in which your perspective may warrant adjustment. In uncertain domains, I believe breadth of perspective may trump depth of
knowledge.

The declining returns to expertise have implications at the individual, company, and even national level. A collection of specialists creates
a less flexible labor force, one that requires constant retraining as technological developments race forward. In this regard, the recent emphasis
in American education on job-specific skills is disturbing. Within a company, employees skilled in numerous functions are more valuable as
business needs change. Many forward-looking companies are specifically
mandating multifunctional experience as a requirement for career progress. Professionals armed with analytical capabilities (e.g., basic statistical

skills, critical reasoning, etc.) developed via a broad diversity of geographic and functional experiences will fare particularly well when competing against those with narrow skills.

Life in the twenty-first century is not about eliminating our dependence on those with deep and narrow expertise. That's simply unrealistic. But we can balance that depth with breadth of perspective that understands the limitations of expert guidance. That means using experts and technologies strategically. They may have a narrow focus, but we can combine their guidance with our broad perspective. What may make sense from their perspective may not be best for our ultimate objectives.

We must also remain in constant and conscious charge of integrating the views of experts and technologies. Each view is by nature incomplete. Only we can see the complete picture. The task of integration is ours alone. As you form your own mosaic, using tiles from experts, always remember that each piece is merely part of the whole story. We must learn to keep experts on tap and not on top.

There are times when it makes sense to outsource our thinking, but this must be a conscious choice, one proactively and mindfully selected. If you haven't seen the TED Talk by Baba Shiv titled "Sometimes It's Good to Give up the Driver's Seat," I encourage you to do so.[9] It's a short talk in which the Stanford professor describes how he and his wife handled a cancer diagnosis—by consciously giving up control of their decisions to a doctor. If you choose to watch it, note the deliberate intentionality of their thinking process. *Outsourcing decisions is not itself a problem, it's the automatic, unconscious default of doing so without thought that concerns me.*

One reason we have stopped thinking for ourselves is that we've become accustomed to doing so. We've had a long habit of relying on others to think for us. It appears timely to reconsider these assumptions.

Consider the following quote:

> A long habit of not thinking a thing wrong, gives it a superficial appearance of being right, and raises at first a formidable outcry in defence of custom. But the tumult soon subsides. Time makes more converts than reason.[10]

This is the opening paragraph of *Common Sense*, Thomas Paine's 1776 essay calling for a reevaluation of the British rule of the American colonies. Paine believed rule by a distant monarch was something that should be questioned, not a default condition. Many Americans had never questioned the king's rule because, well, he had always ruled. Paine was asking Americans to reconsider their basic default assumptions about governance. He wanted them to stop and think for themselves, to question why they were willing to defer blindly to a faraway king.

I continue to be struck by how relevant Paine's message is today. Just because mindlessly outsourcing our thinking to expertise has not been thought wrong, many believe it right. It's time to reevaluate this belief and question how things should be rather than adjust from where they are. We need to think for ourselves.

The Book: What You Can Expect

While it would be fabulous to write a book that empowers its readers to improve their health, wealth, and happiness, my purpose in writing this book is more modest. It's to increase our awareness of the thinking we've outsourced to others and to provide a path to reclaim control. The book hopes to not only explain how we got into our current situation of blind obedience and mindless deference but also to empower readers with tools and strategies to escape from it.

Part 1 of the book provides context, explaining how and why we landed in our current predicament. The explosion of knowledge, driven largely by science but also specialization, lays at the foundation. On top of the information flood we face, there has also been an explosion of choice offered—in virtually all walks of life, ranging from the color and fit of the jeans we buy to the genre, length, and style of the movies we watch. The result has been a never-ending and insatiable quest for the absolute best choice, a twenty-first-century ailment popularly known as FOMO, the dreaded fear of missing out. Social media and the artificial intelligence algorithms have the potential to exacerbate this FOMO. And because of ever-increasing expectations and the hope for an ever-distant optimal decision, we run headlong toward experts, technology, and rules to help us achieve this elusive ideal.

Part 2 explores the ramifications of these developments. It begins with the logical specialization that has emerged among the community of advisors that has arisen to help address our decision anxieties. The result is a siloization of virtually all walks of life and the elevation of focus as an absolute and unconditional positive. After discussing the promise and perils of focus, the book considers how some actions can drive the very outcomes we seek to avoid. In the course of our now-habituated blind obedience to the people, technology, and systems, we've developed a learned dependency on them. Our intellectual self-reliance skills have withered.

Part 3 offers a how-to guide to reclaiming our autonomy. Having been made aware of the perils that accompany the outsourcing of thought, this section begins with a call for metafocus, namely a focus on where we focus, before suggesting that the narrow focus of experts often misses our objectives but achieves theirs. The key is to think for ourselves, to not blindly outsource our thinking to others. But to avoid overconfidence in our own thinking, and to calibrate ourselves, we must learn to adopt multiple perspectives, to empathize with the views of others. When we adopt and acknowledge perspectives other than ours, we are more likely to appreciate the limitations inherent in any one view (including our own). The key is to triangulate. We must retain control of our minds, utilizing the insights of experts and technologies but not automatically deferring to them. Answers are rarely black or white; life today demands independent thinking and judgment rather than rigid rules. This book provides a set of principles and practices that can help readers zoom out and reorient toward connecting insights across silos domineered by experts and technologies.

Part 4 paints a path forward. Living off the grid on a pond in Concord, Massachusetts is an antiquated image of self-reliance. We need a modern adaptation for our interconnected, rapidly changing and technologically

advancing world. Embracing ambiguity and learning to navigate ubiquitous uncertainty is essential to modern life. To do so, we must rede-
velop our sense of imagination and begin thinking in scenarios that
bring the probabilistic nature of modern life into full relief. We also
need to be more aware of the default operating assumptions we make
and take a step back, think for ourselves, and balance the benefits of
depth with the underappreciated value of breadth.

PART ONE

LOSING
CONTROL

As scientific progress and technological advancement continue at a breathtaking pace, we often find ourselves overwhelmed with information to process and choices to make. This explosion of data dangles the possibility of an optimal decision, leaving us with constant low-grade regret and a fear of missing out on the best option. In our quest to optimize choices, we run headlong to those who promise to assist us, to those who claim to know more about a domain than we do. But by turning to experts, technologies, and rules, we cede control of our lives, relinquishing autonomy to those with a narrow focus and inability to appreciate the entirety of our decision context.

CHAPTER 1

Data, Choice, and FOMO

As I prepare to begin writing this book, I'm finding it difficult to think for myself. There's just so much information. I'm staring at a few stacks of books, seven piles of printed articles (each between two and three feet in height), three piles of magazines (sorted into business, technology, and general news publications), and two stacks of newspapers that I promise myself almost daily that I'll skim. Every week, the piles seem to grow, despite my best efforts to make them shrink. The reality is that I'm drowning, quite literally, in information.

Who Can Keep Up?

Scientific and technical advances have overwhelmed us with information over the past two centuries—and the pace of data generation has been accelerating. The growing pool of knowledge demands constant diligence and unimaginable regular effort merely to keep up. Stop for a moment and think about the number of books that exist today. The most recent estimates suggest that there are around 135 million books that have been published.[1] And it's not just the number of books that's overwhelming. The number of scholarly articles published since 1665, when the Royal Society first began publishing its *Philosophical Transactions*, now exceeds fifty million and is rising daily.[2] It's ludicrous to think anyone might be able to digest even a large fraction of this knowledge, let alone *all* of it.

There's simply just too much information to process, and this fact is very distressing and depressing. The anxiety generated by this information overload has been called everything from data asphyxiation to cognitive overload to data deluge to information fatigue syndrome. But we don't like turning the hose off, either.

Recent research suggests that some people develop a deep and debilitating anxiety from being *disconnected* from these sources. Forty-five percent of respondents to a recent survey in the United Kingdom noted that they feel "worried or uncomfortable" when they are unable to connect with their email or Facebook.[3] Ever travel to a foreign country where wireless data services are prohibitively expensive? Whenever I do, I notice myself looking for Wi-Fi, simply to reconnect. It's irrational, but the feeling is real. I worry about what I may be missing. Connected or not, you're going to feel overwhelmed. It's impossible not to. It's life in the twenty-first century, a life in which we're all asked to drink from the proverbial fire hose while not allowing a drop to drip. There's simply no way to keep up.

It wasn't always this way. For thousands of years, there have been people believed to know everything. Somewhere in the last few hundred years, as our insights and understanding grew more voluminous, the feat of knowing everything became insurmountable. So, who was the last person to know everything?

Know It All

A strong candidate is Thomas Young. Born in 1773 in Somerset, England, Young read widely from an early age. By the age of twenty-one, he was a fellow of the Royal Society, Britain's preeminent science society with origins dating back to 1660, and had presented a paper that set the foundation of our current understanding of human vision. By his early thirties, as a practicing doctor, he had delivered a series of lectures that his biographer, Andrew Robinson, described as "covering virtually all of known science, which has never been surpassed in scope and boldness of insight."[4] Over the course of his life, Young made important contributions across a wide range of fields, including physics, physiology, engineering, music, and philology (the study of language in written historical sources—I had to look that up, not being someone who knows everything). He studied over four hundred languages, which allowed him to lay the groundwork for deciphering the Rosetta Stone. And oh, before I forget, he also took on Isaac Newton and demonstrated that light was as much a wave as it was a particle.

When not moving human knowledge forward at a breakneck pace, Young advised leaders on matters as diverse as the introduction of gas lighting in London, the proper mathematics necessary to understand risk in life insurance, and the relative effectiveness of various shipbuilding methods.

In Young's story, we see a tension between pursuing breadth and depth. Knowing that all of us have limited time and attention, we tend to be skeptical of those who seem unfocused and contribute in numerous arenas without really committing to any. Recognizing the suspicion held by society toward those with multiple interests, Young made most of his contributions anonymously, trying to minimize the risk of being considered a jack-of-all-trades. He feared that, if his wide-ranging interests were public, they would scare patients away from his medical practice. Even then, depth was valued more than breadth.

In 1973, the London Science Museum designed an exhibit to celebrate Thomas Young's two hundredth birthday. The organizers noted that "Young probably had a wider range of creative learning than any other Englishman in history. He made discoveries in nearly every field he studied."[5] Any wonder why Andrew Robinson titled his biography of Young *The Last Man Who Knew Everything*?

Specialization and Collaboration

The type of information being produced today is increasingly complicated and specialized. It's becoming more important to have some prior understanding in order to digest new information or to make meaningful contributions. The former chairman of British Mensa, a club for those testing well on IQ examinations, notes that the sheer magnitude of knowledge today is so large that if you really want to understand your topic thoroughly, and if you want to speak with authority, then it's important to specialize.[6] A tight focus has become the ruling mantra of the day. And as piles of knowledge have accumulated, it's taking longer for new contributions to be made.

Indeed, scientists and inventors make major contributions at older and older ages. In a paper entitled "Age and Great Invention,"[7] Benjamin Jones of Northwestern University explored the ages at which Nobel laureates conducted the pioneering work that earned them their awards. He found that the mean age of great achievement for both Nobel Prize winners and great inventors rose by about six years over the course of the twentieth century. Jones also measured the time it takes for researchers to begin contributing to their fields. He found that, on average, the great minds were active in research at age twenty-three at the start of the twentieth century, but at the end of the twentieth century, great minds were active in research at age thirty-one.

But does it matter what kinds of thinking these scientists were doing? Jones found a difference between those who were theorists and those who were experimentalists.[8] Conceptual innovators tend to do their best work at earlier ages, while concrete fields favored late-peaking experimental innovators. Jones explains that the most important conceptual work typically involves radical departures from existing paradigms. When an individual is first exposed to a paradigm, before he or she fully embraces it, she is best poised to identify flaws or areas for opportunity. That is, the early-stage conceptual researcher is more likely to look at the big picture, to see links between previously unconnected dots.

In another research project, Jones found that among inventors, the age at first innovation is trending upwards at 0.6 years per decade.[9] Inventors are taking more time to study before producing their first innovations. The number of people listed on each patent is growing 17 percent per decade, and that specialization—measured as the probability of not switching fields between innovations—is increasing at a rate of 6 percent per decade. It takes more people, with more education and focus, to produce a single novel invention.

The trend of increasing team size is present in science as well. According to *Sciencexpress*, between 1955 and 2000, the number of authors listed on articles in the sciences increased from 1.9 to 3.5.[10] The research also found that articles with multiple authors were cited more often at an increasing rate. Another study confirmed the trend of increasing team size in medicine.[11] Across five of the field's most prestigious journals, it found that the mean number of authors per article increased from 4.66 to 5.73 from 1993 to 2005.

At the top of this totem pole is research about large-scale complex science experiments involving multiple nations and billions of dollars in research budgets. How many authors do the research papers emanating from these efforts tend to have? Ready for it? Thousands. That's right, some science experiments have gotten so complicated that their team size is measured in the thousands.

A gigantic international research effort has been underway in Switzerland with the Large Hadron Collider (LHC) at CERN, the European particle physics lab. Costing $10 billion to build, the particle accelerator smashes protons together, generating a billion collisions every second.[12] In May 2015, members of the experiment's two major collaborations published a joint paper in *Physical Review Letters*.[13] Number of authors? Five thousand, one hundred, and fifty-four! That's right. More than five thousand people. At the time, the paper broke a world record for the most contributors to a single research article. The article took twenty-four whole pages to list the contributors—and only nine pages to communicate the research! Imagine how specialized each of the 5,154 contributions must have been.

Using the same logic as above to decompose per-author contribution percentages, we find that authors writing about CERN had an on-average contribution percentage of 0.02 percent. If we believe Jones's finding that research team sizes are growing at 17 percent per decade, it's only a matter of time before we see papers with ten thousand or more authors. The specialization train is barreling forward, showing no signs of slowing anytime soon.

For someone who typifies this modern mantra of specialization, let's turn to an individual who spent an entire fifty-year career focused on one pursuit—understanding why cells of some underwater creatures glow.

Osamu Shimomura, Ultraspecialist

Our flag-bearing monomath is Osamu Shimomura. He was born 155 years after Thomas Young, and six thousand miles from Young's British birthplace—in Japan. He was sixteen when the United States dropped the atomic bomb on Nagasaki. At the time, he was living just fifteen miles from the center of the blast. Although hit with a large amount of radioactivity, he beat the odds and survived, going on to get a degree from what is now the Nagasaki University School of Pharmaceutical Sciences. He received his PhD in organic chemistry in 1960. As a scientist, Shimomura became as specialized as it gets. After receiving his PhD, Shimomura moved to Princeton University where his work focused on a single organism: *Aequorea victoria*, a beautiful, transparent jellyfish that gives off a green glow. Shimomura was fascinated by the jellyfish's bioluminescence and wanted to understand how it worked. Soon, he had isolated the protein, aequorin, that was responsible for the glow, publishing his early finding in a paper titled "Crystalline Cypridina Luciferin."[14] (I don't know about you, but a title like that is unlikely to grab my attention.)

Nevertheless, after identifying the protein, he needed large volumes of the protein to study. So what did he do? Every summer, when academic obligations were lighter, Shimomura would head to Friday Harbor in Washington state, where there were plenty of these jellyfish. "Our schedule was to collect 50,000 per summer, in one or two months," he said. "Nineteen summers, and we collected a total of 850,000."[15]

One puzzle was that the protein Shimomura isolated gave off blue light, but the jellyfish glowed green. Shimomura helped show how this shift happened. He and his colleagues isolated the green fluorescent protein, which absorbed the aequorin's blue light and shifted its color, from the jellyfish.[16] In subsequent years, Shimomura would go on to study the chemical properties of this protein. The application of green fluorescent protein (known among scientists as GFP) in molecular biology would revolutionize the field starting in the 1990s, as researchers started using it as a marker to track what's happening in cells. According to the Royal Swedish Academy of Sciences, the protein has a "miraculous" property that lets it "provide universal genetic tags that can be used to visualize a virtually unlimited number of spatio-temporal processes in virtually all living systems."[17]

To understand the magnitude of GFP revolution, let's think about the tracking of whales. In the world before we had GPS transmitters that we could attach to the whales, we simply didn't know what they were doing. Sure, we saw whales in Alaska in the summer and near Hawaii in the winter, but were they the same whales? Without the ability to track specific whales across time and location, it was simply impossible to know. The GPS trackers on whales are the equivalent of the GFP attached to cells, enabling scientists to track specific cells in living systems.

In 2008, for his work on the green fluorescent protein, Shimomura shared the Nobel Prize in Chemistry. In the words of the Royal Swedish Academy of Sciences, "Without the pioneering research of Shimomura . . . it is likely that the GFP revolution would have been delayed by decades or even remained one of the hidden secrets of the Pacific Ocean."[18] Shimomura never intended to revolutionize biology. He was too specialized for that. As he put it, "I don't do my research for application or any benefit. I just do my research to understand why jellyfish luminesce, and why that protein fluoresce."[19] The GFP revolution was a fringe benefit of Shimomura's narrow focus.

From Data Deluge to Optimization Ordeals

Today, our society has many more Shimomuras than Youngs. Why's that? To begin, it is a direct result of our attempts to cope with a massive stock of knowledge and its increasingly rapid growth. But it's also a result of simple cash—our society tends to pay more for focus than broad perspective, at least in most professions. A specialized lawyer, doctor, or investment banker is usually paid more than a generalist. And part of that comes from the belief that today's data deluge offers great chances for optimization. Let's now turn to the choice conundrums that emerge from this ever-present quest for maximization.

For most of human history, scarcity was the norm. We battled for limited food, sought scarce shelter, and even fought for the most desirable spouse (well, I guess we still do that!). Economics—the study of how to allocate scarce resources—arose to make sense of these dynamics. In the late eighteenth century, the economist Adam Smith suggested that the "invisible hand" of self-interest would guide a diverse set of workers, merchants, and others to produce an optimal outcome for society as a whole.[20] By this, Smith meant that every person would pursue their own goals, maximize his or her own satisfaction, and, in doing so, inadvertently behave in a way that helped achieve an ideal distribution of resources.

Adam Smith's writing embraced the messiness of reality. As the discipline matured, though, economics left behind the complex stew of human interactions in favor of simpler models. For economists, people became hyperrational pleasure-maximizers. And so off we went, with every man "busily arranging his life to maximize the pleasure of his psychic adding machine," as American economist and historian Robert Heilbroner put it.[21]

Our world today is complex. We have many options, and, more importantly, we are aware of just how many options we have. When we choose between options, there is a human instinct—the one that economics as a field relies upon—to try to choose the best one. But attempting to optimize in the face of uncertainty and interconnectedness is challenging and doesn't always happen. Analysis paralysis is more common by the day.

Choice Conundrums

Choice explosion exists in every aspect of our lives, even when we're just selecting a movie to watch—something that should be fun. Home entertainment has had a truly awe-inspiring increase in options. Surely, pleasure-seeking *homo economicus* is excited by these possibilities, right? There was once a time when in-home entertainment was limited to whatever was on TV. Oh, and there were only five channels. But then, as bandwidth to the home increased with cable infrastructure, the number of options for in-home entertainment grew. Weekly periodicals such as *TV Guide* sprung up to help consumers navigate which channels were showing which shows when. And that was when consumers had dozens of channels to choose from.

While channels were increasing, we also got more choice with the invention of recording devices such as the VCR, which allowed us to watch not only live TV but anything that had previously aired. Eventually, the video rental store came along. If you needed a movie for the evening, you were confronted with shelves upon shelves of options—thousands of videos with no differentiating qualities besides their titles. You couldn't even see the covers, since many stores replaced them with their own generic ones. At that time, your only hope was to go to the "staff picks" shelf and defer to the advice of loyal employees. The choices were overwhelming then, but it was all dwarfed by what came next.

Today, cable companies routinely offer hundreds of channels, as well as hundreds of thousands of on-demand movies, shows, and even radio stations. There are channels catering to the unique interests of cooking, sci-fi, nature, business, and sports enthusiasts. You can get standard-definition, high-definition, or even 3-D displays. Add in the explosion of streaming content across numerous platforms (from Netflix to AppleTV to Disney+), and today's consumer has multiple-millions of options to choose from. You could watch pretty much any movie or TV show created in human history—all without leaving the comfort of your couch.

Is all this choice making us happier? Are we really better off?

We tend not to question the value of choice. Everyone's different—so with more options, it's more likely we'll find something perfect for us—right? Standard economic logic suggests that more options are always better. For many, this makes intuitive sense: you can always ignore the extra possibilities if they don't improve your happiness, so new options can only improve satisfaction. But that doesn't seem to be the case in real life.

Movie Melancholy

At least once a month or so, my wife, Kristen, and I decide to watch a movie together after our kids are asleep. Thanks to the selection of movies available at our fingertips, we don't feel like we have to just accept whatever's playing that evening. We feel empowered. We have choice and plenty of it.

Except here's what typically happens. Whoever gets to the couch first will begin scanning new releases, inevitably watching a preview or two. Given the average trailer is around three minutes or so, approximately six minutes was spent searching. But if my wife beat me to the couch and I arrive after she's already seen a preview or two, I insist on watching what she's seen. I don't want to negotiate against a Harvard Law School graduate who practiced as a litigator for the prestigious Boston law firm of Ropes & Gray until I know what she does. I simply need to be on similar informational footing.

The chance of us agreeing on one of the first three options is about as likely as winning Powerball. Nah, that would be optimistic. It's more like the chances of winning Megamillions and Powerball in the same week of a leap year when there was a crescent moon. So the search continues. There's this nagging feeling throughout that the perfect movie exists for our particular mood at this particular time—why wouldn't it? After all, there are an ungodly number of options available, surely one is perfect.

So we search and search and search. Eventually, we settle—probably about forty-five minutes after we began—on a movie that doesn't really excite either of us (how could it, given our expectations of perfection?) but doesn't really bother us either. Because of the time it took to select the movie, though, I'm exhausted and doze off within the first hour. At which point my wife is angry. She feels abandoned.

"I agreed to this movie because you seemed more interested in it than the one I wanted to see," she's likely to argue. Half asleep, I tell her to just stop the movie and start the one she wanted to see.

"Fine."

I've known my wife since the early 1990s when we were both under-graduates at Yale, and the one thing I've learned since then is that "fine" does not mean fine. It means something more akin to "I'm mad at you, but I'm too polite to tell you." So what do I do? I go to sleep, only to learn the next morning that Kristen fell asleep halfway through the movie she did want to watch, having watched half of a movie she didn't want to watch. She went to sleep angry and frustrated by the whole experience and, as most married people will likely understand, assumed I was the cause of this distressing evening . . . rather than the million options offered by Xfinity. (Hmmm, I wonder if there are other couples suffering from Xfinity's choice explosion—perhaps there's a class action possibility here?)

At least in our case, choice wasn't helpful. The research suggests Kristen and I are not alone. A growing body of research has shown that there are significant downsides to choice—which is why filters to narrow our focus have become so important. It turns out that, often, when presented with, say, hundreds of bags of potato chips, we don't always automatically calculate which has the perfect size, flavor, shape, price, and healthiness, and thus pick out the option that generates the most happiness. Instead, we are often paralyzed. We hesitate and decide we didn't want chips in the first place. Or once we choose a bag and have the chips, we can't help but think of how another choice may have been better. Choice, anxiety, and regret are close cousins.

A number of experiments have bolstered this insight. In the most famous one, researchers set up two different displays of jam in a grocery store. One offered six types of jams; the other twenty-four. More shoppers stopped when there were more jams, with 60 percent of passersby sampling one of the twenty-four offered, compared to 40 percent for the six-sample display. But more choice was paralyzing. Thirty percent of those exposed to six options made a purchase, compared to only 3 percent of those who saw twenty-four samples. With too many options, shoppers didn't sort through and find the perfect one. Instead, their eyes glazed over and they moved on. Further, there was likely a nagging suspicion among the 3 percent that they chose poorly.

It's not just shoppers who act this way. In one study, researchers offered students the option of writing an essay for extra credit. They were divided into two groups. One was offered six possible topics to write about; the other was presented thirty ideas. Fourteen percent fewer students in the latter group (presumably overwhelmed by choice) chose to complete the optional assignment.[22]

Analysis paralysis also occurs in domains other than shopping and school. Even when people are managing their money—where you'd think they'd be at their most rational and patient—they fall victim to analysis paralysis. Companies that offer retirement savings plans often provide their employees with a set of mutual funds in which to invest their money. One researcher found that for every ten additional mutual fund options that were offered, participation in the program fell by 1.5 to 2 percent.[23]

A proliferation of options does not equate to freedom or wellbeing, as economists once believed. A horde of choices overloads our focus systems, leading to paralyzing anxiety. It's why the super-supermarket in the *Simpsons* is called Monstromart and has the tagline, "Where Shopping Is a Baffling Ordeal." Or why the movie *Idiocracy* portrays its dumbed-down future as containing a Costco as large as a city, filled with miles of shelves, a law school, and even its own internal mass transit system.

A Tempting Tyrant

Barry Schwartz is a psychologist who writes about the paradox of choice. One day, Schwartz walked into a store to buy new jeans. He was asked if he would like slim fit, easy fit, relaxed, baggy, or extra baggy jeans. He was then asked if he'd like stone-washed, acid-washed, or distressed. Button fly or zipper fly? Faded or regular? And what color?

Schwartz decided to try them all. Soon, he had become so focused on finding the ideal perfect fit that the act of buying a pair of jeans turned into a daylong affair, a complex decision in which he was forced to invest time, energy, and no small amount of self-doubt, anxiety, and dread. Before these jeans options were available, buyers settled for an imperfect fit, but at least they'd buy a pair of jeans within five minutes. Now, without a filter to narrow his focus, Schwartz became overwhelmed in the face of countless options. Schwartz's dilemma sounds identical to how my wife and I feel when picking a movie.

Schwartz suggests the costs of trying to make the best decision often outweigh the possible benefits. He goes further to suggest overwhelming choice probably also affects our mental health: "Clinging tenaciously to all the choices available to us contributes to bad decisions, to anxiety, stress, and dissatisfaction—even to clinical depression."[24]

Anxiety arises when we have an overwhelming set of options. But it also can come from a seemingly opposite situation: when we're confronted with nothing. At these times, we're reminded that there is an almost infinite number of choices lurking; we simply must be missing them. Our awareness of all the possibilities we might never even get a glimpse of—let alone have the privilege of dismissing—summons the omnipresent specter of modern living, the fear of missing out, also known as FOMO.

Having some choice is doubtless better than no choice. Indeed, choice and freedom are related concepts. Free choice is what enables markets to work and has powered human ingenuity for thousands of years. It generates competition and is, in many ways, the bedrock upon which liberal democracy has been built. But have we taken a good thing too far? Schwartz suggests so: "At this point, choice no longer liberates, but debilitates. It might even be said to tyrannize."[25]

Social (Media) Unrest?

During 2019, incidents of social unrest sprung up across the globe. Consider a sampling of the events: Chile experienced mass protests in the streets of Santiago, Bolivia's military deposed its leader, Catalonians took to the streets to seek independence, yellow jacket protesters filled the streets of Paris, anti-Iranian demonstrations took place in both Lebanon and Iraq, Russia endured mass protests, and citizens of Hong Kong pushed back against pro-Chinese policies in the city-state. Other countries rocked by social protests included Algeria, Britain, Guinea, Kazakhstan, and Pakistan.

While most of the attention on the topic of social media and social unrest tends to focus on the mobilizing and coordinating power of the technology, might it be possible that the social media is exacerbating society's FOMO? Yes, economic inequality reached a tipping point, inspiring the poor and disenfranchised to rise against the wealthy and powerful. And of course social media brings like-minded people together: The *Economist* magazine suggests "its use tends to create echo chambers and thus heighten the feeling that the powers-that-be 'never listen.'"[a]

But might social media be having an impact far greater than mere validation of feelings? Could social media actually be intensifying the protesters' feelings of being left behind? Just think about the topics you might share on social media. . . . I'd bet you're very unlikely to post about losing a job, while you'd be very likely to share news of a promotion. If everybody does this, social media presents an image of the world as being far more positive than reality. Anyone living in reality that fails to understand the biased world presented by positive-only posts will then feel like they're uniquely worse off than most. Might that increase anxiety and a feeling of desperation, leading some into the streets to reset the social system?

a. "Economics, Demography, and Social Media Only Partly Explain the Protests Roiling so Many Countries Today," *Economist*, November 14, 2019, http://www.economist.com/international/2019/11/14/economics-demography-and-social-media-only-partly-explain-the-protests-roiling-so-many-countries-today.

FOMO

While information overload may have defined the 2000s and choice overload the 2010s, my bet is that the ever-dreaded FOMO may become the anxiety that characterizes the 2020s. It's a natural consequence of our interconnected lives, social media, and the overwhelming choice that is bluntly and obviously available to us with little to no effort. You see, the more options we have and the more options we are aware of, the more likely we are to regret the choices we make. Just as with my movie melancholy, the allure of nirvana remains ever-present, even if unattainable.

And while more choice inevitably leads to FOMO, our highly interconnected lives (through social media and other communication and sharing platforms) intensify this problem. MIT Professor Sherry Turkle notes that FOMO drives a constant fear that something better exists somewhere else. In her book *Reclaiming Conversation: The Power of Talk in a Digital Age*, Turkle describes the feelings of Kati, a young woman who seems to typify this condition: at almost any party Kati and her friends attend, someone seems to always be texting friends at other parties to figure out whether they're at the absolute best party. As Kati describes it, "Maybe we can find a better party; maybe there are better people at a party just down the block."[26] Recalling the exploding choice problem, Turkle concludes: "Nothing Kati and her friends decide seems to measure up to their fantasy of what they might have done."[27]

The social lives of many today exist on the back of Silicon Valley infrastructure, which structures our motivations. When we act, we are increasingly preoccupied with how it will be reflected in our friends' feeds. Given the heavy dependence on electronic interactions, accruing likes turns into an arms race. A CNN report described adolescents anxious to join the "100 club"—meaning that a post of theirs accrued one hundred likes or more.[28] It is not uncommon to hear of people doing all sorts of atypical, attention-seeking actions for the likes. The street artist Banksy depicted these dynamics with an image of a boy crying with symbols for no comments, no likes, and no follows hovering over his head.[29] At the current pace, note Peter Singer and Emerson Brooking, "the average

American millennial will take around 26,000 selfies in their lifetime"—many to generate likes. They go on, highlighting how "in 2016, one victim of an airplane hijacking scored the ultimate millennial coup: taking a selfie with his hijacker."[30] The zeal for likes is so strong that in most years, more people die from selfie accidents than shark attacks.[31]

If you're like me and don't understand the logic of the previous sentence, blame the generation gap. I asked some younger folks in my life about why the quest for likes would lead people to die. The way they explained it is this: As more and more people take photos, competition for likes steepens. Therefore, if you can take photos in crazy situations—say, a selfie as close to a moving train as possible, with a live grenade, or while springing down the streets of Pamplona while being chased by bulls, to name just a few examples that resulted in death[32]—and live to post, tweet, or share the tale, then you will get lots of likes.

And don't think this is just for the young among us. In 2016, fifty-one-year-old Oliver Clark died after falling 130 feet after jumping to get the perfect picture of himself with Machu Pichu.[33] In fact, a *Washington Post* article reporting Clark's death noted that less than twenty-four hours prior to his demise, a South Korean tourist fell more than 1,600 feet down the Gocta Waterfall in the Amazonas region in northern Peru. Other selfie accidents mentioned in the article include the death of a Japanese tourist who fell down stairs at the Taj Mahal, tourists being gored by bison in Yellowstone Park, and the drowning of seven men in the Ganges River.[34]

Entrepreneurs have taken notice of this quest for likes. In an article titled "Please Like My Vacation Photo. I Hired a Professional," the *Wall Street Journal* noted the boom in Instagram tours that cater to the needs of those focused on generating the perfect perception online.[35] In addition to helping clients change shoes and outfits while on the tour, many will also find ideal lighting conditions to secure the like-generating shot. In some cases, they may even help create an image that differs from reality. The article notes that "judging from Instagram, the picturesque Hindu temple that houses the Gate of Heaven in Bali is surrounded by a serene body of water. But the reflection . . . isn't a pool; it is actually a piece of glass." The reality is that glass that provides the reflection obscures the gray paving stones that are filled with tourists waiting to pose for that very shot.

Caring deeply about perceptions and prestige is nothing new. But it is amplified, accelerated, and bent into a new shape by social apps, which emphasize instant, one-dimensional quantifications of social interaction and appreciation. *Our relationship with social media encourages a focus on appearances over experiences.* Humans have always been vain, but now the medium of our vanity gives us immediate, addictive feedback. And there is medical evidence that the instant feedback is like a dopamine drip, always bringing us back to seek more. Our focus on the instant gratification of likes blinds us from taking a more holistic approach to social well-being.

And knowledge of these distracting influences on our well-being does not necessarily prevent us from being absorbed by their overwhelming power. I know, as I fell victim to the seductive allure of accumulating likes. In 2014, I began writing a weekly comment on geopolitics and geo-economics. It was a fun way for me to congeal my thinking on a range of issues, and posting it online allowed me to connect with others who seemed to care about those same issues. But in January 2015, I was convinced by one of my readers (I had dozens of them who regularly read and engaged with my content) to post my views on LinkedIn. "The LinkedIn community will love your comments, so why not post your views where people are already going rather than trying to get readers to come to you?"

It seemed to make sense, and so I began putting my weekly comments on LinkedIn. At first, the number of views jumped up from dozens to around a hundred. By the middle of 2015, I regularly had one thousand people reading my stuff, and by the end of 2015, my audience had grown to tens of thousands. LinkedIn then honored me as their #1 Top Voice for money and finance, something that fueled more readership in 2016. During the year, I had several pieces that drew hundreds of thousands of readers and many thousands of likes. I soon found myself stressing about headlines that would draw readers or topics that might generate likes. Bottom line, the tail had begun to wag the dog. What began as a process of writing to help crystallize my thinking had turned into a quest for likes, views, and shares.

So what did I do? After being honored again in 2016 as the #1 Top Voice on LinkedIn for finance and economics, I quit. That's right, I stopped cold turkey. Rather than let popular sentiment drive my writing on a regular schedule, I chose instead to write a monthly reflection piece for my mailing list. As I stopped tracking whether it generated likes or views, the burden of writing reverted into the joy of expression.

Dating Data

For those seeking love today, abstaining from social media is likely not an option, as potential partners are increasingly turning to apps for dates. Given the superficial dynamics of dating—whether online or offline—social apps make searching for love online more convenient and may actually expand our horizons in ways that could result in concrete, meaningful relationships. The difference is, with online dating, the "online" part ends when the relationship begins, unlike with social media friendships. *Not* using dating apps largely condemns us to the narrow focus of our immediate friendship networks, workplaces, and serendipity in local bars.

Consider these facts: Many Americans meet their significant others and spouses through friends. According to a 2012 study, roughly 30 percent of straight couples met this way, which has been the leading path toward a relationship in the post–World War II era.[36] Another popular way to meet a potential spouse is at work, a phenomenon that began in the 1960s as women entered the workforce. But since the 1990s, the number of couples meeting through coworkers or at work has been falling.[37]

Given the importance of choosing a life partner, the data is actually quite shocking. Why's that? As noted by online commentator Tim Urban on *Wait but Why*, choosing a life partner is a big commitment that shouldn't be trivialized. In fact, Urban says that the choice is really about "your parenting partner, your eating companion for about 20,000 meals, your travel partner for about 100 vacations, your primary leisure time and retirement friend, your career therapist, and someone whose day you'll hear about 18,000 times." Urban concludes, "This is by *far* the most important thing in life to get right."[38]

But society tends to work against us by placing a stigma on intelligently expanding our search for potential partners. Urban argues that people are often still timid to say they met their spouse on a dating site—that instead, "The respectable way to meet a life partner is by dumb luck, by bumping into them randomly or being introduced to them from within your little pool." He notes this perspective is counter-productive. The obvious conclusion, according to Urban, is that "Everyone looking for a life partner should be doing a lot of online dating, speed dating, and other systems created to broaden the candidate pool in an intelligent way."[39]

And although this logic is sound, it also comes with some downside effects. While it allows us to zoom out from the focus of our immediate social surroundings, it condemns us to being overwhelmed by the overload of potential matches, making us anxious as we seek to optimize. This tendency can leave us with unnecessary feelings of dissatisfaction with our partners. Surely the perfect match exists, right?

In our quest to optimize, we're giving up the pretty good to search for the ideal. The result is higher anxiety, more confusion, and rising discomfort with trivial challenges within relationships. As one online dater put it, "I find it insanely overwhelming . . . at what point do you stop swiping?" While another confessed: "Sometimes I worry that the love of my life is on a different dating app."[40]

Indeed, some research into online dating trends has suggested exactly this. One study found that married couples who met first online were three times as likely to divorce as couples who met in person.[41] Might this be because of a nagging feeling that an ideal match exists? There's a lot of anecdotal evidence on the anxiety and the corresponding FOMO that comes with online dating, explored by Aziz Ansari in his book *Modern Romance*, and the *New York Times* opinion section, among others.[42]

Connectivity Conundrums and
Data Distractions

People are so focused on their phones that it's endangering their lives. According to the *Daily Mail,* 43 percent of young people in the United Kingdom have walked into someone or something while checking their mobile phone.[43] The situation is so bad in Japan that a cellular operator ran a public service advertisement warning against mindless pedestrian smartphone use. The ad claimed that 66 percent of people have bumped into another person while using a smartphone, while 3.6 percent of people have fallen from a train platform when texting while walking.[44]

This constant connection with our phones is not just endangering our lives, it's also putting public safety professionals at risk. An April 2019 study by the National Safety Council and the Emergency Responder Safety Institute found that 71 percent of drivers take photos or videos when they see an accident, and 16 percent of these drivers *admitted* (how many people do so but didn't admit to doing so?) that they either struck or nearly struck a first responder in the process.[45] The same survey revealed that 60 percent of drivers posted their videos to social media (presumably to generate likes?) and 66 percent sent emails—all while driving through a traffic-filled accident site. The need to stay connected and online at all times is literally threatening our lives and those of the people around us. And yet we continue. . . .

Even if you wanted to try to just partially disconnect to slow the tidal wave of information coming at you, there are increasing social pressures that lead people to distrust those with no social media presence. As Evgeny Morozov has pointed out,[46] it is more and more common for journalists to casually imply that if you don't have an online profile, you're a deviant or have something to hide. You could be ostracized just for trying to avoid notifications!

We are worse off when we allow ourselves to be distracted by notifications. Cal Newport argues in *Deep Work: Rules for Focused Success in a Distracted World* that we cannot enter "deep work," in which we focus on a cognitively demanding task for a long period of time, when we receive constant interruptions.[47] Unfortunately, our workplaces value constant communication and accessibility, which is in direct opposition to enabling employees to produce cognitive products at their highest levels. The average employee receives over 300 emails a week, checks their email thirty-six times per hour, and takes up to sixteen minutes to refocus after handling a new message. Further, workers are interrupted on average fifty-six times per day, switch tasks twenty times per hour, and spend two hours per day recovering from distractions.[48]

Distraction is now a universal competency, as Joshua Rothman wrote in "A New Theory of Distraction" in the *New Yorker* in 2015. We see distraction as a way of asserting control, of regaining our autonomy from any situation that could trap us—a conversation, a movie, or a walk down the street.[49] But there are real downsides to distraction. In 2013, researchers at King's College Institute of Psychiatry in London reported "unchecked infomania" (the constant use of email and other social media) led to a temporary ten-point drop in the IQ of the study's participants—twice as much as pot smokers![50]

Cognitive Crutches

Overwhelming choice generates a nagging sense of regret. But this is the complete opposite of how some economists believe humans act. In reality, we humans are not the rational, utility-maximizing robots that some economists believe we are. In fact, we are so consistently irrational that the whole field of behavioral decision making exists to better understand how we think. The godfathers of this field are Amos Tversky and Daniel Kahneman.

A key insight from their work is that how choices are presented to us impacts the selection we make. Kahneman describes this "framing effect" in *Thinking: Fast and Slow*.[51] And it's backed up by evidence. For example, researchers found that subjects had higher opinions of meat described to them as "75 percent lean" than those described as "25 percent fat."[52] The power of framing can affect almost all walks of life, from organ donations to medical treatments. For instance, in countries where people have to check a box to be an organ donor, between 4 and 28 percent of people become donors. By contrast, if asked to check a box to *not* be an organ donor, between 86 and 100 percent of people become donors.[53] How is this possible? Framing.

In medicine, doctors are more likely to choose treatments presented in terms of survival rates than those presented in terms of mortality rates. In one experiment, doctors were given information about outcomes for two different lung cancer treatments: surgery and radiation. When the doctors were told that for surgery "the one-month survival rate is 90 percent," 84 percent of them preferred it to radiation. By contrast, when they were told "there is 10 percent mortality in the first month," only 50 percent favored it.[54] The options were fundamentally the same, and yet framing dramatically affected how expert doctors responded to them.

As we've seen in these cases, the framer sets our field of vision and in doing so can exert influence toward a specific choice. As Kahneman explains, "A physician, and perhaps a presidential advisor as well, could influence the decision made by the patient or by the President, without distorting or suppressing information, merely by the framing of outcomes and contingencies."[55] In a world of overwhelming choice, we throw our hands up in despair, hoping for someone to present some authoritative optimization strategy and thereby grant enormous power to decision aids and focus filters that frame our choices.

Kahneman and Tversky also showed how we get fixated on seemingly irrelevant numbers in ways that bias our decision making. In one experiment, a researcher spun a number wheel in front of an audience and then read the randomly selected number aloud. He then asked the audience what percentage of African countries were members of the United Nations. Audience members' guesses tended to cluster around the randomly selected number, even though they knew it had no relevance to the question being asked. For instance, they found that if the random number was ten, then the median audience guess was 25 percent; when the random number was forty-five, the median guess was 65 percent.[56] People tend to stick with what they see and hear, even if it's totally irrelevant. This phenomenon, which they called anchoring, confuses our decision making.

The anchoring effect illustrates the stakes of managing focus. Whatever the baseline in our field of view happens to be, it will profoundly affect our ultimate choice—even though we know in our rational minds that it shouldn't. As we encounter new information, we adjust up or down from this baseline. But the psychologists' research shows that we adjust insufficiently. If someone asks us if global GDP per capita is higher or lower than $100,000, even if we receive further information that suggests an answer closer to $12,000, we will insufficiently adjust downwards from the initial high baseline. How our baselines get set is thus key to how we decide if something is high or low, good or bad— thoughts that in turn drive our choices. As you might imagine, this reality allows those to whom we may turn for advice or guidance to exercise tremendous power over our choice.

Another cognitive bias that focus managers exploit is loss aversion. In comparing outcomes, humans feel more pain from losses than they feel pleasure from equivalent gains. As Kahneman, Knetsch, and Thaler note, in gambling on coin flips, people often need the possibility of winning as much as $200 before they are ready to accept a potential loss of $100.[57] Economists would call such behavior irrational.

Attempting to harness these cognitive biases, I often began my classes by letting my students know that everyone in the class currently has an A. I then proceeded to tell them that they would lose their A unless they did a spectacular job on each and every assignment, came prepared for each class, and were engaged in class discussions. Acknowledging that I have a biased and small sample, my trick seems to work. Most retain a good grade. Whether my framing matters is impossible for me to answer, but I do find students more engaged and committed than before I adopted this approach.

The bottom line is that we humans are not as rational as some decision-making models assume. In fact, homo sapiens differs from *homo economicus* in many ways, but most visibly when it comes to how we actually make choices. The cognitive crutches we've developed (called heuristics by psychologists) help us to make choices quickly and often correctly, but we can also be misled when we let our default methods take over and blindly follow them.

Nobel Laureate Herbert Simon suggested that we humans suffer from what he called "bounded rationality," in that our ability to optimize is limited by (1) the information at our disposal, (2) the capacities of our mind to calculate tradeoffs and optimize with them, and (3) the limited time we all have to make decisions.[58] This reality means optimization is almost universally unlikely; yet the very promise of it creates widespread decision dilemmas as the unachievable quest for the perfect decision continues unabated. Simon's solution was simple: we should learn to "satisfice" rather than maximize,[59] meaning we should be willing to make choices that are "good enough" to meet our needs, even if a better choice might be possible. We'll return to this concept later in the book when we discuss goals-based investing.

The proliferation of options does not appear to have increased our satisfaction; rather, the explosion of choices appears to have made us more anxious, paralyzed, and regretful. Choosing has gone from an expression of preference to an anxiety-filled drama in which even trivial selections can generate doubt and regret. This paradox of choice drives demand for anything that can mitigate its symptoms.

Is it any wonder that we willingly outsource our thinking to those who claim an ability to guide us through the deluge of data toward a seemingly optimal choice? Paradoxically, our faith in choice, which was supposed to empower us, has led us to rely more on others. And in so doing, we've given up an in ordinate amount of control.

CHAPTER 2

Outsourced Thinking

Our constant struggle to optimize often leads us to recognize the costs and difficulties of trying to know everything. So what do we do? We run headlong into the arms of experts, technologies, and protocols (or rules) that offer the possibility of salvation. Expert individuals, like doctors and lawyers, are people to whom we often defer because of their domain knowledge. And the embedded expertise in technologies allows algorithms to guide our thinking just as a person might, albeit in less noticeable ways. Lastly, there is extended expertise, by which rules are used to control the thinking and actions of those in organizations. Let's explore each of these three forms of expertise and how they can impact our lives.

Experts

It is often easier to let people—experts, for example—act as viewfinders, focusing our attention on what they think matters. These individuals are granted authority through degrees and licenses—think doctors with MDs, pilots with certified pilot licenses (CPLs)—or sheer reputation. By outsourcing our focus to them, we willfully let them take control over our field of vision, blind to what they leave out. We let them frame our decisions. Many of us don't even think about it this way, and we mindlessly follow their guidance. At the very least, we should think about, and ideally ask about, what other variables might be worth considering.

Draft Pick #199

Tom Brady, for years the superstar quarterback of the New England Patriots, is often called the greatest quarterback of all time by sports writers and commentators. He has played in numerous Super Bowls, won the league MVP and Super Bowl MVP awards several times, and has broken lots of NFL records. My kids grew up watching Sunday football as a sporadic but enjoyable pastime, but when Brady was on, they almost always watched. And in the ultimate testament to his success, they grew up expecting to see Brady in Super Bowl each year—and for most years, they were right.

But the Tom Brady we know almost wasn't.

All manner of talent-identifying experts decided Tom Brady didn't have what it takes to succeed in the National Football League. Countless coaches, assistants, scouts, and sports media analysts passed him over. The result: he was the 199th pick in the NFL draft the year the New England Patriots signed him. Just for reference, most of the attention during a draft is paid to the top twenty-five picks, as they tend to represent the most promising talent entering the league that year. Brady sat on the bench for a year until a teammate's injury gave him the chance to play. That simple event led to his meteoric rise to one of professional football's most successful and accomplished athletes.

Brady had been passed over by lots of teams, teams run by professionals who should have been able to identify the upside offered by recruiting Brady. How did they miss his potential? Might it have been too much focus on expert opinion? In fact, throughout the sports field, overrelying on expert judgments is a widespread problem, as many teams defer their assessment of an athlete's potential to seemingly objective data from algorithms and professional scouts.

The NFL Combine is a set of times and scored physical drills that attempts to "put players on an even playing field by standardizing the drills and measurements taken."[1] They measure an athlete's physical attributes such as height, weight, hand size, and arm length. This data is then combined with performance data: an athlete's speed is measured via a forty-yard dash, jumping ability via a vertical jump, and so on. Brady was unremarkable in a physical sense. When it came to his performance stats, however, he definitely stood out. He had the shortest vertical jump and was the second slowest in the forty-yard dash of the class of 2000.[2]

Experts then combine an athlete's results and summarize the scores on a scale of 0 to 100; Tom Brady was given a score of forty-five for his size, zero for his speed, thirty-three for his agility, and nineteen for his quickness. The professional judges, who were tasked with gauging a player's potential in the NFL, seemed to agree: Brady didn't have what it took to succeed in the NFL. In aggregate, Brady's overall rating, also out of a possible one hundred, was twelve. The grade put on his final NFL Combine report was an F.[3] Oops.

The Goblet of Rejection

J. K. Rowling's series of stories about the magical world of Harry Potter have sold hundreds of millions of books, grossed billions at the box office, and are the inspiration for several popular theme parks. Quite simply, the Harry Potter series became the most lucrative stories in the history of human communication. Most estimates suggest the revenues associated with the series top $20 billion, a sum that has made the once homeless author a billionaire.

But the stories of Harry, Ronald, Hermione, Lord Voldemort, and others may never have seen the light of day. Why's that? Because all the experts to whom the story was first sent rejected it as too long, noting that children wouldn't have the attention span to finish it. Rowling collected dozens of rejections before seeking the help of literary agent Christopher Little, a name she chose because it sounded like a children's book character. But while composing a rejection letter to Rowling, an assistant was struck by the illustrations and spurred the agency to take on the author . . .

. . . and then publishers began sending the rejection letters to Little rather than Rowling. It was only when Little got desperate enough to ask Bloomsbury Publishing Chairman Nigel Newton for a personal favor that things started looking up. As noted by Aren Wilborn in *Cracked*, a multiplatform satire brand, "Newton did something that apparently never occurred to other children's book publishers, which was to show it to an actual child."[4] Newton handed the transcript to his eight-year-old daughter who read it within hours and demanded more. Sensing an opportunity, he offered Rowling a nominal advance and set the initial run for five hundred copies—not exactly a ringing endorsement of expert judgment that foretells insight into one of the best-selling book series of all time.

The rest, as they say, is history. While the achievement of the series is indeed remarkable, it's also stunning that such blockbuster success was missed by almost every expert judge. One might have expected literary experts (those skilled and experienced in identifying and nurturing talent) would have seen potential in the story and developed and promoted it, even if not efficiently or quickly. Not so.

Technology

In addition to people, we also outsource our thinking to technology. Often, the worst consequences of our overreliance on technology products arise from rigid rules embedded in them. The problem is that technological systems can't think for themselves. A computer system can't doublecheck whether something makes sense.

Even when we're not conscious of it, technologies constantly determine what passes into our field of view. They frame our decisions for us. Sure, I could search for a second opinion. But it would take up precious time that most of us don't have. Who even goes to the second page of a Google search? Ninety percent of clicks from searches come from the first page. Five percent come from page 2, and only 1 percent from page 3.[5] Thirty-three percent of searchers don't make it past the first result! Time considerations aside, the fundamental problem is that we often forget the subversive process of focus management that comes with using these technologies.

Dangerous Directions

The downsides of blindly relying on algorithms are exemplified by what happens when small errors surface in navigation software. GPS navigation aids allow us to take our focus away from navigating—sometimes with disastrous results.

In 2008, a bus carrying the Garfield High School softball team crashed into a pedestrian bridge in Seattle, sending twenty-one kids to the hospital (luckily, with only minor injuries). The driver's GPS had routed him under the bridge, even though it was too low for a bus. Why didn't he pay attention to the low bridge as he approached it? One reason, perhaps *the* reason, is because the driver outsourced his thinking to the technology. An algorithm had given him the route, so he didn't stop to think about the bridge's height. You see, the GPS had a "bus" setting. . . .

The driver and the bus company had not considered the possibility that the system could mislead. As the president of the bus company put it, "We just thought it would be a safe route because, why else would they have a selection for a bus?"[6] The bus setting gave them a false sense of security.

In a similar case in 2013, Apple Maps routed drivers across an operating runway at Alaska's Fairbanks International Airport.[7] Drivers mindlessly continued beyond road signs warning them of the active runway and drove onto the airport grounds. Listening attentively and focused on those directions, the drivers stopped thinking about where they were actually driving. To prevent a real disaster and loss of life, airport officials quickly erected barricades to prevent more of the same mindless and very risky outsourcing of thought to GPS-dictated directions.

And in one of my favorite examples of GPS-managed attention, a man drove his van up a small hiking trail (labeled by locals as a glorified goat path) until the system announced he should turn around.[8] At that point, he was halfway up a mountain and couldn't turn around. A heavy-lift helicopter was deployed to rescue him and get the van off the trail. Clearly, looking out the window, rather than listening to the computer-generated directions, would have been more productive.

Blind reliance on technology can literally lead us astray. Lest you think this is just an American problem, consider an experience I had in South Africa. I was invited to address a large audience in Johannesburg, and on the day prior to my speech, my hosts had arranged for me to appear on various TV shows to discuss the global economy and its implications for South Africa.

I was scheduled to appear on CNBC's *Powerlunch Africa* show and was told the studio was not far from my hotel. Given the warm climate, my hosts had a member of their media relations team members drive me to the specific building and exact location. Fighting a bit of jetlag, I asked if we had time for a cup of coffee (it was more than an hour before I was scheduled to be on air) and the poised woman obligingly stopped when I spotted a coffee shop. As we sat and talked about the likely questions I would be asked, we suddenly realized that I was scheduled to be on air in approximately twenty minutes. She seemed nervous so I asked her if there was a problem. She said there was no problem, but she felt we should probably walk as the traffic had grown substantially while we had chatted. She put the address into her phone's mapping app and off we went.

Fifteen minutes later, I was sweating like I had just run a marathon, and her app said we had another two kilometers to the destination. We picked up the pace and after making a left turn, found ourselves on the same block that we had gotten coffee. The studio was literally 100 yards from the cafe. I ended up postponing my interview for a bit to accommodate a cool-down period during which I consumed Gatorade and used the hand blowers in the bathroom to dry my shirt. Having sprinted in a circle before a major media appearance, I was so disturbed that I had to investigate what happened. I asked to see her phone . . . and noticed she had set the GPS directions to "driving" rather than "walking," meaning she blindly took me on a four kilometer circle because of one-way streets.

In what may be the most extreme case of pushing back against the impact of mindless reliance on artificially intelligent navigation systems, one Italian town recently banned Google Maps after too many people had gotten lost while following the directions provided by the app.[9] Salvatore Corrias, the mayor of a seaside town on the island of Sardinia, said that "too many sedans and small cars get stuck on impassible paths."[10] An article in October 2019 noted the town had conducted 144 rescue missions in the prior two years. To combat the growing problem, the town has contacted Google and has placed signs alongside roads that read, "Do not follow the directions of Google Maps."[11]

Deadly Dependence

In 2014, *Vanity Fair* featured a gripping story by William Langewiesche that described the crash of Air France 447; titled "The Human Factor,"[12] the article showed how blind reliance on technology resulted in a (potentially) needless loss of lives. Air France 447, an Airbus 330 that boasted new technology to constrain pilots to within the plane's capability limits, took off smoothly at 7:29 p.m. and hugged the Brazilian coast before setting off across the Atlantic. As the plane moved offshore, the cockpit received a message from the dispatchers in Paris: a line of thunderstorms was developing directly on the charted course. Pierre-Cedric Bonin, the pilot flying the plane, grew nervous, but the pilot in charge, Marc Dubois, expressed little concern.

The plane was on autopilot, heading toward Paris at 550 miles per hour, 35,000 feet above the sea. They were about to enter the Intertropical Convergence Zone, an area near the equator where thunderstorms are common. After dodging some bad weather, the pilots found themselves flying through a barrage of ice crystals. The turbulence wasn't particularly unusual, but ice crystals bombarded the windshield.

At 11:10 p.m., the cockpit's pitot tubes (a technology that measures air speed) failed, suggesting the plane's speed had suddenly dropped dramatically. The dashboard also hinted that the plane had lost a bit of altitude. The autopilot system, which required airspeed data, disengaged. Alarms sounded. The pilots were now actually flying the plane, free and clear of automated controls.

Bonin immediately pulled the plane up to gain altitude, which reduced the speed. A stall warning came on, generating even more confusion in the cockpit. As a plane slows down, it loses lift, threatening its ability to stay aloft. To regenerate the speed necessary to maintain lift,

Bonin would have to lower the nose of the plane. But, in the heat of the moment, that's not what he chose to do. Instead, Bonin continued to pull up on the stick.

Another pilot, recognizing the speed indicators were malfunctioning, encouraged Bonin to point the nose of the plane down. Despite answering with, "OK, I'm going back down,"[13] Bonin merely lowered the rate of ascent. The plane continued to lose velocity.

Eventually, the pilots lowered the nose enough that the climb leveled off. The plane was neither gaining altitude nor losing speed. If they had lowered the nose another few degrees, they would have been back where they started. But that's not what happened. Instead of lowering the nose, Bonin again pulled back on the stick. The plane ascended, generating a cacophony of stall warnings in the cockpit. The airspeed indicators were now working. After repeated stall alarms, the plane stopped ascending around 38,000 feet in the sky and started falling with its nose up. The plane began barreling toward the ocean at 3,900 feet per minute.

The plane rapidly fell below 35,000 feet, its plunge rate accelerating to 10,000 feet per minute. The nose was so high that the computers began rejecting the data as invalid. Warnings stopped. But as Bonin tried pointing the nose down, the warnings again rang, leading him to again pull up. The descent rate increased to 15,000 feet per minute. The plane continued to plunge toward the ocean.

Four minutes and twenty seconds after the airspeed indicator failed, Flight 447 belly-flopped into the Atlantic Ocean. All 228 passengers died. Sadly, in this case, the consequences were deadly.

Protocols and Rules

In addition to people commanding our attention and technology hijacking our thinking, rules manage our focus and frame our decisions. They limit what we and the people around us can do, and they give us a false sense of security. In taking options off the table, they narrow our focus on what remains. In trying to prevent undesirable outcomes, they make us overconfident that they have been successfully ruled out. Rules, it seems, are a means of embedding managerial expertise into a set of procedures that employees are asked to blindly follow.

Bureaucratic Blues

Of all the organizations blinded by overfocused rules, the Division of Motor Vehicles (DMV) looms largest in many Americans' minds. The average American gives the DMV as much respect as racist, drug-dealing sex offenders who evade alimony payments. Visiting the DMV is not a particularly enjoyable experience, either. Most Americans would probably prefer a root canal.

Try typing in "DMV horror" or "DMV nightmare" into Google and you'll get hundreds of thousands of hits within half a second or so. Many are so disturbing and ridiculous you simply can't help but laugh. And they're all the result of an overreliance on rigid rules: broken vision machines resulting in people being listed as blind in an official government system; typographical errors that can't be corrected because the system doesn't allow for changes; or bureaucratic shuffling that infuriates some and necessitates blood pressure medication for others. Go here, get that, talk to them, fill out this form, submit that. If you're still not entertained after reading several of these accounts, jump on YouTube, type in "DMV crazy," and you'll be presented with tens of thousands of videos of Americans who lose their composure in the face of DMV frustration.

Consider this story of an employee who couldn't look beyond the color of a book that she had to consult. Here's the situation, which took place in April 2000.[14] A person purchased a used car in California that was manufactured in 1981. He lived in Nevada, so he went to his local DMV in Henderson to register his vehicle. He arrived prepared with the signed California title, inspection documentation, proof of Nevada insurance, and all other paperwork filled out. To assess a fair tax on the purchase, the state of Nevada needed to determine the current market value of the car. DMV protocol is to use the Kelley Blue Book value or to adjust the original manufacturer's suggested retail price (MSRP) for depreciation since it was made. The problem: the Kelley Blue Book available to the clerk didn't have car values going back to 1981 models.

So the clerk was stumped, because she blindly followed the DMV's rigid rules. The car's owner noticed a NADA guide (a similar price estimation manual produced by the National Automobile Dealers Association, but one which goes back further in time) behind the counter and asked the clerk to consult it. She refused to do so, insisting she had to get the *blue book* value, and the NADA book is not blue. Frustrated, the customer tried another route. He explained that the car would be completely depreciated at this point and offered to pay the minimum tax.

The clerk rejected the offer and suggested the car owner try getting the original window sticker. His response: "The former owner is dead! I bought the car off his surviving family! There is no way that I can provide you with such a document."[15] She couldn't move on, insisting on a blue book value or an original purchase price. Those are, after all, the DMV's rules. The clerk concluded that there was nothing further she could do and motioned for the owner to leave, noting that there were other customers waiting.

After a heated standoff, a supervisor eventually entered the scene and located the original MSRP for the car in the NADA guide. Even then, the clerk insisted that she could not use the price because it wasn't from the *blue book*. The supervisor explained that *blue book* is just a phrase for used car and truck prices because it's the most commonly used book. After several agitating hours, the customer's paperwork was accepted in its original form.

Recently, Kristen (yes, my patient movie-watching companion from chapter 1) and I encountered a silly set of rules. We went out with our kids for an early dinner, so early that those without children might have confused it with a late lunch. Our destination was a relatively nice Italian restaurant. It was almost completely empty. But when we asked for a table for four, the very pleasant host looked down to consult his computer. Two minutes later, he lifted his head and said, "It'll be about thirty minutes." My wife and I laughed. We merely looked over his shoulder at the three tables with people and the other twenty-seven or so empty tables. My watch read 4:20 p.m. Thirty minutes might as well be seven hours when you're with two hungry kids.

I started to say "Thanks, maybe another time . . ." but my wife couldn't help herself.

She said, "I'm sorry. I may be mistaken, but it appears you have tables available. Are you expecting a mad rush based on reservations?" (This wasn't as cynical as you might think. . . . We do, after all, live in a family-oriented suburb of Boston and young families eat early.)

The host said that he was not allowed to sit more than fifteen people in any thirty-minute window. He then pointed to the twelve people in the dining room and indicated that we would tip the balance to sixteen, and that was against the rules. He needed to pace arrivals so the kitchen wouldn't "get slammed." After I suggested he could consider two children the equivalent of one person, he leaned in and whispered, "We're not that kind of restaurant. . . . We don't cut corners." His focus on following the rules led to the perplexing situation where four hungry diners were sent away in the name of delivering a good dining experience.

Rigid rules may exacerbate and intensify, rather than mitigate, the very risks the experts are trying to minimize by imposing the rules. The restaurant rule was probably to ensure a good dining experience, but it instead annoyed four potential customers.

Sick Systems

In late September 2014, Thomas Eric Duncan returned home to Dallas from a trip to Liberia, ground zero of a raging Ebola epidemic.[16] He suffered from severe abdominal pain and had a high and rising fever. Concerned, he went to Texas Health Presbyterian Hospital Dallas, where he was subjected to a battery of questions and simple diagnostic tests. When his temperature was taken, it registered 103 degrees.[17] Despite the media frenzy describing the rapidly spreading disease in Africa, and the news that was dominating virtually all of the American media, Ebola was not seriously considered as a possible cause of his ailments during this first visit. His travel history was not given adequate attention. A mere thirty-five minutes after the concerning thermometer reading, health–care workers sent him home when his temperature dropped to 101.2 degrees, as the rules indicated that was the correct course of action.[18]

He later returned to the hospital and was admitted a second time, now with his family saying they believed he had Ebola. He had all the symptoms. Despite these conditions, hospital protocols did not dictate elevated caution until a confirmed diagnosis had returned from the labs. And so, anyone around the infected patient was no more protected from Duncan than if he had the flu.[19]

Eventually, Texas Health Resources, the parent company of the hospital, announced Thomas Eric Duncan was America's first confirmed Ebola patient. Americans on Main Street panicked alongside those on Wall Street. Cruise ship and airline stocks plunged as fears of enclosed public travel escalated. Trips were cancelled. The fear was palpable.[20]

Amidst the chaos and confusion, Nina Pham, a twenty-six-year-old nurse working at the hospital's intensive care unit, was assigned to care for Duncan. To reduce her risk of exposure to the deadly virus, based on what she could learn from the internet, she donned protective gear, leaving only her neck and hair exposed. A little over a week later, Duncan died.

Shortly thereafter, Pham woke up with a fever, checked herself into the hospital, and tested positive for Ebola.[21] At the same time, the US Centers for Disease Control (CDC) was closely monitoring another nurse, Amber Vinson, who had cared for Duncan along with Pham while he was sick; she had even put a catheter in him while he was in the midst of extreme vomiting and uncontrollable diarrhea. As a result of being in close direct contact with two confirmed Ebola patients, Vinson was asked to check in with the CDC twice a day.

While on a trip to Cleveland, Vinson developed a slight fever. According to CDC protocol, she was required to check in with the center before boarding any flight, so before returning to Dallas, she called the CDC. The representative asked Vinson for her temperature. She reported 99.5 degrees. The decision rule had a no–fly trip point of 100.4 degrees. As a result, Vinson was cleared to board Frontier Airlines Flight 1143 along with 132 unsuspecting passengers. Less than thirty hours after boarding that flight, Vinson was diagnosed with Ebola.[22]

Let's recall that Vinson was asked to report to the CDC twice per day *precisely* because she had been exposed to two confirmed Ebola-infected people. Surely the CDC representative might have asked her to stay put for another twenty-four hours to see if her temperature was rising or falling. Yet the focus upon her body temperature blinded the agent from seeing the very obvious context that demanded an abundance of caution. Nina Pham and Amber Vinson both recovered from Ebola. However, because of a mismatch between rules and the situation at hand, they unnecessarily contracted the deadly disease and, just as avoidably, needlessly exposed others to an elevated risk of contracting it. The system was designed to prevent this exact risk, but it failed because judgment and common sense were overrun by adherence to a strict protocol.

Outsourcing Thought and Attention

An explosion of choice in modern society has increased pressures to focus and filter. Realistically, to make choices, we defer to the opinions of experts or friends, we follow rules of thumb, we use recommendation algorithms—any kind of filter that we think will help us choose well. "Nobody ever got fired for buying IBM," the corporate IT cliché goes. Even if the IBM system falters, that's IBM's fault, not yours, since who *wouldn't* choose IBM? As Keynes wrote, "Worldly wisdom teaches that it is better to fail conventionally than to succeed unconventionally."[23]

Making conventional choices minimizes regret (and may protect your career), even if it isn't the best option given your needs. But in the process of culling, we often cede power to filters in ways we aren't mindful of. Our decision frames are set by others, and we forget to keep track of what options and factors we ignore, opening ourselves up to unnecessary risks and missed opportunities. We are ill-equipped to notice when we're being misdirected by our filters, since they define our very field of perception. The key is to take a step back and ask: What are you losing when you narrow your option set?

We must relearn how to think for ourselves. This does not mean that we cannot rely on others; life today is simply too complex to not do so. But it does mean we should be mindful when doing so. Blind reliance is a recipe for disappointment.

PART TWO

THE
RAMIFICATIONS

L ife is complex, and there is simply no way any of us can know everything. The volume of information available at our fingertips is overwhelming, driving us toward experts and technologies that offer to overcome our choice anxiety and fear of missing out. Unfortunately, the very nature of expertise—in all its forms—is that narrow depth is prized over breadth. One impact is widespread specialization, leading to siloed thinking and blinding focus that often produces the very outcomes we seek to avoid. And as we develop a dependency upon expert insight, we fail to think for ourselves as we obediently follow the guidance offered.

CHAPTER 3

The Promise and Perils of Focus

Given the deluge of data, explosion in choice, and the now constant fear of missing out on the perfect decision, it is not surprising that we have run into the arms of experts, technology, and protocols. There's comfort in outsourcing our thinking and the belief (hope?) that those who know more will guide us toward optimal choices. Those with a focus on our area of interest will obviously know more about the decision we need to make than we do, so why not defer to them?

Let's stop and think for a moment about focus. Who doesn't appreciate and praise focus? It's the key to getting things done. It's what allows you to overcome the urge to procrastinate, the allure of YouTube, and the constant distractions of colleagues, friends, and family. (In fact, as I'm typing this paragraph, I currently have Microsoft Word set to Focus mode so that I don't see anything but the text I'm typing.) In today's complex society, with data and messages constantly bombarding each of us, focus offers the possibility of salvation. Focus seems to be the key to coping with life in the twenty-first century.

The Hocus Pocus of Focus

But there are significant downsides to our unprecedented level of zoom. By focusing, we filter, and thus ignore. In focusing mindlessly, we blind ourselves to risks and opportunities. To restore self-reliance in the twenty-first century, we need to be mindful of our focus. Focus is a variable that needs to be managed intentionally, just like time and money. And we must always remember that focusing means ignoring, because with limited attention, an overallocation in one domain means insufficient attention in others. Researchers have confirmed that the more intensely we focus on something, the more likely we are to ignore anything that's not immediately relevant to that focus.[1] They call this *inattentional blindness.*

In perhaps the most famous of the research experiments, psychologists Christopher Chabris and Daniel Simons created a video of two groups of people walking around in a chaotic pattern and passing basketballs to each other.[2] One team wore white shirts, the other wore black. The test asked participants to count the number of times a basketball was passed between players wearing white shirts in the midst of several players wearing black shirts. Most of the study participants were pretty accurate, meaning they got within one or two of the correct number of passes, but that wasn't the point of the experiment. The psychologists weren't actually interested in the ability of people to count passes; rather, the passes were intended to draw the participants' attention. And most participants took the bait. They focused on the ball.

The real topic of the study was to investigate whether people can be blinded by focus. In this case, about half of the participants were. You see, about halfway through the video, a student dressed as a gorilla walks into the scene. She stops in the middle of the players, faces the camera, thumps her chest, and then proceeds to leave the scene. The gorilla is in the scene for slightly less than ten seconds.

After the video, researchers ask the participant how many passes they observed and whether they noticed anything unusual about the scene. They even ask if there were any other players. Eventually, the participant is asked if there was a gorilla in the middle of the ball-passing players. About half of the people that get asked this question respond with shock and amazement. That's right, about 50 percent of people don't see the gorilla. (When I first saw the video, I didn't notice the gorilla either.)

What the heck is happening? Half of the people don't see a gorilla that enters the scene, stops, looks at them, thumps its chest, and then walks off? Really?

Yup, really.

By focusing intensely on the number of passes and dedicating one's attention to the counting of them, the cognitive and visual systems have little spare capacity to observe unexpected things. Remember my suggestion that focus helps us ignore? Well, that's exactly what happened in these experiments. Intense focus on counting passes led to ignoring the gorilla.

These findings have been replicated globally by dozens of research teams running similar experiments on people of all walks of life. About half fail to see the gorilla. Humans seem to have a set amount of attention, and giving it away is a zero-sum game. As noted by French sociologist Emile Durkheim, "Concentrating the mind on a small number of objects blinds it to a greater number of others."[3]

Chabris and Simons later introduced a twist to their videos. They wanted to test the hypothesis that we have a fixed supply of attention and to explore the implications for multitasking. They asked study participants to separate the number of aerial passes from the number of bounced passes, meaning that counters had to keep two tallies running throughout their observation. The results speak for themselves. The extra attention demanded by the task led more people to miss the gorilla, approximately 70 percent. Simply put, more focus, more ignoring, more blindness.

An interesting side note is that the ability to multitask may differ based on gender. A study published in the journal *BMC Psychology* found that men were slower and less organized than women when switching rapidly between tasks.[4] The study compared women and men in two tests. One compared 120 women and 120 men in a computer test that involved switching between tasks involving counting and shape recognition, and it showed that men were significantly slower than women when the tasks were mixed up. The second test gave forty-seven men and forty-seven women eight minutes to complete a series of paper-and-pencil multitasking tests more relevant to everyday life (e.g., locating restaurants on a map, answering a phone call, finding a lost key), and it showed that women were more organized under pressure.

When I shared this fact with my wife, she laughed and said, "Is that news to you?" while she planned our children's activities for the week, managed a staff of forty via text, secured visas for three of her foreign employees, and coordinated details of a multimillion-dollar construction project. All things considered, though, man or woman, it seems that we'd be best off not trying to allocate our limited focus among multiple tasks at once. It has been estimated that only 2 percent of people can multitask without a decline in performance.[5]

But multitasking or not, the fundamental reality is that as we focus intensely, we ignore intensely. And in the domain of health, this can lead well-meaning medical professionals to break the Hippocratic oath.

PSA Problems

Let's now look at prostate health and the medical community's focus on the prostate-specific antigen (PSA). The PSA test is a simple blood test that is believed by some to identify prostate cancer years before it might otherwise be found. Compared to a digital rectal exam in which a doctor sticks his finger into a man's rectum to feel the prostate directly, the PSA test offers less discomfort as well as the holy grail of preventive care—early detection. It's not hard to understand why the PSA test took off. In addition to being less invasive, it allowed doctors and their patients to focus on one variable, the PSA score. All attention was soon channeled toward this supposedly predictive variable, lessening the focus on other important considerations.

But here's the problem. By identifying prostate cancer up to eleven years before it might otherwise be detected, the PSA test led to invasive biopsies with accompanying risks and unintended side effects. For many, the treatment proved worse than the disease. The focus on early detection led to many more identifications, and once they have been identified as having prostate cancer, most patients want to treat it immediately. The watch-and-wait approach is psychologically challenging, especially given the numerous stories of how early detection can save lives.

In *Overdiagnosed: Making People Sick in the Pursuit of Health*, doctors H. Gilbert Welch, Lisa Schwartz, and Steven Woloshin document significant evidence that the diagnoses of prostate cancer have been directly related to efforts to find it.[6] More PSA tests, more biopsies. More biopsies, more cancer. More cancer, more treatment. The more we focus on finding something, the more we find it. And, surprise, surprise, we also become increasingly blind to the costs of treatment.

But the costs of overdiagnosis are very real: "Everyone knows the potential benefit of cancer screening: you may avoid death from cancer. Relatively few understand the more likely harm: you may be diagnosed and treated for a cancer that was never going to bother you."[7] The downsides of overtreatment can be quite significant.

In his book *Less Medicine, More Health*, Welch explains that we can think of the variety of cancers as a barnyard pen of rabbits, turtles, and birds.[8] Rabbits are ready to hop out at any time: you want to catch them before they escape. Rabbits are the potentially lethal cancers, which might be stopped by early treatment. The most aggressive cancers are like birds: they have already escaped by the time you look for them, and there's not much you can do. The rest are like turtles, which aren't going anywhere. The turtles are the indolent, nonlethal cancers. Early screening helps with rabbits, but not with turtles (which are unlikely to be threatening) or birds (which are likely untreatable). Different cancers have different ratios of rabbits, turtles, and birds.

Prostate cancers tend to be heavily dominated by turtles, meaning that screening reveals many of them, but this revelation does not save many lives. Let's consider some basic facts: the lifetime chance of death from prostate cancer is approximately 3 percent, and the median age of those who die from prostate cancer is approximately eighty. The lifetime risk of diagnosis of prostate cancer, however, is approximately 16 percent, and the median age of those who are diagnosed with prostate cancer is approximately sixty-nine. Clearly, there is a disconnect. Many of the cancers being identified don't really matter. Welch and colleagues conclude, "The fastest way to get prostate cancer is to be screened for it."[9] And therein lies the problem. *In many cases, screening and identifying prostate cancer is not helpful.* Many of the individuals who are identified as having prostate cancer are likely to die from some other cause. Given this fact, might the costs of pursuing a treatment and the risks of side effects such as impotence and incontinence outweigh the uncertain benefit?

In one of the most interesting and persuasive articles I have read on the topic, a group of researchers published a study in *European Urology* that investigated the prevalence of prostate cancer in men that died in Detroit from accidents.[10] Basically, they looked at men who had died for effectively random reasons, which gives their research tremendous power. And what the study showed is that prostate cancer rates rise with age in an almost linear manner. Nine percent of men in their twenties had prostate cancer, 40 percent of those in their forties, and more than 80 percent of those in their seventies. But merely having cancer may not matter. In fact, the data seem to suggest that most men appear to die *with* prostate cancer; fewer die *because* of it.

Further, there is significant evidence that our commitment to screening and early identification has resulted in more aggressive cancer-seeking efforts. While standard prostate biopsies had involved six needles and six samples, studies have been conducted using eleven, twelve, and thirteen samples. Guess what was identified as a result of the more active search? More prostate cancer. In fact, one study took patients that had been deemed cancer-free through three different biopsies and subjected those patients to saturation biopsies involving thirty-two simultaneous needle samples—resulting in *14 percent of individuals who had been deemed cancer-free being labeled as having prostate cancer.*[11]

The authors of *Overdiagnosed* believe that over a million men have been overdiagnosed and been subjected to the anxiety of having cancer. Welch, Schwartz, and Woloshin suggest that their best guess is that for every man who benefits from screening by avoiding a prostate cancer death, somewhere between thirty and a hundred are harmed by overdiagnosis and treated needlessly.[12]

Let me repeat that so your focus on reading didn't blind you into filtering out this shocking fact. Somewhere between thirty to one hundred men are *needlessly* treated for each necessary procedure. All because of a disproportionate focus on screening and early diagnosis.

The head scientist who discovered PSA, Dr. Richard Ablin, wrote a widely cited *New York Times* op-ed entitled "The Great Prostate Mistake" in 2010.[13] Ablin bluntly stated the "test is hardly more effective than a coin toss . . . and can't distinguish between the two types of prostate cancer—the one that will kill you and the one that won't."[14]

Ablin's piece in the *New York Times* was so widely discussed that he published a book-length treatment of the topic titled *The Great Prostate Hoax*.[15] Ablin says the book is an apology to every man that has undergone unnecessary procedures and currently endures side effects resulting from the focus on the PSA test. He suggests his discovery has ruined marriages through unnecessary impotence, decreased self-esteem via avoidable incontinence, and resulted in millions of anxiety-ridden, psychologically scarring, and emotionally driven decisions of what to do about something that might not matter.

How did this happen? Why did we become overly reliant on a narrow indicator that can affect so many lives? We took a simple process that began with symptoms (i.e., there was an issue causing concern) and attempted to preempt it with predictive screening. The medical community became so focused on early identification of prostate cancer that it failed to adequately consider the potential irrelevance of many of the identified cancers. They were so focused on catching animals trying to escape the barnyard that they didn't realize they were catching lots of turtles that would never have made it out. Sure, the system on occasion did catch a rabbit, but only between 1 and 3 percent of caught animals.[16]

What if the PSA test was only used as originally intended—to monitor the progress of a cancer that was previously identified because of the symptoms it caused or the physical abnormalities it produced? By focusing narrowly on the tests, we've lost touch with what is medically prudent. *"Having cancer" does not matter unless the cancer itself matters.* Needlessly treating men for prostate cancer imposes certain costs with the unknowable possibility of a potential gain.

Doctors and patients should focus less on a single indicator like the PSA score and think more holistically about a patient's health, life, and risk of complications from any potential treatments. The fundamental problem is that depth of focus is blinding us from breadth of perspective. Common sense mandates we consider the context, yet as the gorilla on the basketball court demonstrates, focus blinds us. It leads us to miss that which is directly in front of our eyes; in this case, less may in fact be more.

Bureaucratic Baloney

Focus leads us to blindly follow protocols prescribed by leaders in all types of organizations. The extended focus through which managers are able to improve team efficiency is not all bad. It allows for consistent decision making, scalable processes, and managerial control. But an unwavering commitment to these systems, be they embedded in technology or manifested in rules, can comically trump common sense. Employee focus on the system and its demands can work to the detriment of the organization's ultimate mission.

The absurdity of many bureaucratically infuriating situations can often be described by the Peter Principle, the theory put forth by Dr. Laurence J. Peter and Raymond Hull in 1969.[17] Peter and Hull posit that an unhealthy focus on how well people are performing in their current jobs drives promotion decisions. Might it be better to consider how well people might perform in the job into which you seek to promote them? The *Peter Principle* dynamic leads everyone to be promoted not to their ideal job, but past it, to what Peter and Hull call their "level of incompetence." Because people will only stop getting promoted when they are performing poorly in their current job, bureaucratic systems eventually become populated by people in positions for which they lack competence and have demonstrated an inability to do the required job well. If they were competent in the position or could perform the job well, they would have been promoted. And once such an individual reaches their level of incompetence, they remain in the position for the rest of their career.

How and why do we keep promoting people past their levels of competence? Evaluators focus too intensely on an employee's success (or lack thereof) in his or her current role and not on imagining or predicting how they would adapt to the promoted position. Likewise, someone who is less suited for her current job may be passed over for a promotion to a job for which she is ideal. Employees develop skills to succeed at their current job but do not usually think about developing competencies for the promoted position. Likewise, human resource departments and training programs could (and should) think about the skills individuals will need in their next position, not the one that they are currently in.

An example of the *Peter Principle* in action was visible during Hurricane Katrina in 2005. The Federal Emergency Management Agency (FEMA) responded to the humanitarian crisis in New Orleans so poorly that the US Congress held an investigation into the series of mishaps that were part of FEMA's operations. It became clear that one part of the problem was experience and capability of those in leadership positions. The leader of FEMA had excelled as commissioner of judges for the International Arabian Horse Association. Deemed a competent professional in that domain, he was advanced into a role with greater responsibilities: director of FEMA. Given the skills needed to coordinate federal emergency response across different agencies, legal authorities, geographies, and jurisdictions, might it have been predictable that the new head of FEMA would have been overwhelmed?

Fundamentally, the *Peter Principle* is about focus. It's about how managers tend to focus too much on how a person is doing in their current job as the means through which to evaluate their potential for their next job. But when we stop and think about it, that doesn't make a ton of sense. Evaluation criteria should be based on future roles. It may mean that some people who are performing poorly in their current position may blossom if promoted.

Wallets versus Bodies

Given the legendary ability of the gambling industry to manage our attention when we enter a casino, it's interesting to note how extreme focus on a single objective led one of the world's biggest gaming companies into missing what may have been the biggest development in the history of the industry—the opening of gigantic Asian markets to global gaming companies.

To illustrate how the difference in focus generated enormously divergent outcomes, consider the strategic approaches taken by the leadership teams of Harrah's Entertainment (later renamed Caesar's Entertainment) and Las Vegas Sands. In 2005, Harrah's was one of the world's largest gaming companies and owned iconic Las Vegas properties such as Caesars Palace, Harrah's Las Vegas, the Rio, and Paris Las Vegas. At the same time, Las Vegas Sands owned the Venetian and had just opened a property in Macau, China. Former Harvard Business School professor Gary Loveman ran Harrah's; the hard-charging entrepreneur Sheldon Adelson ran Las Vegas Sands. Loveman focused on existing Harrahs customers; Adelson adopted a wider lens to look for future customers.

I wrote my doctoral dissertation on Harrah's Entertainment and their meticulous attention to customer service.[18] They knew how to differentiate treatment among the tens of millions of customers in their Total Rewards loyalty program. Loveman had studied the retail industry and developed a focused strategy: rather than spending lots of money attracting new customers with fancy spectacles and grandiose properties, he directed his organization's focus on extracting as much money as possible from its existing customers' wallets. They planned to gain loyalty by treating their best customers really well. Everyone from hotel reception clerks to casino cage employees and pit bosses learned to differentiate among customers based on their loyalty status. Loveman's focus worked well; the company's performance was so noteworthy that it drew the attention of private equity firms, which took the company private in 2007.

Meanwhile, Adelson pursued an entirely different strategy focused on increasing the number of customers. He didn't care about extracting as much as possible from existing customers' wallets. Instead, he sought to increase the number of people that went through his casinos. In pursuit of this strategy, Adelson focused on getting conventioneers into his properties, rather than retaining loyal—sometimes, hopelessly addicted—gamblers. Adelson also looked globally and was drawn to Asian markets as they opened up to foreign gaming companies. He bid for and won concessions to develop gaming properties in Macau and Singapore.

Roll the clock forward. Harrah's went through a Chapter 11 bankruptcy reorganization and was renamed Caesar's Entertainment. Yes, the bankruptcy was in large part driven by the crippling debt load the company acquired during its top-of-the-market leveraged buyout, but missing the enormous growth opportunities in Asia didn't help. And Sheldon Adelson became one of the richest men on the planet.

While there are lots of reasons why this transpired, one particularly powerful explanation comes from the different foci of the companies. While Caesar's intensely focused on growing its share of its customers' wallets, Las Vegas Sands tapped into millions of new wallets. In 2005, the largest gaming market in the world was Las Vegas. Today, Asian markets are many times the size of the Vegas market. Might the intense focus on existing customers that Loveman and the Caesars team adopted have blinded them to burgeoning Asian opportunities? Adelson's seemingly less focused approach enabled his team to identify a gigantic opportunity and seize it.

Blinded by Focus

While it's important to manage focus, we also need to understand that those upon whom we rely tend to operate within their own area of focus. As such, we need to be aware of the limitations of the advice and guidance they provide. And unfortunately, recent research shows that experts are less accurate predictors than nonexperts in their area of focus. Over the course of decades, social scientist Philip Tetlock asked experts to make predictions. He then went back and checked how they did. What he found is both counterintuitive and extremely insightful. Comparing expert success to that of well-informed and uninformed nonexperts, as well as to simple statistical models, Tetlock found that the experts did not do much better than the nonexperts, and everybody lost out to the simple models.[19]

The more in-demand the experts were, the more overconfident they became. Tetlock even found that amateur forecasters made better predictions and were less overconfident in their predictions than the ultra-focused professional experts. Yup, that's right. *Focus increases confidence while clouding judgment.* Perhaps Peter and Hull's explanation in *The Peter Principle* is correct: Might it be that many experts have reached their level of incompetence, so their advice is nonsensical or irrelevant?[20]

Examples compiled by Christopher Cerf and Victor Navasky in *The Experts Speak: The Definitive Compendium of Authoritative Misinformation* take the reader on a romp through expertise that is accompanied with unwarranted confidence.[21] *Business Week* reported on November 2, 1929, that the Wall Street crash wouldn't lead to a depression because the economy was "stronger than ever before."[22] Ken Olsen, president of Digital Equipment Corp, declared in 1977, "There is no reason for any individual to have a computer in their home."[23] Jeff Jacoby, musing in Boston's *Sunday Globe* about flawed predictions, recommends: "Really smart people are gearing up to tell you what to think. Hear them out, if you like, but remember: There's an excellent chance they'll be wrong."[24] Remember, Steve Ballmer, then CEO of Microsoft, laughed at the iPhone when it launched—"That is the most expensive phone in the world and it doesn't appeal to business customers because it doesn't have a keyboard!"[25]

Just as narrow focus can be costly, so too can shifting one's focus have significant upside. Indeed, the outsider view can often be better in the business world, as those outside the core management team may come with fresh ideas and ask questions about critical assumptions being made

by the insider team. In fact, a 2017 analysis of companies that have strategically repositioned found a common attribute of CEOs who oversaw
successful transformations: they had experience that appeared unrelated
to the business they were transforming.[26] The most transformational leaders held no prior experience in their industries, such as Jeff Bezos, who
reinvented retail but had come from finance.

In *The Outsiders*, William N. Thorndike Jr. profiles unconventional
CEOs, including Katharine Graham, whose path to becoming chairman
and CEO of The Washington Post Company was highly unusual.[27] When
she was forty-six, her husband died, and she unexpectedly took over his
role as CEO of The Washington Post Company in 1963. She was suddenly the only female chief executive of a *Fortune* 500 company. From
the time of the company's IPO in 1971 until she stepped down as chairman
in 1993, the compound annual return to shareholders was 22.3 percent,
compared to the S&P at 7.4 percent and her peers at 12.4 percent. She
outperformed the S&P by eighteenfold and her peers by over sixfold.
Upon entering her new position, she spent a few years settling into the
position, familiarizing herself with the business and her team. Four years
in, she made her first significant personnel decision.

Four years after that, in 1971, Graham chose to run the Pentagon
Papers even though the Nixon administration threatened to challenge the
company's broadcast licenses.[28] In 1972, the *Washington Post* began investigating Republican campaign improprieties with Graham's full support, ultimately leading to Nixon's resignation and the first of eighteen
Pulitzers for the *Post* under Graham's leadership.[29] She brought Warren
Buffett onto the board when he was an unknown quantity, she began
buying her own stock when no one else was thinking along those lines,
and she diversified the business via acquisitions in other industries.

In the early 1980s, McKinsey advised the company to halt its buyback
program; but Graham, with Buffett's help, came to her senses after two
years of following their advice and resumed the repurchase program.
When she stepped down in 1993, The Washington Post Company was
the most diversified among its newspaper peers, earning almost half its
revenues and profits from nonprint sources. And just as outsiders may

bring a different focus to a company and their strategies, so too can those who struggle with focus management perform at extremely high levels.

Some of what we ignore may be crucial to leaps in progress. Scientist Albert Einstein, Olympian Michael Phelps, entrepreneur Walt Disney, JetBlue founder David Neelmann, entertainer Whoopi Goldberg, business mogul Richard Branson, and former US president John F. Kennedy all were diagnosed as having focus disorders.[30] All of these prominent figures suffer(ed) from a deficit of attention management skills. Might their focus disorders have enabled breakthrough thinking that helped advance science, sports, the arts, business, and government? Just think of all the possibilities that are at risk of being extinguished by our love affair with deep focus.

If you've recently been on a casino floor, I'd encourage you to go by a roulette wheel. Decades ago, serious roulette players were handed paper cards to keep track of prior numbers to help them decide which numbers were more or less likely to come on the next spin of the wheel. Today, modern technology and data analytics have enabled very slick electronic displays that describe the percentage of black and red numbers that have recently come up, the hot numbers and the cold numbers, and so on. Surely the casino has the interests of the gamblers at heart when they conduct all this detailed analysis for them, correct? Actually . . . not quite.

You see, it turns out that every number has the exact same probability of hitting with each spin of the roulette wheel (assuming, of course, that the wheel is fair and hasn't been tampered with to produce a higher probability of certain outcomes). All of the data provided by the casino is . . . well . . . completely irrelevant. But by presenting it, gamblers are made to feel the endeavor of betting has an analytic component to it rather than being merely a game of chance. And so many a gambler will wait for the presented percentages to tip in their favor before betting. Yet while the data presented is historically accurate, the probability of all future roles is identical . . . making it a game of pure luck. Why focus on distributions that don't matter? By outsourcing their focus to the casino's technology, gamblers are led to bet when they might not otherwise have done so, thereby supporting the construction of bigger, grander, and more inviting casinos (complete with more modern focus management technology to channel your focus).

. . .

Managing focus is not easy. Our attention is limited, selective, and a basic part of our cognitive systems.[31] But focus also blinds, raising the stakes of how we manage our attention and necessitating the need for each of us to understand the limits of our knowledge and perception. Too much focus and you suffer from tunnel vision and ignore a great deal, some of which may have been useful. Too little and you become a scatterbrained generalist, a jack-of-all-trades and master of none. The key is to actively and intentionally manage our focus in a manner appropriate for our own objectives.

We need to be cognizant of our own focus but also the focus of those upon whom we have chosen to outsource our thinking. And when it comes to the omnipresent technology in our lives, we must open our eyes and take notice of the subtle, hidden, and influential management of our focus by algorithms and artificial intelligence. We are prone to enter focus bubbles in ways that might not have been possible without technology. When we outsource, we give up the framing of key decisions.

Just think about how historical in-person shopping experiences for books differs from today's more common online experience. Sure, online searching is much easier than shuffling through bookshelves. In fact, algorithms will even feed you suggestions of other books that you may find interesting. Fabulous, right? Showing you what you'd likely want to buy. . . . Another way to think about it is that sifting through bookshelves may lead you to find books on different topics, enabling fortuitous discoveries that enable differentiated thinking. The online algorithm focuses on your immediately revealed preference as indicated by your searches. Neither is necessarily better, but if we're unaware of the costs that accompany the benefits of online search, we're prone to miss possibilities.

Likewise, I am a big proponent of reading physical periodicals. Why's that? Because the use of online news alerts and information portals actively manage our focus. They channel our attention toward topics we've expressed an interest in via our clicking, just like the use of online book shopping manages our focus via recommendations of books purchased by others like us. By flipping through a newspaper or magazine, we are forced to skim headlines. The result is exposure to a broad range of topics and news on potential areas of interest that didn't make it through the technological focus filters. Actively choosing to consume information from non-filtered sources also has another big benefit: it generates exposure to a diversity of opinions and views, allowing us to at least partially depart from the echo chamber of consuming news that agrees with our own views.[32]

Later in the book we'll revisit the topic of focus management; but for now, let's turn to see how a narrow focus and siloed thinking process can lead to the very outcomes we seek to avoid.

CHAPTER 4

Unintended Blowback

Thinking in terms of systems rather than parts is useful when considering focus. A system is a connected collection of parts that interact, complete with feedback loops that send ripples across a network. As a result, doing something in one area of the system has the potential to generate dynamics in another. And while many describe these impacts as unintended consequences, systems thinkers see it differently, recognizing and expecting consequences in other areas. To systems thinkers, these are just consequences.

For example, how most people think about seat belts and safety is a great systems example. Conventional, nonsystems thinking suggests that when everyone wears a seat belt, the bodily harm suffered by those in auto accidents will be lessened. Wearing seat belts is an absolute positive, a good thing to do. But a systems thinker doesn't see the world the same way, rather thinking about the potential impact of wearing a seat belt. Might it be possible that wearing a seat belt makes you feel safer, so you are therefore more aggressive (and therefore riskier) in your driving? Could removing seat belts from cars make drivers safer? Systems thinking opens the door to understanding how interactions among parts changes our analysis of the whole, often leading to counterintuitive and surprising insights.

Getting What You Don't Want

In *Foolproof*, Greg Ip shows how focus can exacerbate and magnify un-intended consequences.[1] He argues that the success of our safety mechanisms, from financial stabilizers to levees, lets problems build up, makes us overconfident, and can lead to even greater disasters later. For instance, preventing small forest fires leads to a buildup of underbrush that eventually causes massive fires. Might it be that the massive wildfires that have recently been raging were due to our fire-prevention efforts of prior years? Or might the *Titanic*'s crew have sailed at top speed through ice-infested waters precisely because they felt the ship was unsinkable? Deepwater Horizon had one of the best safety records in BP's fleet of drilling rigs . . . might that have made its management team overconfident?

In finance, could long periods of calm lead banks to take on more risk? In fact, economist Hyman Minsky developed what he called the financial instability hypothesis, an argument that periods of stability generate instability, as it incentivizes actors to take on greater and greater risk as they remain oblivious to mounting vulnerabilities.[2]

When there are more safety measures, people engage in riskier behavior, because they divert their attention away from what is being protected against. On icy roads, studded tires do not reduce accidents as much as expected, because people drive more cautiously when they don't have them and more recklessly when they do. Hines Ward, a former Superbowl MVP who spent his entire career with the Pittsburgh Steelers, suggested football players would be safer if they didn't wear helmets, for similar reasons. "If you want to prevent concussions, take the helmet off: Play old-school football with the leather helmets, no facemask," Ward said on NBC Sports.[3]

Just think of the faith you place in yourself to multitask while driving. Ever talk on the phone while driving? Fifteen states have deemed this activity risky and now mandate that drivers either use a headset or speaker system so that they can keep their hands on the wheel at all times.[4] The federal government provided $17.5 million in grants during fiscal year 2013 for states with primary enforcement laws against distracted driving. But these policies miss the point.

The lesson of the invisible gorilla is that our *cognitive bandwidth* is fixed. By deploying attention toward one activity that requires focus, we become less effective at noticing unexpected developments, let alone processing them—even when they're directly in front of our faces. The hands-free calling mandate makes sense to the extent that we have physical limitations and cannot drive a car safely with one hand holding a phone.

But because it is our attention that's scarce, hands-free policies don't actually address the problem. In fact, by suggesting that hands-free calling while driving is safe, policies may be encouraging individuals to talk while barreling along a highway in a six-thousand-pound vehicle moving at seventy-five miles per hour. The unintended consequence of these safety policies might be roads that are less safe. In this case, the hands-free driving policy is focused on the wrong culprit. The culprit is cognitive multitasking, not motor multitasking. Interestingly, the United Kingdom tries to focus on the cognitive overload and has granted police the power to stop drivers if they believe that they are distracted by their hands-free mobile phones.[5]

Taking to heart the insight that people should not cognitively multitask while driving vehicles (and the logic of systems thinking), one city in the Netherlands adopted the policy that "unsafe is safe."[6] To force people to zoom out, Drachten removed all road signs, only leaving in place simple, easy-to-follow rules. Drachten also has zero traffic lights.[7] As a result, drivers pay attention when they drive, rather than mindlessly following signs. In response to the change, road safety *improved*; Drachten saw accidents at one intersection fall from thirty-six in a four-year period to two accidents in the two years after the lights were removed.[8] Drachten's result may seem surprising, but it shouldn't be if you think about the role of focus via a systems-oriented perspective.

In fact, some have hypothesized that we humans have a set tolerance for risk, something the late Gerald Wilde, formerly a professor of psychology at Queen's university, termed *risk homeostasis*.[9] What this practically means is that any reduction in perceived risk for an activity will result in humans pushing the envelope a bit further. Seat belts? Drive faster. Helmets? Hit harder.

Focus on Fat, Cholesterol . . . Lipitor?

Devotion to focus and specialization creates a perfect storm when it combines with the maximization logic we explored earlier. In medicine, an emphasis on optimization is focused on an easily measured metric— age. Everyone seems to want to live forever, and that's driving the ever- increasing emphasis to screen for potential problems and to nip them in the bud earlier. Indeed, dedication to screening, a manifestation of the optimization logic, is driving what many agree has become an epidemic of overdiagnosis.

This dynamic is encouraged by a professional ethos among doctors that prizes specialization. As H. Gilbert Welch and colleagues write, "Because these doctors care greatly about the conditions they specialize in, I be- lieve they sometimes lose a broader perspective. Their focus is to do everything they can to avoid the bad events associated with the condi- tion; their main concern is not missing anyone who could possibly ben- efit from diagnosis and treatment. So they tend to set cutoffs that are expansive, leading many to be labeled abnormal."[10]

On top of that, putting faith in increasingly sophisticated technolo- gies also compounds focus, further exacerbating the problem of overdi- agnosis: "Our diagnostic technologies are of such high resolution that we are discovering more ambiguous and surprise abnormalities. Both can lead to a cycle of more follow-up testing—including more scanning— revealing even more ambiguous and surprise findings."[11] But discover- ing more and more fine-grained abnormalities does not necessarily lead to better outcomes; what it does lead to is higher costs, false positives, and potentially unnecessary treatments.[12]

If you're like most Americans, you probably head to your doctor for a check-up every year . . . and he or she most likely checks your cholesterol levels. If your doctor has told you that your cholesterol levels (or more specifically your bad cholesterol levels) are higher than ideal, you're not alone. The US Centers for Disease Control estimates that 73.5 million Americans have been diagnosed with high cholesterol.

Perhaps your doctor suggested that a cholesterol-reducing drug like Lipitor might be useful. If you took Lipitor, you're again not alone. Between 1996 and 2012 (when it went off patent), Lipitor became the world's best-selling drug of all time and generated more than $125 billion in sales. It's an astronomical number! It also reflects the drug's widespread effectiveness in lowering cholesterol; after all, doctors wrote prescriptions for 29 million patients (a population greater than Australia!) and wouldn't have done so if it didn't work, would they?

Well . . . it depends on what you mean by *work*. Here are two key facts: First, *Lipitor works for lowering cholesterol.* Yup, that's right, it gets the job done. In fact, it's not just Lipitor but the whole class of statins that work by blocking an enzyme produced by the liver that plays a key role in generating cholesterol. Second, *Lipitor doesn't actually prevent heart attacks.* If you're reading closely, you'll likely want to stop and reread my last sentence. It's not a typo. Statins in general *do **not** prevent heart attacks. In fact, research suggests you'd have to treat 50 people with statins to prevent one heart attack, and that you'd have to treat 890 people to prevent one death. As noted by Dr. Mark Hyman, "it's just not a very effective drug."[13]

But wait! You'd be correct in noting the seeming contradiction between my first fact—that statins lower cholesterol—and my second fact—that they don't generally prevent heart attacks. Both statements are true. But it's a question of focus. What if I told you that heart doctors are so focused on lowering cholesterol that they rarely consider the side effects of doing so? (Every drug has side effects; remember that Viagra was originally supposed to help lower blood pressure!) The side effects usually associated with statins include liver injury, memory loss, diabetes, and muscle damage. And again, if you felt some of these side effects while taking the drug, you wouldn't be alone. More than 17 percent of patients reported some side effects!

Lest you think this is merely legal mumbo jumbo, simply a laundry list of potential adverse consequences to protect the drug companies, which would rarely actually impact patients, you should know that the FDA recently demanded that labels on statins acknowledge the medication increases the risk of developing diabetes.

So let's get this straight: You go to the doctor for a routine examine. You learn your cholesterol is higher than what is deemed a healthy range. Your doctor recommends you begin taking cholesterol-reducing drugs, noting that millions of patients have had success by doing so. She then tells you she's taking Lipitor herself and that every cardiologist she knows also takes the medication.

"It's safe," she notes as she hands you a script. You leave thankful that modern medicine has a solution to help with your condition.

You begin taking the statin and voilà! Your cholesterol drops. God bless modern medicine! But then you get your blood sugar levels tested. Uh-oh . . . they're very high. Your doctor says you have type 2 diabetes . . . and with it comes an elevated risk of . . . drumroll please . . . heart attacks. It was not until 2015 that the connection between statins and diabetes was openly discussed. In fact, a March 2015 story on National Public Radio explicitly asked if cholesterol-reducing drugs merely trade heart disease for diabetes.[14]

Most doctors genuinely believe that lower cholesterol levels are healthier than higher cholesterol levels. And again, that's true, if all else is equal. The research often cited is the Framingham Heart Study that began in 1948 and has tracked the health of more than five thousand residents in the Boston suburb.[15] Sixteen years into the study, researchers noted a correlation between heart disease and cholesterol levels. What they found was that the average cholesterol level of patients with heart disease was 11 percent higher than healthy patients. But heart disease struck some people with very low cholesterol levels and didn't afflict some with very high cholesterol levels. These facts were dismissed as anomalous at the individual level; the real insight came from the population-level analysis— or so we were told. "Avoid consuming fat and cholesterol and you'll live longer," emerged as the mantra of the day.

The food industry then rapidly developed low- or no-fat options that were cholesterol free, in what some have called the Snackwell's phenomena.[16] Fat and cholesterol were removed from foods to create heart-healthy options, butter was replaced by cholesterol-free margarine, and so on. What didn't get much notice, however, was that processed carbohydrates and sugars replaced these fats . . . and in the long run, these tended to be more important drivers of heart disease than cholesterol! Oh, and let's not forget that years later we found that margarine's trans fats weren't exactly great for your health either.

In 1996, the situation was perfectly primed for a pharmaceutical answer to the question of how to lower one's cholesterol: enter Lipitor. Food was too confusing for most Americans to understand, but a pill? It's like the big red buttons now sold at most Staples office supply stores that state "That was easy!" when pushed. Take this pill, eat what you want, and your cholesterol will drop. Patients (and doctors) signed up in droves. And it worked. Cholesterol levels fell.

But more Americans today suffer from heart disease than ever before. Jonny Bowden and Stephen Sinatra, authors of national bestseller *The Great Cholesterol Myth*, explicitly state that "the standard prescription of low-fat diets and statin drugs are contributing to a health crisis of monumental proportions."[17] What?!?! How can that be? Well, my first fact was that statins works at reducing cholesterol . . . but my second fact was that it doesn't prevent heart attacks. Let's investigate this second fact.

As luck would have it, the side effects are far more substantial than originally recognized. At this stage, I could get into the marginal propensities to develop heart disease and diabetes based on a Bayesian analysis of family histories, existing a priori medical conditions, and multivariate regression analysis accounting for lifestyle as best I could, but rest assured I won't. Let's just say that if you are narrowly focused on the heart, rather than the general condition of the body, then you claim success when cholesterol levels drop.

But if we think of a human body as a system that includes other organs (such as the liver and the pancreas) and substances other than cholesterol (like insulin), then we need to take a wider lens. The liver is the body's detoxification engine, so might it face additional pressure when facing a foreign substance like a statin? In fact, it appears that rising liver enzyme levels (a measure of stress on the liver) is a side effect of taking statins. The focus on cholesterol is misguided, even if well-intentioned. Yes, lower cholesterol—all else being equal—lowers your risk of a heart attack. But statins are a far cry from the "all else being equal," as they tend to affect your liver, increase your risk of diabetes, and possibly have an impact on muscles and nerves. All else is definitively *not* equal. And shouldn't we be treating the whole body, not just the heart? Isn't the human body a big, interconnected system?

If we look at how statins work, we find they target the HMG-CoA reductase enzyme. (Ha! I said I wouldn't drown you in statistics but I never agreed to not use obscure medical jargon! I'll make that promise from here forward.) This enzyme controls cholesterol manufacturing in the body; the drugs target it. But insulin (the hormone that helps the body convert blood sugar into energy) also controls that enzyme. In some patients, insulin levels then compete with the drug—placing additional pressure on the pancreas and increasing the likelihood of insulin resistance. What this means is that it might be easier to control one's cholesterol level by controlling one's blood sugar level. But wait, the food industry just did the opposite! It removed cholesterol and fat and added sugar! Oops.

Despite the booming market for cholesterol-lowering drugs, our heart disease burden is as large as ever. According to the CDC, more than 600,000 Americans die each year (approximately 25 percent of all deaths) from heart disease, and it's the leading cause of death for both men and women in the United States.[18]

I'm sure these facts will enrage some patients taking cholesterol-lowering statins. In fact, speaking of rage, that seems to be a side effect in at least a few cases. Here's a quote from a 2011 *Slate* article:

> Patient 1 wanted to kill someone. Normally even-tempered, the 63-year-old man found himself awaking with uncontrollable anger and the desire to smash things. His violent impulses

started after he began taking the cholesterol-lowering statin Lipitor and they vanished within two days of quitting the drug. Patient 2 developed a short fuse after he started on Zocor, another popular statin. The 59-year-old felt an impulse to kill his wife and once tried, unsuccessfully, to do so. His violent tendencies subsided within a few weeks of stopping Zocor. Patient 3, a 46-year-old female, became unusually irritable while taking Lipitor, repeatedly blowing up at her husband for no reason. Like the others, her uncharacteristic behavior disappeared after she quit taking statins.[19]

Before readers run home to see if their spouses are covertly taking Lipitor or prepping a Lipitor-induced insanity defense for plotting to kill them, let's think about the fundamental disconnect that our struggle with heart health exposes. The human body is a delicately balanced system of interconnected parts, and while it's useful to have specialists that understand the individual elements extremely well, it's also critical that someone looks at the whole.

So let's reevaluate the problem of focusing too much on cholesterol. Most of us are relying on experts (doctors) who in turn depend upon data (such as cholesterol levels) that emerge from technologies (lab tests and their algorithms for preliminary interpretation) and are understood according to certain rules (i.e., threshold concern levels) that have been determined by the medical systems in which they operate.

Might it be that by our focus on diagnosis and prevention of heart disease is a contributing factor in the very rise of the disease that our efforts sought to prevent? Might a systems-oriented, feedback-focused thinker approach the problem differently? Does our reductionist approach miss critical connections that impact the whole?

PTSD from . . . a Diagnosis?

I had the pleasure of speaking with Trisha Torrey, a woman who developed post-traumatic stress disorder (PTSD) from a misdiagnosis, some years ago.[20] Trisha's story continues to haunt me to this day, and it should frighten everyone and anyone who's ever interacted with the modern healthcare system. Here's what happened. At the time, Trisha was a fifty-two-year-old self-employed marketing consultant who discovered a golf-ball sized lump on her torso. "It didn't hurt—it was just there," she noted. But as anyone in her shoes would likely do, she contacted her family doctor and went to see him. Unable to identify the lump, he sent Trisha to a surgeon that afternoon, who immediately removed it and sent it out for further evaluation. He promised to get back in touch as soon as he heard from the lab. After about a week of anxiety-filled waiting, Trisha called the surgeon's office to check on the status of her biopsy. The Independence Day holiday, she was told, had delayed processing. Another week went by before she received a devastating phone call.[21]

"When the surgeon finally called me with my lab results, he told me that I had a very rare cancer called subcutaneous panniculitis-like T-cell lymphona known as SPTCL," she told me. Worse, Trisha noted that the surgeon went on to describe that the lab results took so long because they felt the need to reconfirm the results with a second lab. Both labs had confirmed the diagnosis, and the surgeon told her he'd set up an oncology appointment for her as soon as possible.

According to Trisha, "as soon as possible" ended up being more than two emotional, fear-filled weeks. She did what anyone in such a position would likely do—she turned on the computer and began reading everything she could find about SPTCL. But in 2004, there wasn't much information about it online because it was such a very rare condition.

"What I did learn was that everyone died. And died fast. . . . I was scared to death," Trisha told me.

The oncologist was discouraging and condescending, rubbing Trisha the wrong way from the very beginning. He sent her for additional blood work and a CT scan, both of which failed to identify anything unusual. Neither test showed any signs of any form of lymphoma. Further, Trisha had no symptoms other than night sweats and hot flashes . . . but as she herself commented, "But hey! I was a fifty-two-year-old woman! Don't we all?"[22] The oncologist dismissed the menopause reference and insisted

her symptoms were being caused by lymphoma. He strongly advised chemotherapy, and quickly. As Trisha said, the doctor told her she'd be dead
within five months if she didn't.

When questioning if the lab results may have been wrong, she was
told that since there were two independent labs that confirmed the results, there was no chance the diagnosis was inaccurate. Devastated,
Trisha told few people besides her family and a very few close friends.
Her business began to suffer, because as she noted, "I was self-employed
and had lousy health insurance, which meant that my diagnosis had now
become expensive, too. . . . Life, what was left of it, was going down the
tubes, fast."

So she decided to reengage her doctors. When she called the oncologist's office, she learned the doctor who had been treating her was out on
sick leave and that another doctor in the office had taken over her case.
When Trisha finally spoke with the newly assigned doctor, he immediately inquired why she hadn't already begun chemotherapy. She told him
she was trying to get a second opinion from another oncologist. His response to Trisha smacked of expert arrogance: "What you have is so rare,
no one will know any more about it than I do!"[23] The statement threw
Trisha for a loop. It awoke her from her previous slumber of mindless obedience and blind outsourcing of her thinking. She decided to dig deeper.

After a few too many drinks with friends later that week, she shared
her diagnosis, and they were floored. One friend felt compelled to call
an oncologist she knew who happened to be treating someone with
SPTCL. He offered to see Trisha if she wanted to make an appointment.

Immediately after scheduling an appointment with the new doctor,
Trisha called her existing doctors and asked for a copy of her medical
records. When she got the records, she did what few of us would likely
do. Rather than merely deliver the sealed envelope to the new doctor,
Trisha started flipping through her file and searched online for every word
and concept she didn't understand. She felt compelled to learn more and
actually read her medical file.[24]

What she found bothered her. The lab results indicated the data was
"most suspicious for" and "most consistent with" SPTCL, but neither of

them was definitive. Further, the second lab report noted that it had sent the biopsy to yet another lab to test for something called "clonality," a condition describing if the cells were multiplying. Trisha immediately called the first oncologist's office and asked for those results. Unable to find them in the original file, they scrambled to find them. When they did, the report said the cells were not multiplying, a finding that basically meant the lump was not cancerous.

Trisha walked into the second oncologist's office empowered. Although still dependent, she was able to claw back control and think for herself. This new doctor sent the sample to some doctors at the National Institutes of Health to confirm (or reject) Trisha's belief that she had been misdiagnosed. Three weeks later, the diagnosis that returned was for inflammation of fat cells—a minor issue that hasn't bothered Trisha since.[25]

While Trisha was no doubt relieved at this new finding, she was also furious. She accused her first oncologists of insisting on chemotherapy so that they could make more money from her, an accusation that she sticks by years later. "I also fault them for never following up on the clonality tests which were so pivotal to getting the right diagnosis."

Since then, Trisha continues to be affected by the experience. She suffers post-traumatic stress symptoms and finds herself uncontrollably crying when she reads, watches, or hears about a person dying from cancer. "After all," she noted, "had I undergone chemo, and survived, they would have told me that I had been cured of a disease I never had. And just as frightening, I found cases of people who had been diagnosed and treated for SPTCL who had died during the chemotherapy—and autopsies had shown they never had SPTCL."[26]

Trisha is a spiritual woman and believes that everything happens for a reason, so she gave up her marketing consultancy and has dedicated her life to patient advocacy and spurring a movement to empower patients. "I'm doing my best to turn those misdiagnosis lemons into empowerment lemonade." As part of this effort, Trisha has gone on to write several books and has helped lots of patients to retake control of their medical relationships.

Superfood Frenzy

It's not just the avoidance of harmful substances like cholesterol from one's diet that is so alluring to those struggling with health. It's equally compelling to add in helpful foods! But it's also the reason we are willing to follow the latest food fad and consume ungodly volumes of kale, blueberries, or other so-called superfoods in a quest for better health. It's all a symptom of excessive focus, of our never-ending quest to find a magic bullet.

In fact, since the 1990 publication of the bestselling book *Superfoods* by Michael van Straten and Barbara Griggs,[27] there has been an explosion of interest in these supposed miracle foods. Amazon returns almost three thousand titles if you search *superfoods*, including everything from cookbooks to diet manuals. Headlines like, "Superfoods You Need Now" are common.[28] There are also lists of lesser known, yet to be identified superfoods. Or suggestions that "stress eating helps, when they're these superfoods."[29]

Superfood companies try to evoke feelings of longevity, and many of these miracle foods are rediscovered from ancient cultures, adding an extra layer of mystery and intrigue to their already seductive stories. Quinoa and its close cousin amaranth were first domesticated, cultivated, and consumed by the Incas.[30] Cacao is similarly associated with the Aztecs and Mayans.[31] This is not to suggest they are not healthy . . . they may be. I'm merely suggesting there is a heavy marketing component to their stories.

These companies get you so focused on the particular health benefits of their specific products that you fail to think about anything else. They also start stretching claims—Marion Nestle, who retired in 2017 as professor of nutrition, food studies, and public health at New York University, described how producers of fruits and vegetables pay for research they can use to market their products as superfoods. For instance, the Pear Bureau Northwest has paid for research and issued press releases about results such as "New Research Indicates Regular Fresh Pear Consumption May Improve Blood Pressure in Middle-Aged Men and Women with Metabolic Syndrome." If pears are superfoods, Nestle concludes, then "*all* fruits are superfoods. Eat the ones you like."[32]

Birthdays are a natural time to reflect on life and make changes. Consider the actions of Jo Abi, an Australian woman who decided to radically experiment with her diet after turning thirty-nine. She decided to eat a diet of only superfoods for three weeks straight. After all, she had heard about the amazing qualities of these foods to improve our health. So she eagerly began her diet. She explicitly articulated what she thought would then occur: "I expected my clothes to feel looser, my skin to glow and a serene smile to be on my face at all times. I expected clear and shiny eyes, rosy cheeks and thicker hair and nails."[33]

Here's what happened. Although Jo at first found the vegetables, nuts, beans, and berries quite appealing, she was soon overcome with massive discomfort. She notes that she spent the entire three weeks in a state of mild nausea and felt the need to always be near a toilet. Initially, Jo dismissed the toilet-dashing behavior as symptoms of her need to detoxify her system, but she soon gave up. "By the end of the third week," she noted, she "was waving the white flag of surrender along with a roll of extra-soft toilet paper." Summarizing her experience in three words, she bluntly called it "butt on fire."[34]

Might Jo's not-so-super experience have been driven by an unwarranted focus on superfoods? I doubt she's alone. The feedback from focus can foil even the best intentions. Consider blueberries, the miracle fruit that tops most superfood lists. They're full of vitamins, soluble fiber, phytochemicals, and antioxidants, they seem to fulfill every dietary hope we have for a food. What's not to love?

It turns out eating too many blueberries has the potential to throw off the balance in your body between antioxidants and pro-oxidants. Professor David C. Poole has found that too many antioxidants may impair muscle function and increase tiredness during exercise.[35] And if that's not enough to have you put down your blueberries, what if you learned that some believe that antioxidants do not prevent cancer and (gasp!) may even cause it?

It's not some scientific quack suggesting it. Nobel Laureate James Watson, of DNA double-helix fame, has suggested that the cure for many cancers may elude us as we use blueberries and broccoli to vacuum up the extra oxygen molecules (known as free radicals) floating in our system. Free radicals targeted by antioxidants, he believes, may hold the key to understanding cancer.[36] WHAT?! Could it be that our efforts to eat away the risk of cancer by gorging on vast quantities of antioxidant-rich foods is actually increasing our risk of cancer?

Not All Superfoods Are Super for All

Consider kale, that leafy green vegetable that established and aspiring celebrities alike swear by.[37] Kale began showing up on lots of menus. Surely, there's something to it, right? Well, turns out it may adversely affect your thyroid function. Oh, it also has the potential to cause kidney stones as it contains oxalate, a substance that binds to calcium.[38] Granted, these are risks that likely only affect a small percentage of the population, but that's precisely the point.

Chia seeds seem uncontroversial though, right? Not so quick. Turns out that they can interfere with the absorption of needed minerals and hurt your digestive system.[39] Goji berries? Nope. They are rich in a compound (dietary saponins) that can increase intestinal permeability in something known as "leaky gut" syndrome. And you'd have to drink thirteen servings of goji berry juice to get as many antioxidants as one red apple.[40]

Writing in *Vogue*, Petronella Ravenshear expressed her discomfort with superfood mania in an article titled "Lifting the Lid on Superfoods." After describing the hype and marketing around everything from chia and goji berries to acai and agave, she suggests we put this "timeless" marketing logic in context: "Do we need to eat little-known berries from far-flung places or the foods of ancient civilizations to stay well? Superfoods notwithstanding, their lives were short and brutal; the average Aztec lived for 37 years."[41]

This is not to suggest there is not some merit in eating these so-called superfoods. I'm merely suggesting that a plan to achieve immortality by consuming twice a day acai-kale-quinoa smoothies with a drizzling of pureed organic, gluten-free blueberries and free-range, fair trade agave may be worth reconsidering. There may be more myth than magic in these superfoods.

One of the main reasons that these supposed magic bullets are so problematic is that our focus on them blinds us to other potentially important factors. We focus so intensely on antioxidants that we fail to consider the pro-oxidants or the possibilities that free radicals could be useful. Superfoods pique our imagination while stealing our common sense. We become blind to alternatives. And worse, we let these supposedly good things box out other things. Recall the goji berry–apple comparison. Thirteen servings versus one apple!

Adding these superhero foods to our diet can create complications and generate the very opposite consequence from that which we seek, as seen with Jo's experience. But the problem is not merely about superheroes that aren't really superheroes. We can also be blinded by an unthinking focus on villains that aren't really villains.

Consider the Gluten

One villain that seems to have captured a lot of consumer attention is gluten. Gluten-free products compete with *non-GMO, local,* and *organic items* for mindshare among today's health-conscious, price-insensitive, and trend-following foodies, yuppies, and self-anointed amateur nutritionists. It's become so fashionable that even Fido and Spot have jumped on the bandwagon, driving sales of gluten-free pet foods to new records. Like all sweeping trends, it has a powerful attractive force that lures innocent bystanders into asking if they too should join the party. The *New Yorker* even ran an article entitled "Against the Grain: Should You Go Gluten Free?"[42] to help readers answer that very question. *Grain Brain* and *Wheat Belly* held strong multiweek positions on bestseller lists.[43]

Like financial bubbles, the herd behavior identified by such popular attention is never sustainable. Here's the big disconnect that captures the essence of the problem: about 1 percent of the population has celiac disease, less than 10 percent are gluten intolerant, and . . . drumroll please . . . almost 30 percent of American adults are trying to avoid gluten.[44] One of the main reasons consumers want to avoid gluten is because it's supposedly healthier to be gluten-free. It's generally not.

The blunt reality is that many gluten-free foods are not healthier for the 90+ percent of the population that doesn't have celiac disease or gluten sensitivity. It's worth noting, for instance, that a Glutino Original New York Style Bagel has 26 percent more calories, 250 percent more fat, 43 percent more sodium, 50 percent less fiber, and double the sugar than a Thomas' Plain Bagel—for a price that (at this writing) is 74 percent higher![45] Further, because many gluten-free products utilize rice flour, they are also at risk of containing higher levels of arsenic than desirable or healthy.[46] Other gluten-free items use corn, sorghum, millet, or amaranth flour—none of which is objectively better than wheat.

Despite these facts, the gluten-free craze gained momentum. Market research firm Nielsen estimated that sales of products with a gluten-free label had risen to over $25 billion by 2016 with more than 10 percent of all new launches claiming gluten-free status.[47] While the trend is impressive, it's largely driven by marketing efforts. Many brands, for instance, added gluten-free labels onto products that never contained gluten. Add a label, grow your sales! Reminds me of internet mania when merely announcing a URL increased valuations overnight. Another sign the gluten-free bubble is nearing its end is the popular backlash against "casual" (versus those with celiac disease) gluten-free diners.

None of this is to suggest that there isn't a real underlying need for gluten-free products. There is, and I know from personal experience. In October 2011, my doctor informed me that a blood test indicated I had heightened sensitivity to gluten. The sensitivity was so high he recommended a gluten-free diet. I protested, suggesting he was overdiagnosing my unhealthy diet.

I asked: "Have you considered *ice-cream-itis*? That's a disease I know I have," admitting my addiction to the heavenly creamy frozen sugar to which I was devoted. I insisted he conduct a genetic test to determine if I had a genetic marker for celiac disease. When the results came back, I was saddened to learn that I indeed had the gene.

I've been gluten-free since 2011, and I genuinely do feel better. I've lost weight, have gained energy, and at least in my own eyes, look younger. My wife doesn't seem to notice, and my kids say that I look older, and come to think of it, I'm also more tired . . . but this is my book and I'm writing my history. So there you have it. Whether you have celiac disease, are gluten intolerant, or just part of the fashionable trend-following crowd, rest assured that this chapter is certified gluten-free! I can't comment on the rest of the book, as it was produced in a facility that also processes wheat.

The two main reasons that our focus on the gluten villain is so harmful are that gluten is not really a villain for all and that by evicting gluten from our diet, we've created a vacuum that sugar, salt, and fat have jumped in to fill—of course aided by packaged foods companies eager to make cookies, crackers, and other gluten-free products taste ever so slightly less cardboard-like. Our focus on gluten blinds us to the additional calories, fat, and sugar. Go gluten-free to lose weight . . . and uh-oh, you're heavier!

It's hard to blame consumers for reacting this way. Even if they do have a good sense of what they should eat in the abstract, it is difficult to practice this, given the overwhelming number of options to choose from and the constraints of time and money. Few of us can comfortably make the time every day to browse, select, buy, chop, season, and roast fresh vegetables. Where should we turn for less perishable and more affordable options? Pasta lasts and is cheap, but is surely not as healthy (especially when combined with the sugary sauce that is marketed to most of us). What about bean-based pasta and low-sugar sauce? Healthier, but six times the price!

Sometimes it feels like the future really may lie with Soylent: complete nutrition in a bottle of bland, milky formula. Nothing to choose and a supposedly perfect solution containing all the nutrients we need. Think of it as baby formula for adults. As it is perfected, perhaps someday Soylent will allow us to remove the variable of choice in some of our meals. Until then, though, we need to reach a better understanding of how to make good choices on a daily basis.

The evidence at this point is overwhelming. By focusing on calories, fat, cholesterol, gluten, antioxidants, kale, and a host of other missing needles has distracted us away from taking a holistic approach to health. We're so busy digging through a haystack searching that we're not asking if we're even in the right barn. We ate less fat, but got fatter. We consumed more cancer-fighting antioxidants, but cancer rates rose.

Louise Foxcroft's *Calories and Corsets* concludes an exhaustive survey of two thousand years of diet advice by calling for a return to the Greek concept of *diata*, from which the word "diet" originates. The concept "described a whole way of life rather than . . . a narrow weight loss regimen. It provided an all-round physical and mental way to health."[48] Is it possible we're so focused on food that we're missing the point? Might we benefit from unfocusing a bit and seeing a wider perspective?

A *New York Times Magazine* story provocatively called "The Island Where People Forget to Die" highlighted how blinding focus plagues American thinking on diet and health. It noted that Americans tend to "focus on exercise and what we put in our mouths," while for those living on the Greek island of Ikaria, "diet only partly explained higher life expectancy" and exercise "played a small role at best."[49] Indeed, it turns out social structures may matter as much if not more than these two variables. In fact, it may be the interaction of the components that leads the system toward the much pursued goal of widespread longevity. We'll return to this later in the book.

. . .

The logic of systems thinking helps us understand feedback loops that a narrow focus can miss. By focusing intensely in one domain, we often fail to see how our actions may create the very problem we are seeking to avoid. We need to step back, zoom out, and look at the whole system rather than just its parts. The sad reality is that many of our supposed solutions are compounding our problems. Consider the current mechanism for treating those struggling with type 2 diabetes. Because these patients suffer from high blood sugar, they are often prescribed insulin to lower it. But they have high blood sugar *while they have high insulin levels*, a condition resulting from insulin resistance.

Dr. Jason Fung has suggested that insulin prescriptions are likely increasing resistance. He notes: "As it turns out, insulin causes insulin resistance. The body responds to excessively high levels of any substance by developing resistance to it." He goes on, highlighting the unintended consequences of the current approach: "We were prescribing insulin to treat it, when excessive insulin was the problem in the first place. . . . As patients took insulin, they gained weight, and when they did, their type 2 got worse, demanding more insulin. And the cycle repeated."[50] A classic vicious cycle.

Or think about how social media, designed to connect us to friends and family members, has compounded the previously discussed fear of missing out. Given the propensity of people to disproportionately post positive images, social media encourages feelings that one's reality is worse than the world experienced by everyone else. The result is that social media now often leads to loneliness, despair, and depression—the very opposite of bringing users together.

A systems approach and an appreciation of the feedback loops that accompany our choices can be helpful. Systems thinking quite powerfully shows the value of stepping back, zooming out, and looking at the big picture. Connections matter, and while most advice we are given is accurate "with all else equal," rarely is "all else equal." In fact, our decisions almost always assure that all else is not equal, so we need to regularly consider the feedback resulting from our actions. And because deep experts and narrow specialists are unable to see the big picture, the task of doing so necessarily falls to us.

CHAPTER 5

Learned Dependence and Blind Obedience

The blunt reality of life in the twenty-first century is that we simply can't keep up with all the information. Dependence on those who know more is a fact of life, but this does not mean we have to blindly follow experts, technologies, or rules. In rethinking what it means to be self-reliant in the twenty-first century, we must learn to work with those who know more about various matters than we do without being blindly obedient or mindlessly submissive.

Motor Maintenance

Every nine months or so, I take my car to the dealership for the car company's regular search for things they can charge me for (also known as its regularly scheduled maintenance). You see, the warranty is only valid if you maintain the car according to the manufacturer's strict maintenance rules. So every ten thousand miles or so, the car goes into the dealership and voilà, a collection of other must-fixes emerges along with a healthy oil change, tire rotation, or other potentially necessary activity.

I distinctly remember the call I received from a service advisor after one such experience. He was very polite and played the role of messenger well. He noted there was good news and bad news. Lovely. Almost verbatim what he seemed to say every year. Perhaps it's a script in the service advisor playbook? The good news was that my car was ready to be picked up. The bad news was they identified several items that should probably be replaced. Can't say I was shocked. But there was a new kicker: if I authorized them to go ahead and replace the flux capacitor and hydroponic boosting emissions light diode that keeps the filament for the ignition alternator governed to within 17 percent of the ideal idling conditions, then the car would be ready at the promised pickup time.

I paused. "Go ahead," I said, feigning autonomy. It's laughable. He knew I'd probably do whatever he said. He had successfully managed my attention to getting my car fixed and back that day. He successfully framed my decision as a choice between fixed and ready on time or not fixed and needing to take more of my time to return. With that framing, the choice seemed obvious (or so I was led to believe). I didn't ask how necessary the repairs were. I didn't inquire if the repairs could wait. I was blind to the alternative of doing nothing.

Frankly, I don't know if they even changed anything—other than the balance on my credit card. The car runs fine, and for that, I guess I'm thankful. But what was I expected to do? A second opinion would cost valuable time and additional money. Which brings me to a critical topic in our discussion of dependence and obedience. *We need to consider the costs and benefits of our decisions to outsource.* For low-cost topics, it may not make sense for me to seek a second opinion. It may, however, make a lot of sense to do so when the stakes are higher.

Trust Me, I'm An Expert

To empower ourselves by mastering focus, we need to understand how blind obedience syndrome spread throughout society. Fortunately, there is ample research to help us. Maybe we'll even develop a vaccine soon.

Imagine that you've arrived in a psychology lab of a leading university to participate in an experiment on memory and learning. Once you arrive, you learn that you are going to play the role of a teacher and that the experiment will test the impact of punishment on memory. You then meet the learner, another volunteer in the experiment. You exchange some pleasantries and then watch as he is strapped into a chair. Electrodes are attached to his arm.

You then enter another room where you are seated at a device that controls the shocks administered through the electrodes in the learner's chair. The professional leading the experiment then places a sensor on your hand and flips the lever labeled "45 volts." You feel the shock. The panel in front of you has switches that are labeled from "slight" to "severe." The voltage switches begin at 15 volts and go up to 450 volts.

The experiment begins and the learner makes mistakes. The experimenter asks you to raise the voltage with each wrong answer. After the shocks rise in intensity, the learner begins complaining and pleading. You look at the experiment leader, who tells you that you must continue. The experiment requires it. At 75 volts, the learner grunts; at 120 volts, he screams loudly; at 150, he demands to be let go. His protests grow more emotional as the voltage rises. By 285 volts, you only hear an agonized scream. Thereafter, the learner is silent.

How far do you go?

For the participants in these experiments, which actually took place in New Haven in the 1960s under the leadership of Yale psychologist Stanley Milgram, 60 percent of the teachers went all the way to the maximum voltage.[1] Even though the learners were merely actors and did not actually receive shocks, the teachers believed the learners were actually receiving shocks. The experiment, it turned out, was never about learning and memory. Instead, it was designed to study obedience to authority.

Colleagues immediately criticized Milgram, suggesting that obedient Yale undergraduates were not representative of people in general. Subsequently, many tried to replicate the experiment with different subjects. The results were confirmed from Princeton to Munich, from Rome to South Africa—and disturbingly with even more significant results than Milgram found, in some cases with as high as 85 percent obedience.[2]

This shocking finding made a huge splash in the field of psychology. Before the experiment, Milgram had asked colleagues, students, and ordinary New Haven citizens what percentage of the subjects they thought would inflict the maximum punishment. The pre-experiment poll yielded an estimate of 4 percent reaching 300 volts and a miniscule percent reaching the maximum 450 volts.[3]

The experiments taught us a great deal about human beings. When someone has power or authority over us, we tend to comply. This is one of the dynamics at work when focus spreads throughout society. We allow experts—or anyone or anything else we perceive as authoritative—to manage focus. We bow to their wishes, usually without protest and allow them to highlight and deemphasize. They frame our choices. We allow them to take options off the table that we didn't even know were ever on it; heck, we let them build the table in the first place.

More often than not, the obedience dynamic is socially useful, not to mention necessary. But it also means that we are disempowered in many situations, almost always in ways we don't notice.

Actually, we can't notice, because our attention itself is being managed. If someone gives you three options and says, "Ok, you get to choose one," how often do you say, "Wait, I actually don't like those options—I'm going to do a fourth option you didn't mention" or, "I'm not going to do anything at all." We generally stay in the spotlight that has been shined for us. Conversely, the people who are deferred to—the experts, and, indirectly, the rule-makers, engineers, and designers—are granted the authority to direct our attention, effectively installing blinders that limit our field of view.

An A-MAZE-ing A-Fib Adventure

Whenever I think about the Milgram experiment and the extreme deferral to men in white coats, I think of my friend Craig Cerretani. Craig is in great shape. At one point, he was drafted by the Chicago Cubs and played professional baseball. Although that was in the mid 1970s, he still works out consistently. And he regularly saw his doctor, religiously complying with recommended tests. But in September 2009, during a routine annual physical examination, his doctor grew concerned by his dangerously irregular heartbeat. Craig's general practitioner immediately sent him to see the chief of cardiology at a nearby hospital. Upon arrival and after a rapid review, Craig was admitted to the hospital that night and closely monitored.

The cardiologist concluded that Craig had atrial fibrillation (A-fib), a condition that supposedly affects between 2 and 3 percent of the American population. A-fib is dangerous because an irregular heartbeat can generate stroke-causing and potentially life-threatening blood clots. The condition can also affect blood pressure.

The cardiologist caring for Craig had all the right credentials. He had helped professional athletes, was affiliated with top medical schools in the area, had completed numerous prestigious fellowships, had published in the most exclusive journals, and ran one of the most successful medical practices in the greater Boston area. He appeared ideal.

After watching Craig and reviewing his test results, the doctor put Craig on a blood thinner that would reduce the risk of a clot-related stroke. When he reported back for a follow-up appointment six weeks later, Craig looked and felt great—and the doctor could tell. After noting Craig's condition, the cardiologist told Craig to stop taking his blood thinning medication.

To decide if Craig should be on a blood thinner, the doctor simply followed the prevailing rules of the medical system. As scary as this may sound, a five-question test known as CHADS2 determines whether to keep a patient on blood thinners. Specifically, the doctor noted that Craig was younger than seventy-five years old, had normal blood pressure, was not diagnosed as diabetic, and hadn't had a heart attack or a stroke. This five-question checklist is the reason the doctor asked Craig to stop taking the pills.

Checklists have tremendous power to help experts mitigate the negative impact of overconfidence. Checklists can force us to pay attention to things that would otherwise not be in our focus, and thus they help us to avoid being blinded in domains as varied as finance, medicine, and aviation. As Atul Gawande shows in *The Checklist Manifesto*, the dramatic advances in medicine over the past decades have brought with them

requisite complexity, opening up the reality that even the most competent doctors will unintentionally skip steps and overlook potential explanations and treatments.[4] A checklist can help correct for the inevitable
oversights that arise when even the seasoned doctors are confronted
with outsized complexity. Doctors may have their focus trained on a
particular line of reasoning, but, if well designed, a checklist can help
ensure that factors completely outside it don't slip away unexamined.

One such factor is family history—which is not on the CHADS2
checklist. One of the key findings from modern medical practice is that
family history matters. Given the awe-inspiring power of genetics, this
is not a surprising finding. Parents provide their children's genetic material. This is not to suggest that other factors don't matter, merely that
family history does.

Well, what if you knew that Craig's father had a stroke at the age of
fifty-five? And what if I told you that Craig was fifty-five years old? I
understand that this doesn't change the answers to the checklist, but
shouldn't it lead one of the world's leading cardiologists to think for himself, rather than merely outsource the decision to a rule prescribed by
the greater medical system?

In fact, many of these medical checklists and rules should be decision-
aides, not decision makers. Why blindly trust the findings of detailed
academic studies conducted on random patients that may or may not have
been paid to participate? When such studies are translated into rules of
thumb, doctors forget to think for themselves about the validity of the
extrapolation from the experience of geographically specific populations
to individuals in a completely different context.

Sadly, you can probably tell where this story is going.

A mere three months after being told by his cardiologist to stop taking blood thinners, Craig had a stroke. He was rushed to the hospital,
where the attending neurologist advised him he was in the midst of a
stroke and recommended immediate administration of tPA, a strong
blood thinner that is accompanied by a 6 percent chance of death. It's
standard operating procedure, the doctor said. Despite slurring his words,
Craig authorized it.

Fortunately, the tPA worked. After two days of careful monitoring in the intensive care unit, Craig was released. Three months later, he went to his previously scheduled cardiology appointment. He told the doctor he had a stroke, at which point the esteemed Dr. Head Honcho Published Chief Cardiologist became very defensive: "But your CHADS score didn't indicate you were at risk."

Craig reminded the doctor that his father had a stroke at age fifty-five, something Craig had told the doctor about on a previous visit . . . and Craig's stroke took place when he was fifty-five.

"But the CHADS rule doesn't factor in parental or family history of stroke. The question is clearly about *your* prior stroke history," protested the doctor.

It seems clear that the doctor outsourced his thinking to a rule. Turns out a simple Google search can identify the origins of this test. It was based on research conducted on 1,733 Medicare beneficiaries aged sixty-five to ninety-five years with A-fib that had not been prescribed blood thinners.[5] What?!?! Read that sentence again, paying special attention to the age band. The research the doctor used never even included people at Craig's age—yet the doctor applied the rule blindly, without thinking, to a situation that was totally different.

Needless to say, Craig found a new cardiologist. This time he sought out someone who specialized in his condition, believing that an A-fib expert will prevent further issues. He eventually found a cardiologist at one of Boston's leading hospitals—extensively published, board certified, and on the faculty of a medical school. And . . . drumroll please . . . a specialist in cardiac electrophysiology, the study of electrical impulses that make the heart beat. As Craig told me, "This guy was perfect. I mean this was a bull's eye, hole-in-one, perfect 10. I felt like I hit the lottery."

So Craig went to see this doctor, who seemed to grasp the situation immediately. Further, the doctor noted that he was running a seminar on A-fib treatment options the following week and encouraged Craig to attend. Craig did, and learned about the hierarchy of available solutions to treat or cure A-fib. Without getting into the gory details, the first step is drug therapy, followed by cardiac shock therapy. (Think of two handheld devices while a doctors screams "clear!") If those two treatments fail to fix the irregular heartbeat, there is a minimally invasive procedure known as catheter ablation in which tiny laser torches are used to manually rewire the heart's electrical pathways. If that third step fails, the fourth and final treatment option for A-fib is something known as a MAZE in which a patient's heart is literally taken out of their body and physically cut to create scar tissue that rewires electric pulses to make the heart beat properly. Any description of a MAZE is beyond frightening to read.

After the seminar, Craig scheduled another appointment with the doctor to revisit his specific case. At this appointment, Craig met with both a cardiologist and a surgeon who had reviewed his records. They recommended a MAZE, noting that since his heart was consistently irregular, the three prior steps to address A-fib wouldn't work. "You're not a candidate for anything else," they said. The surgeon spoke with authority, "We see this all the time, you're a perfect candidate. Nothing else is going to work for you."

While listening, Craig noticed that the cardiologist appeared to have more questions. But because he was just the cardiologist, he wasn't expert enough or of high enough status to question the surgeon. As Craig told me, "The cardiologist clearly didn't want to step on the surgeon's toes and wouldn't directly answer the question of whether a MAZE was appropriate for me . . . he hemmed and hawed, explained and qualified, while the surgeon bluntly said that I needed a MAZE."

After the meeting, Craig went home and watched a YouTube video of a MAZE procedure. Here's how he described it to me: "You're on a heart-machine, they take out your heart, they cut it! It's crazy! They take your beating heart out of your body! I'm scared, I can't sleep, it's frightening, but what the fuck!? He's the doctor! I mean the surgeon who is the world's expert authority on A-fib. He must know, right? He's learned everything. He's the expert . . . and he's recommending it. Who am I to question him?"

But Craig did question him; the cardiologist's discomfort nagged Craig into seeking another opinion. Craig was stressed out, in fact, so anxious he had probably elevated his risk of a heart attack! Imagine that, a cardiologist-induced heart attack! Craig talked to friends who eventually sent him to Dr. Jeremy Ruskin, who Craig describes as "maybe five feet tall, quiet, thoughtful, and intense."

Within the first few minutes of meeting him, Dr. Ruskin asked, "What are you doing here? Why are you here?" Craig then explained his tale of woe that brought him from a routine physical to a recommended MAZE. Dr. Ruskin noted that, although a MAZE may ultimately be necessary, it's better to start with less invasive procedures. Craig was immediately comfortable with Dr. Ruskin and instinctually bought into his recommended approach. They tried drugs, some shock therapy, and eventually resorted to ablation. About an hour into a seven-hour minimally invasive procedure, Craig's heart started beating normally. It's been normal since.

Craig's story is fascinating and disturbing on many levels. It's a story of the godlike power that experts seem to have over our minds. When his cardiologist took Craig off of the blood thinner, why didn't Craig throw his hands up and say, "Hey doctor, are you sure that's wise given that my father had a debilitating health issues at fifty-five . . . and I'm now fifty-five?" Why not? Because doctors know best! Right?

And most of us, I suspect, would defer to the unwarranted conviction that a MAZE was necessary and would work. We'd trust that drug or shock therapy wouldn't work because that's what the expert specialist doctors are saying. But how hard is it to ask the question of, "What happens if we try and it doesn't work? Are there any residual negative effects of attempting it?" In this case, the answer would likely have been "No."

In fact, it was only Craig's hyperalert people observation skills that led to his positive outcome. The minor observation of cardiologist discomfort in the presence of the surgeon may have helped Craig avoid the risks of open chest, open heart surgery. And the video of a MAZE procedure shocked Craig into thinking for himself. Once he did, he realized that experts had taken over his health. He was not just on autopilot following expert advice; he was a hostage on a plane hijacked by experts that were deferring to automated decision trees.

One of the real takeaways from Craig's story is that star doctors may not always be ideal for your situation. In fact, it may be that top doctors are bad for your health. How's that? A 2015 article in *JAMA Internal Medicine* reviewed over a decade of data involving tens of thousands of patients with acute, life-threatening cardiac conditions.[6] What the researchers found is counterintuitive, but consistent with Craig's story. When senior cardiologists were out of town, patients did better! The data indicate that high-risk patients with heart failure or cardiac arrest had up to 30 percent better survival rates when the top doctors were at national cardiology meetings. Might it be that our unwavering faith in Dr. Head Honcho Expert Specialist, MD, PhD, is misguided? Are we letting our necessary and acceptable dependence on experts turn into unnecessary blind obedience?

Japan in Jeopardy

The problems caused by hyperfocused systems are magnified when employees actively embrace subservience to hierarchy. Japanese society has long worshipped at the altar of efficiency, with all the risks that accompany it. Individuals are deemed less important than the group, and employees are trained and retrained to never act without appropriate approval or authorization from those above—a dynamic that dampens independent thought across all walks of society. Many in Japan explicitly learn not to think for themselves.

On the afternoon of March 11, 2011, Japan's extreme focus on group primacy, deference to authority, and rote obedience to workplace rules nearly turned a natural disaster into a nuclear catastrophe. It began at 2:46 p.m. when a magnitude 9.0 earthquake hit approximately 230 miles northeast of Tokyo in the sea.[7] In the Fukushima prefecture, astute fisherman had sensed doom and, as they often did during such events, quickly got in their boats and headed out to sea. They understood it's easier to ride over a swell than to survive a crashing wave. Some headed inland toward the mountains, recalling that earthquakes often cause tidal waves.[8]

But at the Fukushima Daiichi Nuclear Power Station, all seemed fine—at least initially. Of the six reactors at the facility, three were already shut down for normal course maintenance. The other three active reactors automatically shut down, as they are supposed to when their foundations shook. The manager, controllers, and regulators watching closely were relieved when the lights came back on shortly after the earthquake. But inside the reactors, workers sensed all was not well.[9]

According to Carl Pillitteri, an American technician who was working in the plant, "I heard that the earthquake lasted six minutes, but for me, it felt like a lifetime. You could feel it under your feet. It was this entire enormous building moving at once. A lot of things were falling. We lost almost every light in the room. The structural steel was moving overhead. The lights were crashing everywhere . . . in one nanosecond, the entire floor went black. . . . I felt within the first two to three minutes of the earthquake that this was going to be significant."[10]

Once Pillitteri and his team escaped the plant, the first wave of the tsunami crashed about one hundred feet from them: "It didn't resemble a wave. It resembled this huge swell of the ocean. . . . The water just came in, wrapped around the walls, and came back out." He headed toward his rental car, which he had parked up the hill to allow for a short walk in on a beautiful clear morning. But as the first wave receded, "a big, black, ominous front came rolling down" the mountain, and it started snowing. The time was 3:27 p.m.[11]

Eight minutes after the first wave receded, another hit. This one was much bigger, around forty feet in height, and barreled over the thirty-three foot concrete wall designed to protect the plant from typhoons. The reactors and generators were immediately flooded. Trucks, cars, and heavy equipment were tossed about like feathers in a windstorm. By 3:37 p.m., two minutes after the big wave arrived, the control room lost power.[12]

Power at a nuclear plant is essential because it is used to cool the radioactive fuel rods. When the radioactive fuel is not continually cooled with pumped water, it has the potential to melt through the rods' protective casings, ultimately boiling off the sitting water around it. The steam in the air then mixes with fuel rods to create a flammable hydrogen–filled environment. Eventually the pressure generates an explosion that can breach containment chambers and release radioactive isotopes into the atmosphere.[13]

When the power failed, then, it was like the fuse of a bomb had been lit. The matter instantly became extremely urgent, warranting immediate attention. By 3:00 a.m., the government of Japan and the management of the Tokyo Electric Power Company (TEPCO), the plant's owner and operator, both understood this risk and felt it prudent to open vents from the reactors to reduce the pressure and minimize the risk of an explosion. The vents would release some radioactive elements, but a mere fraction of what would be released in an explosion. Everyone involved understood this was a necessary evil to prevent a total meltdown.[14]

But by 7:00 a.m., the vents had not been opened. Plant managers were following protocol, confirming that local residents had left. No one would acknowledge the big white elephant in the room until Prime Minister Naoto Kan literally flew to the plant by helicopter and demanded TEPCO open the vents. Opening the vents proved critical in limiting a far worse disaster from unfolding—but only barely. The focus on limiting radiation leaks blinded many to the possibility of a complete meltdown and explosive release of far more radiation.[15]

The chief of the plant then proceeded to assemble what he called a "suicide squad" to open the vents; by 9:00 a.m., three teams of two were assembled and headed toward the vents. The first team managed to open the vent slightly, the second team had to turn back due to the radioactive pressures emanating from the slight opening, and the third team abandoned the mission.[16]

On March 12 at 3:36 p.m., almost exactly twenty-four hours after the second wave of the tsunami had knocked out power to the control room, Reactor #1 exploded, disrupting all efforts to restore power to the plant's other reactors. Radiation levels now became untenable for any relief efforts and over the next several days, two other reactors suffered radiation-releasing explosions. The situation seemed dire.[17]

Because it would render it permanently useless, the decision to flood a multibillion dollar nuclear reactor with seawater carries enormous weight. Yet seawater has the potential to prevent a meltdown. It's also an admission to anyone paying attention that the situation is spiraling out of control.[18]

So when TEPCO executives began injecting seawater into the facility four hours after the explosion, the decision must have been seriously considered. But they hadn't sought the prime minister's opinion. As it happened, the prime minister was discussing the use of seawater with Haruki Madarame, the chairman of the Nuclear Safety Commission, that afternoon. The two had considered the possibility of recriticality, a low probability occurrence in which heat generation accelerates as the fission process resumes while the fuel rods are in water. The prime minister was warned the probability of this happening was "not zero."

TEPCO's liaison in the prime minister's office conveyed to TEPCO management that the government seemed to be against seawater injections. So the TEPCO manager then ordered Masao Yoshida, the plant manager, to suspend the seawater operations. When later asked to defend this order, TEPCO's Executive Vice President Sakae Muto, noted that the liaison had said that "was the atmosphere or the mood" in the prime minister's office. Even the former head of the Cabinet Security Affairs Office, Atsuyuki Sassa, found this disturbing: "Mood? Is this a joke? Making decisions based on mood?"[19]

Fortunately, Yoshida did what is nothing short of remarkable in a society as regimented as Japan. He ignored the order and kept pumping the seawater. He bluntly disobeyed the orders of his superiors. He thought for himself instead of robotically following the orders issued. While the prime minister's office had been focused on the low probability risk of recriticality, Yoshida concentrated on the immediate dangers of neutralizing the rods through flooding.[20]

In retrospect, experts agree that the seawater was the only way to keep cooling the reactor, and not doing so would have risked a more severe meltdown and the release of more radiation. Several months after the explosions, Yoshida explained his rebellious actions to a reporter, noting that not pumping in seawater would have made the already bad situation much worse. "Suspending the seawater could have meant death" for those at the plant, in the surrounding areas, and possibly even Tokyo. His actions almost certainly prevented the evacuation of Tokyo's 13 million residents.[21]

Lest you think Masao Yoshida is somehow different than you or me, think again. By all outward appearances, he was a normal person. At the time of the explosion, he was a fifty-six-year-old, hard-drinking, frequent smoker who enjoyed cooking Italian food.[22] He took pride in his work and understood in the moment of crisis that he bore huge responsibility. He saw his job as not merely to execute orders from Tokyo but rather to help save the lives of those at the plant and beyond. He saw the big picture, refusing to be blinded by the focus that hierarchy and rules demand. He focused on the mission, not the task. And most importantly, he trusted himself. Yoshida is an unsung hero who saved many lives. Some believe his act of disobedience was in fact the only decision that prevented a total meltdown of the reactors and a complete uncontrolled release of radiation that would have affected Tokyo and quite possibly most of the country.

You'd think he'd be a national hero, right? Given the Japanese equivalent of the Congressional Medal of Honor? Nope.

In return for these courageous actions, TEPCO management gave Yoshida a verbal reprimand for defying orders. Yoshida took an early retirement from TEPCO in late 2011 after being diagnosed with cancer of the esophagus. He died in 2012. It is believed the cancer was unrelated to his experience at the plant.[23]

Sadly, Yoshida is not typical in Japan, TEPCO, or even in any of today's large organizations. Shortly after the accident, and for the first time in Japanese history, the government ordered an independent investigation into what happened.[24] The committee charged with investigating the events produced a scathing report that was released in July 2012.[25] Kiyoshi Kurokawa, a professor of medicine at the renowned University of Tokyo School of Medicine, was charged with leading the investigation. His summary of the accident's causes was about as blunt as one can be: "its fundamental causes are . . . reflexive obedience; reluctance to question authority; devotion to 'sticking with the program'; groupism, and insularity."[26]

At the press conference announcing the results, Kurokawa warned that, "Had other Japanese been in the shoes of those who bear responsibility for this accident, the result may well have been the same."[27] I disagree. Without Yoshida at the helm, I fear the result may have been much, much worse. Further, I'm not so sure how Japanese this problem actually is. Sure, the cultural homogeneity and societal devotion to groups over individuals may have exacerbated the situation; but frankly, I think Kurokawa's insight regarding Japan may be far more broadly relevant than he recognized. Don't most of us blindly follow rules, the advice of experts, and the opinions of authorities?

Is it possible that he has put his finger on a far more universal problem? Every time I read the report, I'm struck by the relevance of the "reflexive obedience . . . reluctance to question . . . [and] devotion to . . . the program" to the world outside of Japan. Aren't those the same conditions that we all find ourselves in with our reflexive obedience to a doctor's orders, a reluctance to question the rationale for a treatment, or the devotion to her status as a medical expert? How about if a mechanic suggests that your car is in urgent need of new brakes—who among us has the chutzpah to question such a recommendation?

It's a little-known fact that nearby Fukushima Daiichi was another plant, Fukushima Danini, which fared even better—also in part due to a leader who thought for himself. Known as "iron-hearted Masuda," the superintendent of the site, Naohiro Masuda, made tough decisions—against the instincts of his staff and supervisors—that saved plant.

Despite the apparent danger, he forced all employees to stay in the plant, because he knew that morale was as important as efficiency, and unity boosted morale. Further, he took a stand against headquarters on multiple occasions. When higher-ups, endowed with a frustrating combination of authority and ignorance, demanded Masuda turn off power that was crucial to monitoring the reactors, he bluntly refused.[28] At another point, when he requested 4,000 tons of water, management in

Tokyo granted him 4,000 liters.[29] Thankfully, Masuda thought for himself and rather than take the fractional allocation he was granted, he went back and demanded more water. At one point, he basically incited what under any other circumstances would be seen as a rebellion. His directive to his colleagues and peers was, "Don't rely on others. Let's do things by ourselves."[30]

Masuda, like his colleague at the other Fukushima plant, is an unsung hero of the crisis. His ability to think for himself saved the plant. In fact, it's believed that his efforts resulted in zero radioactive emissions from the plant.[31] How many of us would bluntly disobey the orders of our bosses rather than blindly hiding behind the cover of "I just work here" or "I was just doing what I was told"? Sadly, fewer than ideal.

. . .

What are we to make of our simultaneously appealing and distasteful willingness to submit our autonomy to people who know more than we do? A large part of the answer is the environment of overwhelming complexity that overloads our ability to cope with the frequency and intensity of the decisions we are asked to make. Outsourcing many of these decisions may enable higher success rates in those domains in which you retain autonomy. Sure, there's a cost to outsourcing our decisions, but there's also a benefit.

After all, for me to invest the time and energy to learn about the technicalities of my car is probably not the best use of my time. Nor is learning about plumbing or about aspects of my body and how it functions. If we are to live in this highly complex world with any semblance of normality, we need to learn to rely on others. The bottom line is that we are all dependent on others to some extent; it's a fact of modern life. But this dependence need not translate into blind obedience. As we turn to those who can help, we must remember their limitations and appreciate other perspectives.

PART THREE

RECLAIMING AUTONOMY

The problem of blind obedience to expertise is that it has become our default condition. To reclaim our autonomy and self-determination skills, we need to think for ourselves. We must begin by understanding the constraints that exist upon the expertise we obtain. Awareness of how our scarce attention is deployed is critical and requires we be cognizant of who or what is framing our choices. But we also need to remain goal oriented, understanding that those with a narrow focus can help with tasks, but responsibility for the mission, however, remains ours. We should also fight back against the tyranny of established wisdom if it isn't applicable to our specific situation. We cannot be expert in everything and different perspectives can help, but we should keep experts on tap, not on top. Depth of expertise must be balanced with an appreciation for breadth of perspective.

CHAPTER 6

Mindfully Manage Focus

One of the most critical practices we can adopt in thinking for ourselves is to become aware of the focus managers that constantly exert their influence upon our lives. Who is framing our decision choices? What options may be left in the shadows of the spotlights others are shining on our behalf? We need to mindfully manage where our focus is channeled and the topics that merit our attention.

Like Magic

Years ago, I had just sat down to dinner at a conference when I noticed a man walking around, greeting people in a random pattern, and eventually making his way to the stage. He was introduced as "Apollo Robbins, Gentleman Thief."

Robbins is possibly the world's most advanced student of focus. He's mastered the art of managing other people's attention, and he does so in such an unobtrusive manner that he's able to empty a person's pockets without them noticing. He's an expert in perception management and uses sleights of hand to demonstrate how diversions can lead to self-deception. Companies, governments, and organizations of all sorts seek his counsel and expertise.

Robbins rose to fame by pulling off one of the most audacious lifts in the history of pickpocketing. In 2001, he encountered Jimmy Carter's Secret Service detail while the former president was having dinner. The *New Yorker* summarized the encounter as follows:

> Robbins struck up a conversation with several of [Jimmy Carter's] Secret Service men. Within a few minutes, he had emptied the agents' pockets of pretty much everything but their guns. Robbins brandished a copy of Carter's itinerary, and when an agent snatched it back he said, "You don't have authorization to see that!" When the agent felt for his badge, Robbins produced it and handed it back. Then he turned to the head of the detail and handed him his watch, his badge, and the keys to the Carter motorcade.[1]

In the years he's been a full-time entertainer, Robbins has managed to take (and return) an engagement ring from actress Jennifer Garner's then-boyfriend Ben Affleck, a thick pile of cash from NBA star Charles Barkley's pocket, and a Patek Philippe watch from former Bear Stearns chairman Ace Greenberg's wrist. For one trick, he managed to extract a man's driver's license from his wallet, replace the wallet, and have the license appear in a sealed bag of M&Ms in his wife's purse.

Robbins's skills have not been relegated to mere entertainment; he's an active educator and regularly shares his perception management insights with audiences, clients, and even the public. He's produced and cohosted a popular television show with National Geographic called *Brain Games*. TED organizers have hailed his talk as a revelation of the flaws in human perception. He's also formed an education and training firm to deliver immersive training in support of experiential learning.

OK, so by now you probably get it. When it comes to picking pockets and other sleights of hand, Apollo Robbins is as close to superhuman as exists on this planet. Having watched him in action, I can say he's amazing. But you're probably interested in understanding, as I was, how he does it. What's his secret?

The key, Robbins told me during a phone conversation, is managing focus.[2] Robbins is always thinking about where people are channeling their attention. He's innately aware of the fact that people have a set amount of attention and he uses that to his advantage. In fact, he even describes his methods in that language. When explaining what he does and how he does it, Robbins told me, "I manage the attention kind of like water flow, and I see where it goes, and then I have to move with that."[3] He even talks about cutting up a target's "attentional pie." Sound familiar? Robbins actively misdirects what little focus we have, thereby leading us to ignore his efforts to take our wallet, unfasten our watch, or empty our pockets.

Robbins goes further than misdirecting our visual focus. He uses touch and voice to distract, noting: "Because you have to make choices between all your senses—your vision, your hearing—all those are coming in at one spot, if I can tap into your priority system, I can now start hacking to re-prioritize certain things so other things will go under the radar."[4]

Read that last sentence again. Robbins is thinking about what we ignore and he uses all the tools at his disposal to do so. A touch on the wrist, a tap on the shoulder, moving a target's body to the left, looking into their eyes. It's all about focus and ignoring. And the anxiety Robbins produces because people know he's going to try to pick their pockets actually works to his advantage. It leads people in his presence to expend more focus upon what he does touch, what he does say, what he does do.

The increased intensity of focus leads to larger blind spots. Think of it as asking you to count the number of basketballs being passed left to right and keeping that tally separate from your count of aerial (but not bounced) passes going right to left. Your chances of seeing the gorilla (discussed in chapter 3) will plunge as the exercise takes larger and larger slices of your attention pie. He assaults your sensory systems and controls your attention. As you focus, you drain your attention reservoirs and lose the ability to see unexpected developments.

As Robbins manages what we feel, where we look, and what we hear, we literally stop feeling, looking, and hearing. Robbins's lessons reveal the importance of mindfulness around focus. What we focus on, we are mindful of. What is outside our focus, we are mindless of. Robbins reminds us to focus on focus. Focus is a variable that needs to be managed intentionally, just like time and money. We fail to do this at our own peril, as the examples in this book show. When we're mindful of our focus, we keep in mind what we're ignoring, making us prepared for the risks our focus creates and the opportunities it ignores.

Susana Martinez-Conde, a researcher at the Laboratory of Visual Neuroscience in Arizona and coauthor of *Sleights of Mind: What the Neuroscience of Magic Reveals about Everyday Deceptions*, has spent a great deal of time studying Robbins's approach to focus. Her research confirms that gorillas are everywhere, and Robbins is a master of producing them. "When Apollo gets on stage, he is making [people] look at things, he is talking to them, he is touching their body, he is coming very close to them and producing an emotional response as he is entering their personal space. . . . It's complete attentional overload."[5]

Attentional overload? Remember that attention is merely one side of a coin; the other side is ignoring. We might as well replace the word *attentional* with *ignoring* because Robbins is effectively creating ignoring overload. He's so stressing our sensory processing capabilities that he might as well disconnect our heads from our bodies, which is why so many people feel utterly powerless and are completely befuddled around him.

New York Times science writer George Johnson wrote in 2007 that, "Apollo, with the pull of his eyes and the arc of his hand, swung around my attention like a gooseneck lamp, so that it was always pointed in the wrong direction. When he appeared to be reaching for my left pocket he was swiping something from the right."[6]

Swinging *attention* like a gooseneck lamp? If that doesn't capture the essence of Apollo Robbins, I'm not sure what does! It should come as no surprise, then, to learn that Warner Brothers retained Robbins as an advisor while it was producing *Focus*, a 2015 movie starring Will Smith as Nicky, a seasoned and experienced con artist who gets romantically involved with Jess, played by Margot Robbie, a woman who wants to learn his skills.

In one scene, Nicky and Jess step outside onto a snow-filled lawn, where Nicky takes off his jacket and begins a short lesson: "At the end of the day, this is a game of focus."[7] At this point, Nicky reveals that he has removed her ring from her finger.

Nicky continues, spinning her like a ballerina: "Now, attention is like a spotlight, and our job is to dance in the darkness." He then shows her that he has taken her watch off her wrist.

Jess is genuinely impressed, but naively so. While she's utilizing her limited attention to figure out how he took her watch, Nicky's on to the next thing.

He continues, "The human brain is slow, and it cannot multitask." Nicky reveals he has stolen her ring again.

Nicky explains that Jess needs to perceive from the perspective of her victim: "Human behavior is very predictable. If I look at my hand, it naturally pulls your gaze, and allows me to enter your space. But when I look up at you it causes you to look directly at me." Nicky now reveals that he's taken her sunglasses.

He then demonstrates the power of sensory focus. Just as visual focus can generate blindness to stuff directly in front of your eyes, so, too, can a person's focus upon a particular body part numb the feelings in other parts. After touching her shoulder, Nicky says, "I touch you here, I steal from here." He then hands back the cell phone that was in her pocket. He then taps the left side of her body, noting, "I tap you here, I steal from here" and reveals that he took the keys out of her right pocket.

Nicky wraps up with, "You get their focus, you take whatever you want." He then hands her back her ring, having lifted it off her finger a third time. She's laughing while shaking her head and smiling.

When I first watched *Focus*, I immediately thought of Apollo Robbins and only later learned that he was an advisor to the producers. In fact, Robbins coached Will Smith and Margot Robbie for over three months, teaching them how to do it for real. Smith says he learned from Robbins that misdirection is not looking in one direction while activity happened in the other direction. Instead, "You can be looking straight at it, and if you're not thinking about it, you won't process it."[8] Sound like the gorilla?

The Dog That Didn't Bark

To untangle mysteries involving the unexpected, let's turn to one of the most famous Sherlock Holmes stories, "Silver Blaze."[9] Silver Blaze is a prized racehorse that disappears on the eve of an important race. Its trainer is found dead the next morning. Sherlock Holmes heads to the scene to help with the investigation. Upon arriving, Holmes dismisses the obvious suspect, Fitzroy Simpson, upon whom Inspector Gregory and the police are focused.

Even though Simpson appeared near the stables the night of the crime inquiring about the horse's capabilities (he was wagering on the race), and his jacket and scarf were found near the trainer's dead body, Holmes notes that Simpson could easily have killed or injured the animal in its stall. There's no reason he would have had to take the horse to the moor to hurt it. And the fact that the horse is nowhere to be seen doesn't support the case against Simpson. Where and why would he hide it?

The police had searched all neighboring stables, but had not found the horse. When Holmes finds the horse, it is in a nearby stable, with its white forehead concealed with dye. Inspector Gregory and the police were so focused on finding the white forehead that they failed to see the otherwise striking resemblance to the missing animal. The color became their basketball passes. The horse was their gorilla.

Holmes then turns to the matter of the dead trainer. The stable boy who was on duty that night had been drugged with powdered opium mixed into his dinner. The meal he ate that night was curried mutton, a spicy dish that concealed the otherwise notable taste of opium. Simpson couldn't have chosen the meal, so Holmes quickly suspects the trainer and his wife.

But there were other anomalies. Rather than hone in on how the trainer had died, Holmes instead looks broadly. He found the trainer had been living lavishly and had a surgical knife in his pocket. There was also the seemingly irrelevant fact that three sheep had gone lame in the prior weeks.

But it was "the curious incident of the dog in the night time"[10] that enabled Holmes to crack the case. You see, the dog didn't bark in the middle of the night, a nonfact that all had overlooked. Inspector Gregory and the police had focused on the unusual events and were thereby blinded to nonunusual events of significance. The dog didn't bark because it must have been the trainer who took Silver Blaze from the stable; for were it not the case, the dog would surely have made noise.

Holmes concludes the trainer had planned to surgically tear some of the horse's muscles in a manner that would impair his racing abilities but would remain concealed from all observers. The trainer must have practiced on the sheep, which is why three of them were lame. And the trainer's wife was wearing expensive dresses atypical for a family of their means. As the trainer was about to maim the horse in the middle of the night, it got spooked and kicked him in the head, killing him instantly.

The short story is a wonderful example of a mystery that is solved by managing focus. The police inspectors can't solve the case, because they are too focused on certain things. They don't have any attention left to expend on topics like the lame sheep, the expensive dresses, or the non-barking dog at night. The police are blind to these developments because they are focused elsewhere. They can't see the gorilla.

It takes an independent, external, and less focused perspective to connect the dots in a conclusive way. In fact, throughout the story, Holmes praises the police investigator as an extremely competent officer but one who lacks imagination. If imagination is the ability to think broadly, letting the mind wander as it creates possible scenarios, then it's probably not a big jump to suggest that Holmes is really criticizing Inspector Gregory for being too focused. Inspector Gregory didn't have the bandwidth to connect the dots because he was so busy digging deeper to generate new dots. He should have unfocused, zooming out and seeing the bigger picture.

Once Inspector Gregory expended his attention on Simpson, the head injury that killed the trainer, and the missing horse's white forehead, he had none left to deploy toward the lame sheep, the curried mutton, or the nonbarking dog. The inspector was blinded by focus.

Shifting Your Focus

We do not realize how much information we broadcast about ourselves. In reality, we are constantly telling the world a ton via subtle and contradictory tells. Consider that pickpockets tend to hang out around "Beware of Pickpockets" signs. Why's that? Because the first thing most people do after reading these signs is to check if they still have their valuables—thereby producing an effective map of their possessions. Here again, focus blinds us. The focus on one's belongings is so complete that we become oblivious to the message we're broadcasting: "Here are my belongings! Inside upper pocket!"

I've been fortunate to have many friends over the years who have entered the intelligence services. They understand the cues we unintentionally broadcast. When I was traveling through several not-so-safe emerging markets years ago, a college friend working in Langley, Virginia, advised against using a security detail. My friend's advice was straightforward: using a security detail draws attention. He also advised me not to register with the US Embassy for a short trip. Why's that? He noted that those lists can and often become targets.

Instead, he advised, "Arrive in ripped jeans with your belongings in a backpack, wear a sweatshirt and sneakers, and, if you're having someone pick you up, ask them to drive an ordinary car and sit in the front seat next to the driver." By shifting my focus from my safety to look through the eyes of the potential bad guys, I believe I reduced the risks associated with traveling in many of the world's most challenging security environments, conducting business in Asia, Africa, Latin America, Eastern Europe, and the Middle East.

Held Hostage by Focus

While focus management is always important, it is absolutely essential in situations involving life and death. Take hostage negotiation, for example. Perhaps more than any other profession besides a professional pickpocket, the hostage negotiator needs to be a master of managing focus. Some negotiators focus widely on the overarching mission of resolution and hostage recovery. Others mechanically follow textbook procedures, narrowly focused on rehearsed steps to negotiate releases.

Consider Michael Schneider, a professional hostage negotiator working for the Antioch Police Department. In July 1993, Officer Schneider was summoned to a situation in which a man had taken his two kids hostage, holding them at gunpoint. Schneider spoke with the man for hours, convincing him to hand over some guns and asking him to take his shirt off as a sign of surrender. He remained committed to securing the release of the children, however long it took. Schneider's captain, though, focused intensely on timing. He pressured Schneider to impose a deadline.[11]

Officer Schneider convinced the captain to give him more time, but ultimately the captain's focus on timing prevailed. He imposed a ten-minute deadline. Nine minutes later the man had killed his children and himself. He was found with his shirt off, suggesting that he had in fact resigned to surrender but changed his mind when rushed. The captain was fixated on controlling the situation and imposing a strict deadline, while Officer Schneider had been committed to a peaceful resolution, no matter how long it took. Time-based tunnel vision may have contributed to unnecessary, tragic deaths.[12]

A similar dynamic was at play in one of the most famous hostage negotiations in recent American history. In 1993, FBI hostage negotiator Gary Noesner was notified through his beeper of an escalating hostage situation at an isolated compound near Waco, Texas. The Branch Davidians, a religious cult led by an authoritarian leader named David Koresh, had secured the grounds with illegal weapons and were supposedly abusing children. Agents from the Bureau of Alcohol, Tobacco, and

Firearms (ATF) had tried to raid the compound on a Sunday, believing that the cult members would be vulnerable, with their weapons locked away on the Sabbath. But the agents had lost the element of surprise after a news crew unwittingly tipped off Koresh's brother-in-law while asking for directions.[13]

ATF officials found out that their plan had been discovered, thanks to an undercover agent who was in the compound when Koresh's brother-in-law rushed to inform the leader of the impending raid. Despite knowing that the Davidians were prepared, the ATF leaders chose to focus stubbornly on the plan they had, rather than adapting to the new circumstances. Unsurprisingly, the raid set off a skirmish, resulting in deaths on both sides. Hostage negotiations began in earnest after bullets flew.

That evening, Noesner took over negotiating with Koresh. He immediately set out to understand Koresh's perspective. Noesner aimed to gain Koresh's trust, in part by exploiting the fact that he was angry with ATF agents and not so much at the FBI, the organization for which Noesner worked. He patiently chatted with Koresh, never implying any bad faith. He tried to empathize with Koresh, and when he understood that no "grand surrender" was in sight, Noesner started to focus on the release of more and more children (and, ultimately, adults). He called this the "trickle, flow, gush" strategy. It began to work, with twenty-one children released in the first five days after this approach was adopted.

But because Noesner was part of the negotiation team, a group that was distinct and different than the hostage rescue team, he was unable to control the actions of the more aggressive agents. The heavy weaponry the Branch Davidians possessed alarmed this other team. They wanted to use a show of force to demonstrate to the cultists that their position was hopeless. As Noesner put it, "While negotiators tried to show understanding and find common ground, the tactical people couldn't help but present a warlike image that heightened tension. An empathetic voice over the phone can only do so much to offset the powerful impression available to the subject's own eyes."[14]

Noesner's job was to manage Koresh's focus, but he was undermined by the tactical team's actions on the ground. It was hard to command the focus of the Branch Davidians when the rescue team was competing with Noesner using armored vehicles. Eventually, Koresh agreed to surrender in exchange for a sermon of his being broadcast on television. When the negotiators followed through, Koresh stalled and finally refused to surrender, claiming later that God had told him to wait.

According to Noesner, his superiors outside of the negotiating team, Dick Rogers and Jeff Jamar, were annoyed with what they believed to be Koresh's intentional deception, deciding then and there that they wanted to punish him. As Noesner explained, their desire to retaliate violated "a core principle of the FBI negotiation program: never confuse getting even with getting what you want."[15] They moved the armored vehicles toward the compound.

This upset the Davidians, who claimed they had not broken any promises. In their minds, they still planned to surrender; God had just told them to wait. Noesner's empathy allowed him to see that those in the compound likely *believed* Koresh's clearly self-serving pronouncements. It only confused things to assume they were acting in bad faith. Still, Noesner persisted in empathetically communicating with Koresh. When he heard on the radio a story about a guitar-shaped nebula, he suggested to Koresh, a guitar player himself, that this might be a sign for him to come out.

Then, inexplicably, the rescue team approved an action to cut off all power to the compound—just as Noesner felt his team had been gaining traction with the cultists, most recently having delivered much-needed milk to the compound. Without power, the milk started going bad shortly after its arrival. This pattern continued, with Noesner making emotional in-roads, and being undermined by the rescue team's aggressive tactics. They continued to cut off their power periodically, installed glaring lights pointed toward the compound, and authorized the blaring of loud music into it. Every such action was focused on accelerating and antagonizing; all the while, Noesner was focused on empathizing.

In the most poignant example of this dynamic, Jamar ordered heavy armored vehicles once again to move forward, but this time they accidentally severed the phone line that the negotiator was using to communicate. After that, feeling pressure to produce results, the rescue team ordered agents to dismantle and remove machinery from around the compound—destroying the cultists' property at a time when the negotiator was trying to establish trust.

Shortly thereafter, Noesner was taken off the case. After that, the situation deteriorated rapidly. His replacement, a devout Christian, tried to argue theology with Koresh rather than trying to understand his perspective. Soon, Noesner's former superiors staged an intervention into the compound. Agents filled the compound with tear gas, smashing holes into the walls to allow people to escape. Within minutes, the Davidians set fire to the compound and committed suicide. Seventy-six died.

Noesner had a radically different focus from Jamar and Rogers. Although all wanted to end the standoff, the latter were concerned with eliciting reactions and accelerating conflict. A rapid ending of the standoff was their primary focus. Noesner, by contrast, tried to understand the perspective of the cultists and take them at their word, believing a slow and steady approach would result in a trickle of innocents out of the compound. His primary focus was a peaceful de-escalation and freeing of the hostages. While it's unclear if Noesner's approach would ultimately have succeeded, it did appear to be making progress. Could it be that the shift to focusing on time was partially responsible for dozens of deaths?

Broken Theories

The power of zooming out is also useful in the domain of policy to understand what policies are driving what behaviors. Think of the focus management act as an iterative process by which each new cycle generates greater and greater insight. Let's turn to the topic of crime and policing policies.

Take New York City, a city that many felt typified the problem of urban crime in the early 1990s. As a kid who grew up in New Jersey not far from the city, I believed New York was not safe and best to be avoided at night. And so when I had the unique opportunity, during high school, to work at Bear Stearns, the (in)famous New York investment bank, my parents were a bit worried. Despite their concerns, I convinced them to allow me to take the internship, which entailed a two-hour commute each way, involving a bus to the city and a walk down Forty-Second Street to Park Avenue.

If my parents had known about this last leg of my commute, I'm pretty sure they wouldn't have let me take the job. The twenty-minute walk passed numerous adult entertainment shops, at least five to ten street-side drug vendors, and what I remain convinced were several organized crime fronts pretending to be convenience stores. The word that comes to mind today when I reflect on the Forty-Second Street of 1990 is *seedy*. It's not the type of place you'd send a sixteen year old from the 'burbs. Somehow, I survived.

And I remember in 1993, as a college student, that the candidate for NYC mayor, Rudy Giuliani, ran a campaign that focused on making NYC safe. As a former prosecutor, Giuliani made crime the defining issue of the campaign and he seemed well-credentialed to clean up the city. As difficult as it is to imagine today, New Yorkers in the early 1990s felt like the city was under siege by criminals, drug traffickers, prostitutes, and other nefarious influences. And these impressions were backed up by hard facts: between the 1960s and the early 1990s, rape rates had risen nearly 400 percent, murder rates were up 500 percent and robbery had gone up more than fourteen-fold.[16] It was in the midst of this environment that the tough-on-crime mayoral candidate Rudy Giuliani rode to victory.

Shortly after winning the election, Giuliani installed Boston police chief Bill Bratton as the commissioner of the New York Police Department. Bratton and Giuliani aggressively pursued "broken windows" policing, a crime-fighting strategy based on a theory described in a March 1982 *Atlantic* magazine article written by James Q. Wilson and

George Kelling.[17] The approach was later made famous by Malcolm Gladwell's description in the *Tipping Point*.[18] The practice focused on stopping petty crimes to create an environment in which little infractions were penalized, telegraphing messages to potential criminals that absolutely no crime was going to be tolerated. Fix broken windows, and the message was clear: people cared. Stop small crimes, and big crimes would not happen.

In addition to punishing robbers and violent criminals, Bratton spearheaded an effort that cracked down on turnstile-jumpers and panhandlers in subway stations, drunks and drug pushers on the streets, and even the window-washing squeegee men who would, without asking, clean drivers' windows and expect tips in return. Crime rates plunged.

Between 1993 and 1996, NYC rape rates dropped by 17 percent, assault by 27 percent, robbery by 42 percent, and murder by almost 50 percent.[19] The Wilson-Kelling theory, put into practice by Giuliani and Bratton, seemed to work. A huge success, right?

Well, it's actually not clear. For one thing, as noted by an article in *Mother Jones*, violent crime had peaked in NYC in 1990, years before the Giuliani and Bretton team had taken control. And, the article continues, "Far more puzzling . . . in city after city, violent crime peaked in the early '90s and then began a steady and spectacular decline."[20] Plenty of other cities didn't practice the broken windows approach to policing, and their crime rates plunged alongside that of NYC. Washington, DC, had seen violent crime fall by more than half, Dallas by 70 percent, Newark by almost 75 percent, and Los Angeles, 78 percent.[21]

Plenty of alternative theories emerged, ranging from economic explanations (the economic boom of the 1990s created new jobs and reduced the motivation for crime) to demographic logics (fewer young men = fewer criminals). In one particularly famous explanation for the plunge in violent crime, *Freakonomics* authors Steven Levitt and Stephen Dubner suggested that the drop in crime might have been due to legalized abortion (*Roe v. Wade* was the landmark 1973 decision to legalize abortion) and the prevention of unwanted babies that would grow up without attention or role models.[22] It made sense that seventeen to twenty years after this ruling that crime would drop, right? But all of these things happened at the same time, making it unclear what actually caused what.

In a persuasive piece of investigative journalism, Kevin Drum analyzed all of the studies relating to these and other theories about why violent crime had fallen.[23] And the dots he connected resembled nothing like the ideas I just reviewed with you. In trying to disentangle the spaghetti-like connections between crime and its causes, he began with guidance from Karl Smith, a professor at the University of North Carolina, Chapel Hill who studies epidemics. Drum summarizes the rules of thumb that Smith gave him to understand epidemics:

> If it spreads along the lines of communication, he says, the
> cause is information. Think Bieber Fever. If it travels along
> major transportation routes, the cause is microbial. Think in-
> fluenza. If it spreads out like a fan, the cause is an insect. Think
> malaria. But if it's everywhere, all at once—as both the rise of
> crime in the 60s and 70s and the fall of crime in the 90s
> seemed to be—the cause is a molecule.[24]

What?! A molecule? Yup. In fact, Drum goes on to review numerous studies that have linked one specific material lead to violent crime, reduced IQs, and even the ADHD epidemic. Drum shows how Rick Nevin, a consultant for the Department of Housing and Urban Development, demonstrated how lead poisoning had produced all sorts of problems in children, but he also showed that 90 percent of the changes in violent crime in America could be explained by changes of lead emissions from automobiles. Did the 1970 Clean Air Act, which very specifically targeted the environment, unintentionally and powerfully impact crime rates as it spurred automobile companies to shift from leaded toward unleaded fuels?

While it's still unclear if all the dots to connect are in fact connected, tracing the evolution of our understanding demonstrates how dot connecting can and should be iterative. With each cycle of triangulation, our insights grow. The key in the case of crime was for policymakers to connect health studies with social studies and econometric analysis to cross the silos of understanding.

Bull Magic

We must gain an understanding of what we know—and, more importantly, what we don't. We spend a large portion of our waking hours at work. Following meaningful personal relationships, our jobs are the most significant potential contributors to life satisfaction. It should come as no surprise that careful focus management is an important factor in success at work. And yet few make a deliberate effort to consider just how over-focus hinders work and how active attention management can unleash potential and success.

One of the most respected coaches in basketball history, Phil Jackson was a master of focus management. He led the Chicago Bulls to six championships in the 1990s and the Los Angeles Lakers to five in the 2000s. His success as a coach relied heavily on his ability to guide attention (both his own as well as his players') in ways that other coaches couldn't.

In his book *Eleven Rings*, Jackson describes his deliberate and direct efforts to manage his players away from tunnel vision.[25] By looking broadly and widely, the players he coached developed a mission-oriented, big-picture appreciation for the context of their actions. They were better suited to navigate the inherent ups and downs of professional basketball than their peers. He taught them to zoom out.

To do this, Jackson forced himself to adopt a broader perspective than that of his rival coaches. While most of his competitors focused on the "Xs and Os" of tactics, Jackson concentrated on fine-tuning the mindsets of his players—developing in them what he calls "the spiritual nature of the game."[26] He taught his players to be mindful.

While most coaches tried to deliver the most exciting pump-up speeches before games, Jackson found that this approach made players lose control of their focus. Instead, he "developed a number of strategies to help them quiet their minds and build awareness so they could go into battle poised and in control."[27] This included having players engage in ten minutes of Zen meditation before games. By helping players to stay in the moment and be mindfully aware of their own thoughts, he encouraged subservience of the *me* to the *we* on his teams. And given how star-studded his teams were, this was a major differentiator.

But Jackson didn't hold them to a single hyperfocused process. He was too sensitive to the blinding power of over-focus. As he put it:

> To strengthen the players' awareness, I liked to keep them guessing about what was coming next. During one practice, they looked so lackadaisical I decided to turn out the lights and have them play in the dark—not an easy task when you're trying to catch a rocket pass from Michael Jordan. Another time, after an embarrassing defeat, I had them go through a whole practice without saying a word. Other coaches thought I was nuts. What mattered to me was getting the players to wake up, if only for a moment, and see the unseen, hear the unheard.[28]

Jackson also made sure to expose his players to a variety of perspectives. For example, he would have "experts come in and teach the players yoga, tai chi, and other mind-body techniques." But the outside insights were not confined to Eastern mindfulness practices. He would invite all sorts of guest speakers to provide new perspectives, including "a nutritionist, an undercover detective, and a prison warden."[29]

He'd also gift players books that he thought would help widen their focus, selecting them based on what he knew about each individual and what he felt might specifically help expand their individual horizons. One year's recommendations included *Song of Solomon* (for Michael Jordan), *Things Fall Apart* (Bill Cartwright), *Zen and the Art of Motorcycle Maintenance* (John Paxson), *The Ways of White Folks* (Scottie Pippen), *Joshua: A Parable for Today* (Horace Grant), *Zen Mind, Beginner's Mind* (B. J. Armstrong), *Way of the Peaceful Warrior* (Craig Hodges), *On the Road* (Will Perdue), and *Beavis and Butt-Head: This Book Sucks* (Stacey King).[30]

Jackson also took advantage of the team's vigorous travel schedule to expose his players to new thinking. Sometimes when they were traveling short distances—between Houston and San Antonio, for instance—he'd load everybody onto a bus to give them a chance to see what the world looked like beyond airport waiting rooms. Once, after a hard loss in a playoff series with the Knicks, Jackson surprised everyone by taking the team on a ferry ride to Staten Island rather than making them go through another round of interviews with the media.[31]

But Jackson didn't constrain his perspective-broadening endeavors to sightseeing. He insisted they meet people from all walks of life and learn to appreciate them all. On one trip, Jackson took his team to visit US Senator Bill Bradley, a former basketball player, in his Washington, DC, office.[32] Senator Bradley shared his thoughts about race, politics, and basketball with the team—shortly after he had just delivered a rousing speech on the floor of the US Senate to highlight issues raised by the Rodney King events. He showed the team how he kept a photo in his office of the jump shot he missed in game seven of the 1971 Eastern Conference finals that basically ended the Knicks' hope of a championship that year. As Jackson said, "Bill kept it there as a reminder of his own fallibility."[33] The message was not lost on the players.

Jackson was keenly aware of how overfocus mixed with personal ambition in confident players to produce a toxic cocktail of hubris and narrowness of thought. Consider that Jackson himself was hyperfocused on individual stats, wanting to break as many individual records as he could. But Jackson understood the risks of this individualistic approach; simply put, it would not lead to championships.

. . .

The fundamental problem with employing help to make decisions—regardless of whether it is from focused experts, algorithms embedded in technology, or bureaucratic rules—is that we tend to *mindlessly* adhere to the guidance of these focus managers. This is a subtle and often hidden way through which we stop thinking for ourselves. Managing focus is a critical role that should be done with intention and full awareness of the constraints facing those upon whom you may be dependent.

Imagine you find yourself on the street in the pitch black and completely lost. Along come experts and technologies wielding a much needed flashlight, but a light that only they operate. By looking at the spots where they shine the light, we gain a view of the terrain and may even find our way. But by controlling the spotlight, they're controlling where we focus—which is not by itself bad. It has the potential to mislead, however, if we blindly assume the spotlight is shining in the optimal spot.

Questions to Ask Yourself

- **Are you focused on the right topics?** Think about your focus and how technologies and experts may be influencing where you pay attention. Is where you focus actually an expression of your interests?

- **What might you see if you moved the spotlight elsewhere? Are there options to consider beyond the ones you've been offered?** Remember that attention is limited and the very act of focusing is also an act of filtering and ignoring. Use caution to not filter out the most useful potential options.

- **What is it that experts and technologies do not (or cannot) know about the context that may change your focus?** Recall that experts and technologies, by nature, are only looking within their area of focus and fail to see the complete picture that you are facing. How might these constraints bias their well-intentioned guidance?

- **Do you have the right level of zoom?** Often our level of zoom may not reflect the optimal degree of focus. Consider zooming out to see a bigger view, and then determine the correct level of analysis to help you address the challenge at hand.

CHAPTER 7

Be Mission-Oriented

There is a difference between battle tactics and war strategy. Battles are important but only insofar as they further the objective of winning the war. A key element of thinking for ourselves in the twenty-first century is to deploy our attention toward objectives and not to be distracted by the many battles along the way. Working with experts and specialists, a necessary part of life in the twenty-first century, comes with an elevated risk of pyrrhic victories that might prevent us from achieving our goals. To mitigate this possibility, we must always be mission-oriented.

Disciplined Disobedience

Military strategists have often warned about the idea of winning battles but losing the war. Given the increasing ambiguity, dispersion, and uncertainty of warfare in the twenty-first century, tomorrow's soldiers are likely to be tasked with quickly making unsupervised, high-stakes decisions that reflect their commanders' strategic intents. That is the logic behind the US Army's concept of "mission command," a doctrine that empowers leaders to think for themselves and align their efforts with the ultimate objective.[1]

General Mark Milley (at the time US Army Chief of Staff) noted that the US Army had become "over-centralized, overly bureaucratic, and overly risk-averse" before commenting these dynamics have created a decision-making culture that "is the opposite of what we're going to need." He even went so far as to call for "disciplined disobedience," something that seems absolutely anathema to military culture. Specifically, he noted "a subordinate needs to understand that they have the freedom and they are empowered to disobey a specific order, a specified task, in order to accomplish the purpose." Milley clarified that such behavior cannot be "willy-nilly" but must be toward a higher purpose. A critical component of the doctrine is that commanders must tell their subordinates the purpose of the orders when they give them.[2] The purpose, it seems, is to empower a mission focus.

A Catholic Girl Caught in the Act

Ann Marie Murphy was a girl from Dun Laoghaire, a small and deeply Catholic town seven miles from Dublin. She grew up in government housing. Her father was a sanitation worker and her mother was a housewife, giving birth to ten children in thirteen years. Murphy was the fifth, and she was noticeably shy and beautiful.[3]

Murphy attended Catholic school until the age of fourteen, at which point she went to work for the Glen Abbey hosiery factory. Working in a room without windows from 8 a.m. to 5 p.m., earning $60 per week, the single girls working at the factory stitched 1,500 pairs of pantyhose per day. It was miserable work, and so after ten years of working in such conditions, Murphy was only too happy to take a buyout offer from the factory.

Unlike most of her colleagues, who left their positions upon marriage and pregnancy, Murphy was single. In fact, she stood out as being attractive, sweet, and mysteriously didn't even have a boyfriend. For the next five years, she failed to find regular employment . . . but then things began to change for the better, and quickly.

Her friend Theresa Leonard had found them work as chambermaids at the Park Lane Hilton in London. Within weeks of arriving, Theresa had started dating a Jordanian named Khalid Hassi, who had a roommate named Nezar Hindawi, a good-looking pipe-smoking journalist.

Murphy and Hindawi began dating. Within months, Murphy was pregnant. Unfortunately for the young, unmarried couple, she had a miscarriage and it created a great deal of tension between the two as they coped with his frequent travel and their infrequent meetings. They managed to stay together and six months later, Murphy was again pregnant.

While the difficulties of raising a child as an international journalist were concerning to Hindawi, he agreed after a few months to marry Murphy. Hindawi suggested they fly to Israel (to the Holy Land) so she could meet his family. The couple began to plan their trip. Hindawi gave Murphy money to buy a ticket to Tel Aviv as well as $150 for a passport and a couple of dresses. Hindawi indicated he would fly separately from her as his company provided him a ticket on another airline.

After weeks of planning, Hindawi arrived at 7:30 a.m. to take Murphy to Heathrow Airport to catch El Al Flight 16. He helped with some last-minute packing of a new, lightweight, wheeled bag, a present he had given her in anticipation of the trip, to help her transit without having to carry her luggage. He also told her to not mention their relationship, as it could complicate her travel, but that he'd see her in Tel Aviv. They then headed to the airport, where he escorted her to security, kissed her on both cheeks, and departed.

The airport security at Heathrow took a bit of time, but Murphy got through without any trouble. Six months pregnant, she visited the restroom and then worked her way toward the gate, arriving forty minutes before the check-in window closed. As is typical for El Al flights, she was then subjected to additional screening. El Al security personnel asked where she planned to stay in Israel. After indicating she was going to be staying at the Hilton and was traveling by herself, the security guard noticed that she had very little cash and no credit cards. Confused by the seeming inconsistency, the interviewer selected her for a more thorough search. Six months pregnant, traveling with inadequate resources and by herself, and apparently on holiday were three dots the El Al interviewer had trouble connecting.

Murphy's luggage was sent through the scanner, tagged appropriately, and cleared for loading onto the plane. They then asked her to empty her carry-on bag, which she dutifully did. The security personnel sent the unpacked bag through the scanner. Again, the luggage was cleared, but in handling the bag for the pregnant woman, the El Al man noted that the empty bag was "significantly heavier than normal."[4] He investigated the zippered bottom and revealed a three-pound slab of plastic explosives called Semtex that had been programmed to detonate when the Boeing 747 aircraft carrying 395 people was 39,000 feet above Greece. Murphy was arrested and taken in for questioning, beginning a process that soon revealed Hindawi's terrorist ties.

The date of the failed terrorist attack was April 17, 1986. The unraveling of the intricate plot has since been known as the Hindawi affair.

Since its first hijacking in 1968, El Al Airlines has become a poster child for the Israeli approach to security. I am intentionally using the word *approach* because it's not a set of procedures that sets El Al apart but rather a philosophy of focus management.

In the wake of September 11, *Fortune* magazine labeled El Al as "the most tempting terrorist target in the world."[5] Yet despite this dubious distinction, the airline has had regular success in foiling terrorist plans, in large part due to their approach to handling uncertainty.

Take the case of the Hindawi affair. Murphy had been screened by Heathrow Airport security, and no one caught the presence of explosives in her possession. Why? Might it have been the fact that she was "innocent-looking"? Perhaps it was her Irish passport. Or maybe the fact that she was pregnant? Could it be that the security personnel screening passengers at Heathrow Airport on the morning of April 17, 1986, thought they knew how A terrorist acted? Or the passport he would be carrying? Or his general body type? Or the terrorist's gender? Might it be that in the midst of so much data, the screeners had become overconfident in their own images of the bad guys to catch?

Likewise, what was it about the El Al approach that led the security team to the explosives and saved the lives of 395 passengers and crew? Might it have been a broader approach to thinking about the risks? Or possibly an awareness that the cat-and-mouse game of terrorism involves an element of surprise, meaning you can't know in advance what to look for? If you didn't know what to look for, why focus on anything? Perhaps an approach that emphasized seemingly irrelevant connections in a quest to paint a mosaic is more effective.

According to former El Al CEO Joel Feldschuh, the airline focuses on "terrorists, not just bombs." This means that the airline doesn't apologize about profiling. In reaction to the civil-liberties-oriented objections, he notes, "Banks and credit card companies in the US already use profiling. . . . It shouldn't be a dirty word."[6] Profiling brings with it the ominous connotation of racism. Indeed, El Al has been sued on multiple occasions for discriminating against Arab passengers. Profiling is a tool for directing focus, and it can be trained on narrow variables like skin color, which understandably is criticized in liberal, modern societies. But profiling according to less obvious variables can be invaluable for catching terrorists.

Zeev Friedman, a former sky marshal and El Al security manager, says that profiling can and should go beyond mere ethnicity to include: "Was the ticket purchased in cash? Is it a one-way flight? Does the itinerary include multiple stops when a more direct route could have been taken? Did the passenger arrive late to the gate?" He goes on to note, "Individually, none of these means anything. It just means we put the passenger in a second category where they must clarify things."[7]

Further, every single El Al passenger is then interviewed by a highly trained interviewer to see how he or she reacts and if he or she is telling the truth. Friedman says that all El Al inquiries are specifically designed to not be answered with one-word answers (requiring more detail than typical questions, like: "Did you pack this bag?" or "Has anyone given you anything to carry?"). El Al passengers must instead utilize full sentences to answer questions such as where they plan to stay, and how, when, and where the ticket was purchased. Friedman notes "It's harder to lie when someone asks you how you got to the airport or where you plan to stay or where you bought the ticket and how you paid."[8]

For many of these questions, the interviewer has the answers in the passenger's records and is observing reactions. If the passenger seems nervous or the answers are inconsistent, as with Ann Marie Murphy, more questions are asked and his/her luggage is thoroughly screened.

El Al security does not stop there—it continues with multiple layers of redundant checks that exemplify an approach that acknowledges the airline can't know everything. All checked bags are x-rayed. If something seems suspicious for any reason, it is placed in a bombproof decompression chamber on the ground to simulate the low-pressure conditions that may be used to detonate a bomb. Undercover and armed sky marshals are on every flight, and in those rare cases that a passenger with a suspicious profile boards a plane after he passes the interview and has luggage that is cleared, the marshal is informed of that person's seat number.[9] Additionally, cockpit doors are reinforced to provide an extra layer of security. Lastly, some El Al flights are even equipped with Flight Guard, an infrared countermeasures system used to divert heat-seeking missiles from the jet engines by emitting diversionary flares during both take-off and landing.[10]

In focusing on terrorists rather than bombs, El Al's whole system of security adopts a zoomed-out approach to attacking uncertainty and deception. It's philosophically organized around the belief that recurring checks increase the probability of catching a cunning evildoer. Yes, it is redundant. Yes, it is resilient. But it is more. It improves with each failed terrorist tactic. (Flight Guard was developed in direct response to a failed attempt to shoot down an Israeli airplane in 2002 using shoulder-fired, heat-seeking missiles.[11]) It hones in on anomalies rather than dismissing them. The El Al security system is designed to be antifragile, to draw on useful nomenclature developed by Lebanese-American risk analyst Nassim Taleb in his 2012 book, *Antifragile*. According to Taleb, "antifragility" characterizes things that actually *benefit* from shocks, volatility, randomness, disorder, and stresses.[12]

Blue Zone Bonanza

Dan Buettner, author of a bestselling book called *The Blue Zones: Lessons for Living Longer from the People Who've Lived the Longest,* is a great example of someone who adopted a mission-oriented mindset.[13] While most health writers tend to focus on details, such as heart health or weight, Buettner instead chose to delve into a study of those who live longest and to figure out why. Health is, after all, about living, and topics such as cholesterol and blood sugar are only of interest insofar as they happen to affect the quality and length of one's life.

The journey that Buettner took is as revealing as his findings. Rather than studying science and working toward health, he decided to look at the world's longest living people for guidance on how to eat. He began with health, trying to understand its causes; but his initial focus was narrowly defined by diet. Most, and it seems Buettner was no exception, assume that diet is the one of the most important factors affecting health and longevity.

Indeed, the motivation behind the popular Mediterranean diet was demographic research that highlighted Sardinia's Nuoro province as having an unusually high concentration of centenarians. Later research went on to identify other hot spots, areas that were soon called "blue zones" because of the concentric blue circles drawn on maps by longevity researchers.

Buettner identified four other areas besides Sardinia in the world, which he profiles in his book. In addition to Sardinia, Italy, he covers Okinawa, Japan; Nicoya, Costa Rica; Icaria, Greece; and, to the shock of many Americans, Loma Linda, California. Over more than a decade of meeting with and observing those living in the blue zones, Buettner notes, "Diet does tend to be an entrance ramp for better health."[14] But he didn't stop there.

It was, of course, curious that blue zones even existed. What did geography have to do with diet and longevity? Well, we have to widen our lens a bit and consider the context. It turns out that community and social networks are a key part of understanding the blue zones.

Social networks have proven useful in explaining all kinds of phenomena, including the spread of obesity. Professor Nicholas Christakis and his collaborator James Fowler showed that an obese friend increases your risk of obesity by 45 percent. An obese friend of a friend does the same by 25 percent, while an obese friend of a friend of a friend raises the odds by 10 percent. If your friend becomes obese, you have a 57 percent increased chance of also becoming obese in that same time.[15] Interestingly, Christakis noted that when this result was reported in the *New York Times*, the headline read, "Are You Packing It On? Blame Your Fat Friends," while the European papers asked, "Are Your Friends Gaining Weight? Perhaps You Are to Blame."[16] American individualism at its finest.

Christakis and Fowler also found similar dynamics in behaviors like smoking, drinking, and voting. That something like obesity could spread as a "social contagion" analogously to how, say, the flu spreads, is a reminder that a strong focus on diet choices misses at least a portion of what is at work.[17] Diet is one piece of the puzzle, and a narrow focus obscures the many other pieces.

So perhaps the blue zones exist because they are filled with people who eat healthily? Is it just about surrounding yourself with others who eat well? Surely networks matter, but community dynamics cannot fully explain the longevity anomalies. Only by continuing to ask about the drivers of the blue zone dynamics did Buettner come to appreciate the complexity of the situation. He stayed focused on his mission, namely that of understanding the drivers of extended longevity. And what he found was only possible because of his mission-oriented approach.

Buettner ultimately notes that a "dozen subtly powerful, mutually enhancing and pervasive factors are at work."[18] Factors such as adequate sleep and regular sex combine with family ties, moderate daily wine consumption, and regular unintended exercise. Add to this mix a strong sense of community and purpose and, voilà, you get a blue zone. Easy to describe but hard to replicate. And that's the key insight—that it's not about any specific food, activity, or even the environment. It's about all of them. "The big aha for me," notes Buettner, "is how the factors that encourage longevity reinforce one another over the long term. . . . For people to adopt a healthy lifestyle, I have become convinced, they need to live in an ecosystem that makes it possible."[19] Turns out, there is no magic bullet.

Shoot for the Goal

Directing our focus in the right place can also help secure our financial wellbeing. Many of us have some exposure to the stock market, either through our retirement accounts or through direct brokerage or financial advisory accounts. And over time, our account balances go up and down. Some years we feel great. Others we don't.

Yet many investment managers tell us that's the wrong way to think about it. Because you can't actually predict the investment returns of an investment type—be it stocks, bonds, commodities, or another asset—we focus on relative returns to determine how well an investment manager is doing. It's how you're doing versus the market that matters, not the actual returns you earned—or so we're told. The practical implication of this is that a 30 percent return in one year is deemed horrible (if the index for that particular asset class was up 40 percent) while a 30 percent loss is considered spectacular in a year when the index is down 40 percent. Stop and think about this for a moment: up 30 percent and you're supposed to feel bad, down 30 percent and you're supposed to feel good? Huh?!

One reason this happens is because of the focus we have on optimizing our returns given the plethora of investment funds we have available. Think of it as modern-day investment FOMO. And virtually all of the evidence points to one disturbing conclusion—most investment managers underperform relative to their benchmark. Why's that? In the most simple of terms, fees. The fees that fund managers charge for their services explain a large portion of the difference.

As Yale's chief investment officer David Swensen wrote in the *New York Times*, companies that manage for-profit mutual funds face a conflict between producing profits for their owners and generating returns for their investors. For-profit mutual funds spend on marketing campaigns to gather assets. Investors in general have suffered below-market returns for decades as mutual fund management company owners enjoyed market-beating results. Swensen condemns this practice, saying, "Profits trumped the duty to serve investors."[20]

But we've known for decades that for-profit mutual funds benefit management, not investors. And yet investors continue to flock to underperforming managers. Why? It's logical to be confused by this dynamic. In an effort to untangle the reasons for why such suboptimal performance persists, I read a paper by my friend, colleague, and coteacher Charles D. Ellis entitled "Murder on the Orient Express: The Mystery of Underperformance."[21] Despite my admittedly biased relationship, I think Ellis's paper offers the best explanation out there for widespread underperformance. In a playful Agatha Christie approach to untangling the mystery, the paper evaluates four suspects—investment managers, fund executives, investment consultants, and investment committees—at the scene of the underperformance crime. The paper's ultimate conclusion is that all are guilty. Remind you of the logic of blue zones? Looking at the parts misses the dynamics of the whole.

Ellis argues that the whole system of interlocking pieces in the investment industry is so narrowly oriented that it's failing to see the proverbial big-picture goal on which it should be focused. Without a change away from the specific tasks of investment management to the ultimate mission of return generation, it's unlikely to improve: "Each participant knows that it is working conscientiously, knows it is working hard, and believes sincerely in its own innocence . . . [and] until they examine the evidence and recognize their own active roles, however unintentionally performed, the crime of underperformance will continue to be committed."[22]

Ellis is right to suggest that the task-focused approach of the industry's key players has hijacked the mission orientation. But what if we push this logic further? What if the focus on maximizing returns is blinding us? Perhaps the basic underlying assumption that more is better is misleading us? Might it be possible to reconceive how we even think about the mission of investing? Is there possibly a good enough solution? Can we satisfice while investing?

In fact, as behavioral approaches have increasingly entered the world of economics and finance, we've seen a shift from maximizing approaches to the satisficing logic mentioned earlier in the book. To recall, Nobel

Laureate Herbert Simon thought it was impossible to truly maximize given we have "bounded rationality," so we should instead try to achieve our goals. The application of this satisficing logic in the investment domain is known as goals-based investing. I know, you're probably asking: What type of investing isn't focused on some goal? After all, doesn't everyone invest with a goal in mind—retirement, college fund for the children, new house?

While true, the logic behind a goals-based approach is more targeted. It's like the old vacation clubs popularized by the savings and loan industry in the 1980s, in which set amounts were saved into separate accounts for the explicit purpose of generating an adequate lump sum for a specific goal. It's more specific than the generic goals of retiring, funding a child's education, or purchasing a new home. For example, a goal might be something as specific as having $210,000 for a child's college education within ten years, given an initial investment of $50,000 and monthly investments of $500.

The pursuit of concrete goals differs dramatically in focus from the conventional college savings plans that lack a specific targeted goal. An open-ended goal lends itself to a focus on maximizing while a targeted goal generates a focus on achieving. Before I explain, let's take a step back to understand why investing is done the way it is.

The basic idea of modern portfolio theory is that there is no free lunch when it comes to investing. That is, for a given amount of risk, there is an optimal portfolio structure that can maximize returns. To get more returns, you need to bear more risk . . . or alternatively, if you bear lower risk, you should expect lower returns. Modern portfolio theory can be summed up very crudely as: there's a tradeoff between risk and reward. It all makes sense, but let's not forget it is logically derived from the idea of maximizing returns, given a specific tolerance for risk.

Goals-based investing originated in the pension industry, where the future obligations of sending retirees pension checks generated specific objectives. Managers of pension funds generally don't get paid more if they exceed the pension's needs, and so some sought to increase the probability of achieving their targeted return, even if it came by clipping the possibility of significant outperformance. Satisficing increases the probability of achieving one's targets, even if it means potentially forgoing an unintended surplus.

Years ago, I had a chance to hear Nobel Laureate Robert Merton make the case for goals-based investing.[23] At the heart of his argument was a shift in focus—away from maximizing and toward the probability of achieving. What if a client had the explicit goal I mentioned earlier of saving $210,000 for a child's college education and genuinely didn't care about earning a penny more? In that case, she can take on meaningfully less risk and also increase the probability of success by cutting off the upside. She could, in effect, sell an option to someone for returns in excess of $210,000 and use the payment she received toward her objective of reaching $210,000. By selling the optimization logic to another and focusing on a satisficing logic for herself, she improves the likelihood of hitting her goal.

For this hypothetical client, what really matters is ensuring that she can, for example, afford her child's tuition when she needs to pay for it. The goals-based approach acknowledges that people have different risk-return preferences for different goals rather than a single overarching one for every aspect of their lives. A college education is so important that they would want to minimize the risk that they couldn't afford it, while they might be willing to take on more risk in saving for a car with the knowledge that they could always get a more modest one than they planned if things don't go their way. The goals-based approach shifts our focus away from fighting battles toward winning wars. Rather than encouraging greed and the fear of missing out on elusive outperformance, it instead channels attention toward our ultimate mission.

Football, Footprints, and the Future

Those not versed in the arcane details of accounting may think of costs as a single category. But, in fact, there are different types to consider. To form a business in the first place, there are a bunch of one-off expenses: for example, buying land, constructing a building on that land, and purchasing specialized machinery to fill it with. These are called capital costs. And they don't just involve physical property like land; they also cover, for example, the development of internal software designed to make the business more efficient or the research required to spin out a new, innovative product.

Once a system is in place, the business also incurs numerous day-to-day expenses. These are called operating costs. They can include regular, re-curring costs like rent and variable costs like wages. They're what it takes to keep a business simply chugging along.

Increasingly, we're also starting to consider the environmental costs of our activities. When we do so, most of us tend to overfocus on the en-vironmental operating costs of our devices. We think about the gas our cars use, the electricity demanded by our devices, or the recyclability of the packaging in which our products arrived. By focusing so intensely on operating costs, we tend to minimize the less obvious environmental costs of *producing* the devices in the first place.

Take the iPhone, for example. The daily battery drain reminds us of the power we're wasting in order to satisfy our addiction to tweets, beeps, and buzzes. Who of us hasn't desperately dashed into a coffee shop just to give our digital sidekicks some extra juice? In focusing on the daily drain, we tend to ignore the total costs.

Using something called lifecycle assessment (LCA), we can calculate the total environmental impact of a device, from manufacturing, through operation, and ultimately on to disposal. Using such analytic methods, we learn that 61 percent of the greenhouse gas emissions emanating from an iPhone's life come from extracting raw materials or the design and manufacturing of the device. Another 5 percent comes from packaging and transporting them all over the world. Operating the phones only ac-counts for 30 percent of emissions. The rest come from disposal.[24] That's right—that daily battery drain accounts for less than a third of the emis-sions associated with your smartphone.

If the source of the environmental impact of the iPhone comes from is shocking, you won't believe what it looks like in cars. Switching the power source for our most important mode of transportation from dirty gasoline to clean-sounding electricity seems like a sound approach to protecting the environment. But the extreme focus on the immediate emissions of cars—the environmental operating costs—blinds us to a bigger problem: the environmental impact from manufacturing the vehicles.

Entrepreneur Kevin Czinger is working hard to widen environmentalists' narrow focus from the operating costs of cars. Rather than concentrating on immediate tailpipe emissions, Kevin's company, Divergent3D, which he founded in 2013, uses LCA to analyze the total environmental impact of the vehicle, from production to decommissioning.[25] The company considers the carbon footprint of both the production of the car as well as the operation of it, rather than retaining a narrow focus on the latter. And he's found that "a far greater percentage of a car's total emissions comes from the materials and energy needed to manufacture a car (mining, processing, manufacturing, and disposal)" than does from the car's operation. To summarize Kevin's words, "how we make our cars is actually a bigger environmental issue than how we fuel our cars."[26]

Kevin is personally familiar with the blinding focus on tailpipe emissions of most environmentalists in the transportation industry. He used to have it himself. A former Yale linebacker, reserve Marine, record label founder, investment banker, and dotcom-era executive at Webvan, he entered the world of cleantech with ambitions to save the environment by disrupting the fuel source of automobiles.

In 2009, he founded an electric car company, Coda. "We thought we were saving the world," he later recalled.[27] But the experience of building the car widened his focus dramatically. As he visited the Chinese plant that produced his electric car, he encountered the severe pollution that surrounded the factory, and he studied the inputs and outputs involved in the manufacturing process. With this new perspective, he realized the environmental costs of operating vehicles were only the tip of the iceberg; the manufacturing impact was beneath the surface. While reducing tailpipe emissions was a worthy task, his ultimate objective shifted to minimizing the environment footprint of the entire process of both building and operating vehicles. Kevin didn't want to win the operating footprint battle but lose the environmental war.

Divergent3D is pushing what is called "dematerialization"—that is, reducing the materials and energy needed to build a car. Divergent3D attempts to disrupt the traditional, capital-intensive factory model of automobile manufacturing. Instead, Divergent3D is developing methods to build cars using 3D printing technologies. Kevin believes his company's approach could reduce the negative environmental impact of car manufacturing by 70 percent. And the stakes are high, because twice as many cars will be produced over the next forty years as were produced over the last 115. Divergent3D's technology will also allow small, flexible, diverse teams of people to design cars on their own with much lower capital requirements; in Kevin's words, it will allow a "democratization of car manufacturing."[28]

Kevin's insight was to see that even the most brilliant innovators could trap themselves in an overfocus on narrow technological solutions to the detriment of a broader rethinking of systemic problems. If the goal was to reduce the carbon footprint of our transportation system, then why not zoom out and focus on that objective, taking into account the whole systems' footprint? By managing his focus and retaining a mission-orientation, Kevin may be reinventing the future of manufacturing.

. . .

Proposing a mindful approach to focusing on goals (rather than generalized optimization or maximization) runs contrary to the conventional wisdom. Regardless of whether we're talking about health care, airline security, or money management, the prevailing logic is to stop illness, identify bombs, and maximize returns. But what if these task-oriented pursuits, using the language of systems thinkers, produce feedback loops that make the goal less achievable? What if the very manufacturing of electric cars accelerates climate change?

The narrow task-oriented approach many of us adopt in our day-to-day decision making can lead us astray. It's important to stop and reconsider the purpose of our efforts. Why are we doing what we're doing? Likewise, in certain domains it may make more sense to proactively satisfice. We need to remember we are trying to win wars, not battles.

Questions to Ask Yourself

- **What's your goal? Do the actions you're taking or the decisions you're making make that objective more or less likely?** Recall that experts and technologies do not have an appreciation of the big picture that you do and may not understand your ultimate goals. Focus on winning wars, not battles.

- **Are there experts or technologies that are trying to manage your focus toward tasks rather than your mission?** Consider having a blunt discussion about your goals and how to increase the *probability* of achieving them. Experts may assume you are seeking to optimize when you may be content to increase the probability of achieving a more modest goal.

- **Might disciplined disobedience be in order?** When noticing expert or technology-driven decisions that are not goal-oriented, consider active pushback to reorient toward the mission.

CHAPTER 8

Think for Yourself

As we've seen, being mindful of how we focus is critical for our wealth, health, and happiness. Expert advice and focus filters are necessary: the world is simply too complex not to highlight some things and tune out others. But when we let experts direct our spotlight, we are likely to lose sight of what lies in the shadows. This is as true for expert opinions from doctors as it is for information that makes it through filtering algorithms designed by coders. As obvious as it sounds, learning to think independently is an important step to restore self-reliance in the twenty-first century.

Over half a century ago, the future Nobel Laureate Kenneth Arrow explicitly explained that "because medical knowledge is so complicated, the information possessed by the physician as to the consequences and possibilities of treatment is necessarily very much greater than that of the patient, or at least so it is believed by both parties."[1] In econo-speak, this knowledge imbalance is called information asymmetry. In plain English, Arrow was saying doctors and patients both believe doctors know more, and therefore, doctors know best. The patient feels that he or she cannot discriminate between treatment options like the doctor can, and so "the patient must delegate to the physician much of his freedom of choice."[2]

Think about the power dynamic between you and someone who wears a white coat, has made you wait because he or she is very important, and has the degrees and fellowship certificates on the wall to visibly remind you of information asymmetry. The doctor is in demand, why else would you be waiting? So it's not shocking that most people retain the belief that "doctors know best." And while that's mostly true, we can and should be more active patients. After all, who is more expert on your body than you?

A particularly cynical friend of mine notes that the strategy some doctors employ to make patients wait is analogous to the strategies pursued by many nightclubs. Long lines filled with eager customers trying to get in are used to telegraph the quality of the club. "Why else would so many people be waiting for an hour in a line with others?" or so the thinking goes. The long wait is a signal to potential customers that the club is very popular and in great demand. Of course, some nightclubs may actually be filled to capacity, but this is unlikely the case for all.

When visiting a doctor, taking advice from a financial expert, or even making a high-stakes decision at work, it's critical that you think for yourself. Don't let information asymmetry intimidate you into turning off your brain. There may be visible power dynamics that also telegraph the knowledge imbalance, but that doesn't change the reality that only you can fully understand the complete context of your decision. The advice and guidance you receive from others are tiles in a mosaic that you are forming—they're inputs into your decision making. Not more, not less. Just inputs.

Wizards and Humbugs

Outsourced thinking runs rampant in the world of investing. Jon Stewart laid bare the dangers of letting others direct our investing attention during one of the most memorable *Daily Show* segments of 2009 in which he interviewed Jim Cramer. Cramer, the host of the popular prime-time financial advice program *Mad Money*, joined Stewart during a weeklong series of discussions about financial markets and the financial crisis.

During the half-hour interview, Stewart took Cramer—and the broader financial news industry—to task for misleading viewers seeking investment guidance. After some friendly banter, Stewart explained why Americans were frustrated with finance and, specifically, financial media. Stewart cited a "gap between what CNBC advertises itself as and what it is and the help that people need to discern this."[3]

To crystallize the idea, Stewart played the promotional advertisement for *Mad Money* while pictures of Cramer wearing a tie with a serious expression flashed across the screen, a seemingly wisdom-filled voice bellowed, "The economy in free fall. Investments on the brink. When you don't know what to do, don't panic. Cramer's got your back!" At which point the logo for the show appeared, reminiscent of a dollar bill: "IN CRAMER WE TRUST" was written across the bill. After the audience had a small chuckle, Stewart spoke directly to Cramer, saying, "We're both snake oil salesmen to an extent, but we do label the show here as snake-oil. Isn't there a problem selling snake oil as vitamin tonic?"

In Stewart's eyes, Cramer had misdirected his viewers. He suggested Cramer was trying to entertain people, but in the process obfuscating the seriousness of investing. The normally comic Stewart then turned noticeably serious: "I can't reconcile the brilliance and knowledge that you have of the intricacies of the market with the crazy bullshit you do every night. . . . I understand that you want to make finance entertaining, but it's not a fucking game."

I was recently reading *The Wonderful Wizard of Oz* to my children and I couldn't help but notice the similarities between Cramer and the Great Humbug. (Perhaps this is because I had recently been reading how *The Wonderful Wizard of Oz* has been analyzed by some as a parable about the perils and dangers of currencies that were not backed by hard assets![4]) But in the children's version of the story, Dorothy discovers that the Wizard is not the magical force she and the Lion, Tin Man, and Scarecrow had been led to believe he was, and so bluntly asks: "Are you not a great Wizard?" to which he replies, "Not a bit, my dear; I'm just a common man."[5]

The Wizard says that he can't "help being a humbug . . . when all these people make me do things that everybody knows can't be done."[6] Reading this line to my children made me think of Cramer as "The Wizard of CNBC," the great humbug of the modern investo-tainment industry.

Stewart seemed to draw a similar analogy. After he highlighted Cramer's obvious duplicity and misguided focus on getting eyeballs rather than helping investors, Cramer agreed that the "goal should always be to try to expose the fact that there is no easy money." But Stewart didn't stop, adding, "There are literally shows called *Fast Money*" on CNBC, to which Cramer sheepishly responded: "There's a market for it and you give it to them." Sound like the Wizard of Oz? Is Cramer the finance equivalent of a common man peddling bran and pins and needles as brains?

The problem is ultimately one of focus. In our never-ending search for magic bullets, we willingly listen to those offering the investment tonic that might cure our woes. By doing so, we're misled and misdirected. We focus on the wrong things. Cramer, CNBC, and most of the financial media complex funnel our attention toward individual stocks and the daily vicissitudes of financial markets. Our focus as individual investors should lie in long-term investing, not whether Cramer's reaction to the mere mention of a stock yields a screaming "Buy, buy, buy!" while he frantically throws a stuffed bull at the camera. Our focus should not be on the daily swings in stocks. Aside from professionals who spend their days and nights studying markets, it's been best to just gain broad exposure at low costs. But that too may be changing, as I'll address in the next section.

Jack Helped Me (and Millions of Others)

I've known Jack for a long time, and I attribute much of my success to his generosity. In 1987, as an eighth-grade student at Mt. Arlington Public School in northwestern New Jersey, I heard about a scholarship program being offered at a boarding school located due west of my family's home in Landing, New Jersey. I had never even contemplated private school. Simply put, my family couldn't afford the option.

But a scholarship was a compelling proposition, and you can imagine my joy when I was awarded a scholarship and supplemental financial aid to attend. I enrolled as a freshman at Blair Academy in the fall of 1988 and began a four-year high school experience that inspired me and gave me much-needed confidence. My time at Blair would not have been possible with the generosity of a single donor—John C. Bogle (Jack)—the father of the passive index fund and the founder of Vanguard. I had the distinct honor of getting to know Jack before I understood what a mutual fund was. He changed my life by opening a world of opportunity.

The best part of Jack's story is that I'm just one of the millions of lives that he's changed. By shifting the focus of America's investing mantra, Jack helped secure the retirement and futures of many people. Here's an abbreviated story of his career and the stunning focus-shift he's enabled.

Jack became interested in mutual funds as an undergraduate at Princeton in late 1949, when he came across an article in *Fortune*. An economics major, he decided to write his senior thesis on the industry.[7] After graduation, Jack secured a job at the Wellington Fund, rising through the ranks and eventually becoming chairman. After being forced out in 1974 following an unwise merger that he oversaw, Jack set out to found a new company. He named it Vanguard after the British admiral Horatio Nelson's seventy-four-gun ship, the *HMS Vanguard*.[8]

Jack made sure that the shareholders in the mutual funds of Vanguard also controlled the company itself, so that the interests of shareholders in the funds and the company were aligned, allowing it to focus on reducing fees. Under this new entity, Jack started the first real index fund, which tracked the S&P 500—inspired by a 1974 article Paul Samuelson wrote calling for the creation of such a fund. Further, Jack's own research showed that most active funds lost out to the S&P 500.

Toward this end, Jack exhibited a mission-oriented mindset. His goal was to offer well-diversified funds at minimal costs, focused on the long term. Rather than getting sidetracked by a task focus, when his initial offering was 93 percent below the anticipated size and underwriters wanted to cancel the deal, Jack responded, "Oh no we won't! Don't you realize that we now have the world's first index fund?" At the time, Jack recalled, the fund was referred to as "Bogle's Folly."[9]

But it ultimately took off, in part thanks to support from Samuelson and others. Today, Vanguard controls some of the biggest equity funds in the world and manages trillions of dollars of Americans' assets. Jack contributed at least three major developments to investing. First, he introduced index funds. Second, he lowered the costs of these funds. And third, he showed the importance of removing the perverse incentive of for-profit mutual fund companies. In doing all this, Jack meaningfully shifted the objective for many investors from beating market returns, eloquently called "a loser's game" by Charley Ellis, to earning market returns.[10] By helping individuals not lose, he helped them win.

Jack's logic was sound: turning off CNBC, focusing on asset allocation, and investing in Vanguard's low-cost passive index funds would allow you to avoid many investment pitfalls. (I'm not sponsored by Vanguard, I promise!)

But I need to insert one (major) caveat. The logic behind passive investing relies on two things: (1) accurate prices and (2) owning everything. But these don't always hold true. Prior to his unfortunate passing in January 2019, Jack was getting nervous about another product available to investors hoping to go passive: exchange-traded funds, or ETFs. First created in 1993, "ETFs have become a marketing and promotional game," he said in an interview with *Think Advisor*.[11] The July 2, 2017 issue of *Things That Make You Go Hmmm*, a newletter published by my friend Grant Williams, who's been active in the finance world for thirty years, was titled "Passive Regression." In it, Grant quotes Jack:

> Through September 2015, shares of the 100 largest ETFs, valued at $1.5 trillion, were turning over at an annualized volume of $14 trillion, a turnover rate of 864%. By way of comparison, the annualized turnover volume of the 100 largest stocks, valued at $12 trillion, is running at $15 trillion for the same period, a turnover rate of 117%. Trading in the 100 largest ETFs thus represents about 89% of such stock trading, up from a mere 7% 15 years ago. Given these powerful data, it is hardly unfair to describe today's ETFs—as a group—as the modern way to speculate in the stock market.[12]

Passive investing is good generalist logic. You can't know everything, so why not own everything? But with the explosion of indices, each one narrower than the last, the logic breaks down. Are you really getting the benefit of passive investing when you invest in an index that tracks small cap biotech companies listed on emerging market exchanges but excluding state-owned enterprises or companies that begin with the letter *w*? It's now possible to invest in the Obesity ETF, SLIM, which tracks the performance of companies positioned to profit from servicing the obese, more than 40 percent of which is invested in two companies; narrow ETFs such as these (and others) may prove useful for speculation, but let's not think they're good passive index investments.

The irony is that the logic that makes passive investing a good idea falls apart when too many people start to do it. Think about it. Imagine a world in which everyone is investing passively. All stocks would rise or fall depending on inflows or outflows. Both good and bad companies would rise with inflows and fall with outflows. The premise that prices are accurate, the foundation upon which the argument in favor of passive investing lies, breaks down. Systems thinkers will not find this shocking.

Prices lose their grounding if everyone invests passively. The blunt reality is that passive investment involves buying and selling stocks *without considering their price*. Stop and think about my last sentence. Does that make sense? Would you really want to buy and sell securities without considering their prices? We're now seeing a drop in active investing overall, which I think is a worrying trend. We want people paying attention to prices! And in fact, it's the active investment community that helps push prices toward their fair values. Without active investors, price discovery processes break down.

Grant describes this phenomenon with respect to fixed income ETFs, which have ballooned in recent years: "Assets which used to be subject to scrupulous credit checks . . . now sit in one-click wonders and, as volatility has steadily fallen, so has the quality control around the bonds which make it into ETFs."[13] Back in 2010, only 20 percent of companies in the S&P 500 had Vanguard index funds with a significant ownership stake (5 percent or more); since then, the number of companies in which Vanguard (and its peers BlackRock and State Street) own meaningful stakes has risen.[14] As fewer people actively choose which companies to invest in, I'm afraid that we'll see the market become more volatile. As the report showed, stocks with the highest passive ownership were more vulnerable to price swings because fewer shares were available for trading.

In many ways, investing successfully over the long term is about thinking for yourself and ignoring the noise. It's about being a contrarian and understanding that most people do not think for themselves, allowing financial media houses to manage their attention. Push back on the allure of hot stocks and the *Mad Money*–inspired investo-tainment industry . . . and think for yourself about what makes sense for your risk tolerance and personal objectives.

"What Do We Do, Boss?"

When it comes to making decisions and thinking for yourself, in no domain are the stakes as high as they are when it comes to fighting terrorism. Jose Rodriguez, the director of the US Counterterrorism Center from 2002 until 2004, faced perhaps the highest stakes decision of his life when he was later traveling in Pakistan.[15] But before I tell you about the call he received, it helps to have some background.

In the tense post-9/11 period, US intelligence authorities were monitoring what seemed like a never-ending stream of plots to attack US interests. Many American allies, including the United Kingdom, shared intelligence and coordinated gathering efforts. By 2006, one specific plot was gaining momentum at an alarming rate.

Here are the facts as they unfolded.

British intelligence services had been tracking a person by the name of Rashid Rauf, who supposedly had been in touch with Al Qaeda leadership in Pakistan. He was a British man from Birmingham and was emerging as the ringleader of a major terrorist plot.

By chance, investigators had the opportunity to covertly open the luggage of Ahmed Ali, one of Rauf's numerous accomplices, when he returned from a trip to Pakistan. His luggage contained a large number of batteries and some Tang, the orange drink powder. These items raised sufficient suspicion that British authorities began what was then the country's largest surveillance operation, employing hundreds of people and dozens of targets. It unveiled a disturbing set of facts, including a person of interest disposing of numerous empty hydrogen peroxide bottles. When the surveillance team followed him, they noticed him meeting with another individual, whose apartment (upon later covert inspection) was a de facto bomb factory. MI5, the British intelligence service, installed recording and transmitting devices in the apartment and later watched individuals constructing explosive devices out of various drink bottles. One of the men was later seen at an internet café, where he spent two hours studying airline timetables.[16]

The widebody plot, as it has since been called, seemed to point to the simultaneous downing of numerous planes that were heading to North America, all being masterminded by Rashid Rauf's Al Qaeda cell. Both the US and British intelligence services were getting increasingly alarmed at the specificity of the rising threat. According to some reports, the British MI5 had infiltrated the group with an undercover agent. The evidence of an imminent attack was mounting.

As former CIA director Michael Hayden recounts in *Spymasters*, a documentary about the American intelligence agency, the US and British analysis of the threat differed a bit with respect to process: "The British wanted to build up as much physical evidence as possible . . . so we're saying 'They've got the hydrogen peroxide' . . . and they're saying 'we need more evidence. . . .'" Hayden continues: "They had gathered up an awful lot of hydrogen peroxide and a homemade recipe to turn it into an explosive and then put it into sports bottles . . . so we had great concern on our side of the Atlantic."

Rodriguez, who reported to Hayden, noted that the stakes were rising every day: "the plotters had already selected the ten flights that they were going to blow up . . . and I said to myself, 'This is imminent!'" In early August 2006, Hayden was in Pakistan with Rodriguez, who at the time was the head of the National Clandestine Service. Rauf happened to be in the country as well. Rodriguez was summoned to a meeting with the chief of Pakistani intelligence and informed that they may have an opportunity to capture Rauf that very evening at a police checkpoint.

Earlier that day, CIA headquarters personnel had explicitly promised the British authorities that the American agency would not capture Rauf. Further, Rodriguez noted at the time, "I was told that Prime Minister [Tony] Blair had spoken with President [George] Bush that day and they had agreed that they needed more time."

Later that very evening, Rodriguez was traveling with the CIA's chief of station for Pakistan, who received a call from the Pakistani authorities informing him that the bus with Rauf was approaching the police checkpoint. The Pakistanis wanted authorization to capture Rauf. The chief of station turned to Rodriguez and asked, "What do we do, boss?"

What would you do? Remember the stakes. Lots of lives. But also that the president of the United States assured the prime minister of the United Kingdom that they would not capture Rauf. In boiling down the situation to its very essence, General Hayden commented, "So Jose, in a very short period of time, has to make a really big decision." Had Rodriguez taken time to phone up General Hayden or to seek permission from Langley, it would have been, as he later noted, "the equivalent of saying 'no' to the operation."

At great personal risk to his career, his reputation, and to the trust that had been built between the British and US intelligence communities, Rodriguez authorized the capture. Despite the protocol of following a chain of command, Rodriguez thought for himself. As Hayden later said, "The decision he made was 'I can't pass up the opportunity to grab Rashid Rauf,' so he does." The plot was foiled, saving hundreds of lives and preventing a global panic.

Weeks later, the *New York Times* revealed that seven martyrdom tapes had been discovered during British raids.[17] Further, digital forensics found files pointing to the specific flights operated by United Airlines, American

Airlines, and Air Canada that had been targeted, all of which were departing from London's Heathrow Airport and were headed, as suspected, to North American cities including San Francisco, Toronto, Montreal, Chicago, Washington, DC, and New York City.[18]

As a result of the British raids and breakup of the cell, information was later revealed during the trials of several plotters that confirmed earlier suspicions. The plotters had planned to use hydrogen peroxide mixtures to create explosives once onboard and to use batteries to detonate the homemade bombs. And so now you know why passengers flying on commercial aircraft in the United States are restricted from bringing more than 3.4 fluid ounces (100 ml) onboard the plane in their carry-on luggage.

The stakes of thinking can be very high, as Rodriguez learned. But had he not thought for himself, or if he had decided to take a permission-driven approach, it's unclear what might have happened. The panic and economic impact of a successful terrorist attack would have been as severe, if not more so, than 9/11. Fortunately, it didn't transpire . . . but it was a really close call, prevented in large part by an official who thought for himself.

The Swensen Effect

As a thirty-something financier with zero experience managing money, David Swensen was convinced by his dissertation advisor, Nobel laureate James Tobin, to return to mother Yale from Wall Street and run the university's endowment. Rather than begin from the approach taken by others, David began with a blank sheet. He went back to first principles, realizing that Yale had a long time horizon, was tax-exempt, and could handle illiquidity. The result was a portfolio that included heavier weights to alternative assets like private equity, venture capital, and hedge funds than his peer institutions. He developed his own guiding light, didn't rely on the thinking of others, and put together an investment approach that made sense to him. David didn't seek external validation. No focus groups, no conventional logic, just independent thinking.

David articulated a boring, sound approach to investing—and I mean that as a compliment! It began with an understanding that there are three sources of investment return in any portfolio: market timing, security selection, and asset allocation. Market timing is choosing when to buy and sell; security selection is deciding which individual investments to make; and asset allocation is the act of spreading your investments across different buckets like stocks, bonds, and cash.[19]

Asset allocation—at what proportions you allocate your money across investment classes—accounts for between 90 percent and over 100 percent of investor returns, compared with security selection and market timing. That number could be over 100 percent because active timing and selection can actually lose you money—when you buy high, sell low, and incur all kinds of fees and taxes.[20] As David explained to my students when he visited my class, "Asset allocation is far and away the most important tool that we have available to us as investors."

The results of David's thinking for himself speak for themselves: the Yale Investment Office has produced one of the best long-term track records in the world of endowment management. But in addition to being a great manager of assets, David is a good teacher both in the classroom and at his office. Former colleagues of his from the Yale Investments Office are running the endowments of MIT, Bowdoin, the University of Pennsylvania, Stanford University, Princeton University, Wesleyan University, and many other endowments and foundations. While some have given David a run for his money in the short run by outperforming Yale, no one has been able to match the Yale Investment Office's long-term track record. The performance has resulted in literally billions of dollars of support for Yale, enabling it to improve facilities, conduct ground-breaking research, and recruit the most promising students from all over the world, regardless of their ability to pay. Simply put, Yale would not be the university it is today had David not thought for himself.

This blunt fact seems lost on those who fail to appreciate independent thinking and fresh perspectives. Sandra Urie, the former chief executive officer of Cambridge Associates, the world's leading investment consultancy to large endowments and foundations, recounted a story to me over coffee that illustrates the point well. She recalled how one of her larger clients asked for her help in recruiting a new chief investment officer and explicitly asked for "someone like David Swensen." Urie responded with "OK, so you want someone in their thirties with no money management experience?" I suspect you can finish the rest of the story yourself.

· · ·

Recall the earlier story of Trisha Torrey. When facing a dynamic as complicated as the one she faced, the only person who had a holistic view of the problem was Trisha. Had she not actively engaged, she likely would have been treated for a disease she didn't have. But there are a host of other disappointments. Why did the surgeon simply assume the lab results were conclusive? Was he too busy to think about them or truly evaluate them? And why not check the ultimate test of malignancy, cell multiplication? Maybe because he didn't need to live with the diagnosis but could simply pass her along to an oncologist? Let's recall that Trisha began with her family doctor, who sent her to a surgeon, who then sent her to an oncologist. Each step is associated with narrowing perspective, deepening focus, and a greater likelihood of being blinded. You can imagine this chain continuing. Rather than crossing siloes and using multiple perspectives, the process got more and more focused.

Trisha's story, unfortunately, may not be a rare anomaly. Medical misdiagnosis is not as unusual as we would hope. Arthur Elstein has estimated that doctors incorrectly diagnose a patient's ailment somewhere between 10 and 15 percent of the time,[21] a suggestion that should petrify all of us. We simply must take control of our own health and think for ourselves.

Trisha overcame a common trap that many of us fall into when we believe we're being thorough. Rather than having a second first opinion, she went out and found a true, unadulterated, independent second opinion. That was a key event in her story, and it wouldn't have been possible without her thinking for herself.

One thing that's obvious from these and many other stories is that great breakthroughs rarely come from adopting other people's thoughts. If

David Swensen had adopted (and maybe even tweaked) endowment strategies of the world's best managers at the time he took over the Yale endowment, rather than going back to first principles, he might not have come up with as innovative and successful a model. Rather than reading Harvard Business School case studies of successful endowment managers, he became the subject of one. As hard as it is to do, we all can and should take the time to think for ourselves.

Questions to Ask Yourself

- **How would you approach a situation if you were a beginner and didn't have prior knowledge?** Rather than relying blindly on convention and/or existing best practice, try approaching the problem from scratch. Revisit first principles and "blank sheet" the ideal strategy given your objective.

- **Are experts helping or hindering your thinking?** As exemplified by the case of Jim Cramer and his info-tainment show *Mad Money*, some supposed experts are more akin to snake oil salesmen than those with deep expertise. Always ask yourself if they're helpful with your specific situation.

- **Have you adopted new thinking or just confirmed existing logic?** Think about Trisha's experience and seek out truly independent second opinions (vs. second first opinions); using existing conclusions to begin your analysis is (by definition) not thinking for yourself.

CHAPTER 9

Triangulate Perspectives

The information explosion that drove today's tremendous specialization shows no signs of stopping. One antidote to joining the ranks of the narrowly zoomed-in and focused is to adopt a generalist approach, one that seeks out multiple perspectives with the hopes of triangulating unique insights. Acknowledging that every perspective is, by definition, incomplete may enable a broader, more flexible, and open-minded approach to empathizing with others. It will also help us navigate the ubiquitous uncertainty that plagues our world today.

The Power of Multiple Lenses

Vantage Point,[1] a 2008 movie starring Forest Whitaker and Sigourney Weaver, is a movie that replays the same twenty minutes surrounding an assassination attempt on the US president and coordinated terrorist attack from different vantage points. Each take is from a different perspective—that of a mobile television studio covering the event, a secret service agent, a local police officer, an American tourist, the American president, and the terrorist group behind the attacks. The viewer appreciates the limits of each viewpoint, only fully grasping who did what when all of the plotlines converge at the end. They show the incompleteness of each perspective. If you haven't seen the movie, I highly encourage you to do so, as it demonstrates just how limited each lens can be.

Other media that have used the same approach include the *Star Trek* TV episode, "A Matter of Perspective," which was broadcast in 1990, centered on a scientist's murder and exploring how those aboard the *Enterprise* perceived reality and remembered events. And most recently, *Sense8,* a Netflix sci-fi series, takes empathy to a new level when eight strangers around the world are suddenly linked mentally. They experience each other's emotions and see what each other see, making viewers acutely aware of the limitations of every perspective.

On a personal level, empathizing and seeing your circumstances in a bigger context can be useful. It's helped dampen my exuberance when I'm on top of the world, and also boosted my spirits during tough times. One situation, indelibly scarred into my memory, took place when I was between jobs. My wife had recently quit her job in the hopes of starting her own business, and we found ourselves in the emergency room with our eighteen-month-old daughter . . . without any health insurance coverage. Life didn't feel so good. Beyond the anxiety of being in a hospital with a young child, there were financial worries. Hospital visits can be expensive. But I knew bad times come and go, and so we persevered, later reading the COBRA paperwork that allowed us to retroactively get covered.

Flip Perspectives

In early 2013, my wife Kristen and I decided to sell our apartment in Brookline, Massachusetts. After we had successfully negotiated our way through a very favorable sales agreement, we went searching for and found a new house we were excited to make our home. But little did we realize that a quagmire of banking rules would almost derail our carefully orchestrated plans. By the time that we had finally identified a home we wanted to buy, I was self-employed. I immediately applied for a mortgage at Bank of America, the bank at which I had my personal checking, business checking, and existing mortgages. I had almost perfect credit and a long history of faithfully paying my bills on time. Oh, and Kristen and I planned a down payment on the new home of more than 50 percent of the purchase price. I figured this was a no-brainer and Bank of America would be thrilled.

Boy was I wrong. After spending about twenty minutes with a mortgage specialist at the bank, I was told that I probably wouldn't qualify.

"You don't have a job," was his deadpan explanation. Fair enough, but I was earning more than when I did have a job, albeit through consulting and speaking engagements.

"Your income is not certain," he added. Again, a fair criticism from his perspective, but I presented him consulting contracts that included monthly retainers and annual commitments.

"Those contracts can be terminated," he said. Yes, that was true. But can't people with jobs be fired? In fact, I explained that I would have to be fired by more than a dozen people, while those with traditional jobs would have to be fired by one.

He emphasized that I had been self-employed less than two years. No denying that, but I had been able to quickly generate income and had contracted increases in some of my consulting contracts. Next year would likely be better.

To make a long story short, he didn't care, ultimately saying, "I'm sorry, but after the financial crisis, we have no discretion on these matters. The rules are the rules." I had the almost identical experience at every bank I approached, where loan officers took out their lending guidelines and blindly followed them. Among traditional lenders, I was *persona non grata*. They were intensely focused on their money and whether they may lose it by lending to me.

Thankfully, I was then introduced to First Republic Bank. First Republic has a different focus than Bank of America or any of the traditional banks. In a refreshing change of approach, the banker I met focused on me and took the time to understand my situation. He asked for a lot of information, which I happily provided. I could tell throughout that his approach was different, but it crystallized when he explicitly noted to me that I had more to lose than the bank did.

"You're an academic teaching and writing about finance, associated with both Harvard and Yale, and your wife is a prominent entrepreneur in the Boston community. Sure, we'll get collateral in your new home to protect us, but frankly, the best collateral we have is your reputation. You're approved." We moved into our current home in the fall of 2013, and because First Republic genuinely focused on me (and the losses I might suffer) they gained virtually all of my business. They flipped perspectives, carefully considering what I had to lose. I've since shut down my business, individual, and mortgage accounts at Bank of America and do most of my banking with First Republic.

Learn Whenever, Wherever, from Whomever

Years ago, I received an invitation from a couple of groups in Omaha to share my views on the global economy. As the son of Indian immigrants who was born and raised on the East Coast of the United States, I had (unsurprisingly) never been to Nebraska, and I jumped at the chance to see another part of America. At the time, I had been studying the global agricultural markets—with a specific attention to the animal protein industry. I reached out to some contacts I had at the Federal Reserve and asked for an introduction to some cattlemen.

"You have got to go meet James Timmerman. . . . He's the chairman of the Omaha branch of the Kansas City Fed and he runs a big cattle operation. I'm sure Jim would be willing to show you around."

And so I called Jim. I told him I was going to be visiting from Boston, that I was a lecturer at Yale University, and that I wanted to learn about the cattle business. He and his brother Gerald offered to meet me for breakfast and show me around their feedyard in Springfield. I was thrilled. Having removed the tags from the cowboy boots I had purchased the night before, I joined Gerald and Jim for a quick bite and tour of the yard. We then went back to their simple office, where something fascinating transpired.

Jim and Gerald were as interested in learning about me and my views of the world as I was about them and their views. Immediately, we began sharing ideas on a wide variety of subjects, from how to spot financial bubbles to the ideal conditions for raising livestock. Although we came from different worlds, all three of us appreciated the value of different perspectives and the possibilities of learning from one another. We've grown to be friends.

Having learned an immense amount about life, business, and the cattle industry from Jim and Gerald, I invited them years later to share some of their thoughts with my students. At this point, I was teaching a class at Harvard called "Humanity and Its Challenges" and one of the topics we studied in the seminar was the sustainability of our food systems. Jim and Gerald helped lead the class through an exploration of the social, technological, and environmental challenges that arose from a booming global middle class that was eating increasing amounts of animal protein. We talked about demographic trends, consumer preferences, water dynamics, and innovations such as lab-grown meat. The students absolutely loved them.

But here's the most interesting part of the story and a lesson we can all learn from the Timmermans. Toward the end of the class, as the students began to put away their notebooks and pack their bags, Gerald stood up and did something that typifies the spongelike learning approach that has contributed to the success he and his brothers have had. He asked: "If you don't mind, would you all be willing to share your views with us? We shared our ideas and experiences with you, but frankly, all of you in this room are the future. What do you think about the future of meat? What would you do if you were in our shoes?"

For the next ten minutes, Gerald and Jim then diligently took notes while the students shared their views. Both were surrounded by students with follow-up questions after the class. By flipping roles and being genuinely curious, the Timmermans have developed an ability to learn from whomever they meet, wherever and whenever they meet them.

Mumbai Murders

Within organizations, the dynamics of rules and other controls have spurred the rise of silos in which focused teams of individuals can digest parts of an otherwise unmanageable whole. But this coping mechanism, driven by the specialization and focus, has created new frictions and risks. By their very nature, organizational silos are designed to channel the focus of a group of individuals toward a particular purpose. But they also prevent the cross pollination and dot connecting that comes from crossing silos and integrating disparate perspectives.

While it's inappropriate to lay blame for the intelligence failure around the November 2008 Mumbai terrorist attacks that killed 166 people and wounded more than 300, admittedly 20/20 hindsight shines a disturbing light on the amount of information and the warnings issued before the attack. The Mumbai massacre, which was so scarring it's often referred to as India's 9/11, included days of coordinated attacks on multiple iconic locations in Mumbai that were frequented by Westerners. The 2019 movie *Hotel Mumbai* captures just how harrowing an experience it was for the city and its visitors. Here are the facts, as reported in a detailed *New York Times* piece titled "In 2008 Mumbai Attacks, Piles of Spy Data, but an Uncompleted Puzzle."[2]

Three separate intelligence agencies had been monitoring the terrorists for months before the four-day siege of India's financial hub that included mass shootings in hotels, train stations, cafés, and other public venues. British intelligence services had been monitoring the actual web browsing of the plot's mastermind and had credible evidence a plot was mounting. Indian intelligence services likewise had picked up specific chatter in early 2008 about a potential attack on Mumbai. And starting in the Spring of 2008, the US Central Intelligence Agency actually warned that the iconic Taj Mahal Palace Hotel might be a target.

Brian Hale, a US intelligence spokesperson explained, "The information identified several potential targets in the city, but we did not have specific information about the timing or the method of the attack."[3] The US intelligence community also alerted British intelligence of their mounting concerns. And then in late September 2008 and then again in October 2008, the terrorist group responsible for the November attacks botched two attempts to get the attackers to Mumbai via inflatable boats by sea. Lastly, the CIA delivered a warning to Indian officials on November 18, less than two weeks before the attacks began, of the location of a terrorist-linked vessel off the coast of Mumbai, not far from where the attacks occurred.[4]

So what happened? While it's easy in retrospect to piece together the facts, the overwhelming noise in the intelligence system clearly prevented the signal from being heard. Consider some of the facts that were known in advance of the tragic events: Zarrar Shah, the digital coordinator of the attacks, whose computer was being monitored by both British and Indian intelligence agencies, showed interest in "small-scale warfare, secret communications, tourist and military locations in India, extremist ideology and Mumbai," as noted by the *New York Times*.[5] And before the attacks started, Mr. Shah apparently was viewing Google images of the Oberoi Hotel and did similar searches for the Taj hotel and the Chabad House, a Jewish hostel that was also attacked during the siege.

It's clear the dots weren't connected, but why not? Were there simply too many? After all, given the volume of data generated by electronic and signals intelligence efforts, how would it have been possible to identify the signal and pattern from within the massive noise? Are silos to blame? Possibly, but it does seem that the US efforts to share information with India met deaf ears.

Even in America, a Pakistani-American who helped the attackers plan the massacre left a trail of suspicion that made it to authorities. The unhappy wife of David Coleman Headley, who scouted targets in Mumbai, told counterterrorism officials that her husband was a terrorist conducting mysterious missions in Mumbai. No one did anything.

One thing remains certain: there were plenty of dots. What remained missing were meaningful connections between them. Triangulating using multiple sources is a key capability that we should all seek to embrace, and while it's unclear if it would have mattered in this specific case, doing so should increase the probability of identifying signals in a noisy world.

Take People as Seriously as
They Take Themselves

For most of the past fifty years, whenever Bob called, POTUS picked up. It's been true for Democrats and Republicans alike. And as a *Telegraph* article phrased it, "Bill Clinton, George W. Bush (four times), and Obama have all decided it was safer to have America's most famous investigative reporter on the inside than out."[6]

You see, Bob Woodward is the world's most influential investigative journalist, period. He's a deep thinker in a world of 140 character tweets and news stories with half-lives in minutes. And although most of journalism tends to be reactive, taking in the news and analyzing it, Bob takes a different approach.

In fact, for the last session of a class I taught in 2016, I had my students read broadly on the work of investigative journalists. I had them read about the work done on Watergate, the Pentagon Papers, and other examples where journalists played the crucial role of bring truth into the open, allowing the court of public opinion and judgment to work its magic. Unbeknownst to the students, I had invited Bob to attend as a guest . . . and given many of them were way too young to recognize him, I merely introduced him as my friend Bob who was visiting campus and wanted to sit in on our class.

The class began with a discussion about the work done by investigative journalists—several students dismissed the efforts as naively righteous, others found it critical for democratic society. But all were stunned when they began talking about Watergate and Bob chimed in. It took about five minutes, but my students eventually connected the dots, so to speak, and realized it was Bob Woodward.

The star-struck students then sat in awe as Bob described his motivation: "I wake up every day and I want to figure out what the bad guys are hiding from us." Why's that? When Bob was growing up, he flipped through the files of his father's law practice. He read about the dirty secrets of seemingly perfect families in his neighborhood and realized then that there was usually a story behind the story—that all is not as it seemed. Bob explains, "To this day, I listen to what people say and try to give them the benefit of the doubt, but at the same time, I always wonder whether there may be a more authentic version, a darker side of people and their behavior."[7]

And it's this philosophy that served him well during his work on Watergate—as he said to me, reminiscing, "Clearly a lot is hidden. We go see people and they slam the door in our faces. . . . The experts are all the people who poo-pooed us." But Bob kept digging. The result, a change in the US presidency and a press that utilizes its power to supplement courts and laws to maintain justice. In fact, when I spoke with the president of another nation about Watergate, he commented to me that Woodward and Bernstein demonstrated to the world that no one is above the law in America, and that "the *Washington Post* did more for the US reputation in the world than any American leader could possibly have done with words or actions."

But Bob's work didn't stop with Watergate. In fact, he's still at it, by using data to find signals of truth in a world of noise. He has no qualms about being an instigator and going after the individuals occupying the highest offices. He holds the feet of the world's most powerful leaders to the fire and follows the story to where it takes him. And throughout, he maintains a (unsurprisingly) deeply skeptical approach: "Sometimes the official story's right . . . generally not, but sometimes it is."

"I try and show people that I take them as seriously as they take themselves," Bob said.[8] And his preparation for the interviews he conducts is stunning. After we had lunch one day at his home in Washington, DC,[9] he handed me the list of questions he had sent to President Obama in April 2010 in preparation for an interview as part of research for what became *Obama's Wars*. He uses them as part of a class he's taught for years.

The more than twenty pages of questions were excruciatingly detailed and indicated not only tremendous preparation on Bob's part but also deep access to information. The following excerpt may help illustrate the level of detail that Bob used in the questions to show President Obama that he was indeed trying to adopt his perspective.

MARCH 18, 2009: On an Air Force One Trip to California, you read the 44-page Riedel strategy review. It said "the core goal of the US must be to disrupt, dismantle, and eventually defeat al Qaeda and its extremist allies."
QUESTION: Your overall reaction to the report? At the time did the goal seem overly broad, especially the "defeat" of the "extremist allies," which seemed to imply the Taliban?

The Riedel report included a "counterterrorism-plus" strategy option that would have maintained a force level of between 25,000 and 40,000.
QUESTION: Why did you reject that?

The second option was a "fully-resourced civilian-military counterinsurgency strategy focused on the Pashtun area in the south and east," specifically keeping the troop level at 68,000 with a later decision on an additional 10,000 that "would be made in the fall and based on our assessment of the situation then."
QUESTION: Why did you decide on this? What was your initial thinking about counterinsurgency? Was it explained to you that with a full-resourced counterinsurgency (about a 1:50 ratio of counterinsurgent forces to population) the 68,000 would not be enough?

On Air Force One, Riedel said the report was necessarily a bureaucratic document reflecting the interagency process, but he would read between the lines for the president. Bottom line: Bin Laden and al Qaeda are as much a threat as the day before 9/11. Al Qaeda leadership was

```
recruiting, training, actively plotting and
communicating.
QUESTION: Your reaction? Why did you approve
fully resourced counterinsurgency in Afghani-
stan? You never used "counterinsurgency" in your
March 27 speech announcing the strategy. Why?
```

Bob was also kind enough to share with me the transcript that came out of his meeting with the president and the nature of the insights he received. In fact, by trying to take the perspective of the US president, Bob earned the respect to not only get an audience with the president but to also have an interactive discussion during which he was able to probe and cite even more evidence that kept the president on his toes during the interview. In fact, at the end of the meeting, President Obama asked Bob if he's ever thought of leading the Central Intelligence Agency, joking that he apparently had better sources than the president.

As this story shows, Bob is successful in part because he tries to adopt the perspective of the person he's interviewing. He lays out the facts that were present at the time and paints a mosaic of the world that the interviewee was likely facing. And then he empathizes without judgment, asking for reactions. The result: Bob remains one of the world's most respected journalists, more than fifty years after he was instrumental in unveiling the criminal dynamics of Watergate.

Diabolical Thinking

One tried and true way to really understand the complexity of an issue is to take the time to really understand the pros and cons of every decision we make. The essence of this approach is captured in an oft-cited quote from Alfred Sloan, the longtime chairman of General Motors. At the conclusion of a senior executive meeting, Sloan summarized the discussion: "Gentlemen, I take it we are all in complete agreement on the decision here." After observing that everyone's head nodded affirmatively, he went on: "Then I propose we postpone further discussion on this matter to give ourselves time to develop disagreement, and perhaps gain some understanding of what the decision is all about."[10]

Management theorist Peter Drucker also noted the value of disagreement: "A decision without an alternative is a desperate gambler's throw, no matter how carefully thought out it might be."[11] Fundamentally, the key is to surround yourself with people who offer disagreement, meaning people who look at the same set of agreed upon data and see it differently, people who come to different conclusions.

Let's take a cue from the Roman Catholic Church here. During the canonization process through which the church declares a person who has died a saint, a canon lawyer is charged with serving as the *promoter of the faith*. Unlike the *promoter of the cause*, whose job it was to present evidence of the departed's worthiness, the promoter of the faith was supposed to take a skeptical view and present alternative explanations of the supposedly godly deeds. Although the position dates back to the 1500s, it's been popularly deployed in many nonchurch contexts via its Latin name, *advocatus diabolic*, "the devil's advocate."

A devil's advocate is generically a person who takes an alternative position for the sake of presenting a counterargument. The person may or may not actually believe in the position adopted, but the value of disagreement and alternative interpretations is why such a position exists. Might all of us benefit from consulting our own devil's advocates prior to making big decisions? Shouldn't we deeply consider alternatives?

Or what about coopting those with radically different opinions from our own? Why not include those who don't agree with us or even with each other? Perhaps we might benefit from adopting a tactic Abraham Lincoln employed, namely engaging his chief rivals as teammates.

In *Team of Rivals: The Political Genius of Abraham Lincoln,* Doris Kearns Goodwin traces internal Republican feuds within the Lincoln administration, exploring the dynamics of a party in the 1860s that was a coalition of politicians who only a few years earlier had been Whigs, Democrats, Free Soilers, or Know Nothings.[12] Goodwin highlights the dynamics among New York Senator William H. Seward, who became secretary of state; Ohio Senator Salmon P. Chase, who became secretary of the treasury and then chief justice of the Supreme Court; and Edward Bates from Missouri, who served as attorney general. From the pre-election debates, we know these personalities each had strongly held views that often differed or completely conflicted with Lincoln's. But rather than generate an echo chamber of like-minded advisors, Lincoln did the opposite. Not only did he include them in his leadership team, but he elevated them to key posts. You might imagine such orchestrated disagreement would yield chaos and paralyze meaningful decision making.

The result was carefully considered decision making in what may very well be the most tumultuous and uncertain time in America's early history. Might slavery still exist in law had the motley crew of rivals not chosen to work together? Lincoln's explicit invitation of those most skeptical of him to join him was genius on many levels—politically, for sure, but also in that it assured him the multiple perspectives so needed to understand the complex dynamics facing the young nation.

In a short interview with *Prologue Magazine*, Goodwin was bluntly asked why Lincoln filled his cabinet with his rivals. Her answer: "He declared that at a time of peril, the country needed to have the strongest men, and he couldn't deprive it of those talents . . . by putting his rivals in his cabinet, he had access to a wide range of opinions, which he realized would *sharpen his own thinking*."[13]

The idea of sharpening your thinking by engaging those with views different than your own is a very powerful way to overcome groupthink and address the biases many of us naturally bring to a discussion of big and important decisions.

Years ago, I was invited to address the top management team of United Technologies, one of the world's largest companies that at the time included such iconic brands and businesses as Otis (the elevator and escalator company), Carrier (a global air conditioning and climate control business), and Pratt & Whitney (one of the world's leading aircraft engine manufacturing companies). To prepare for my talk, I read everything I could find about the businesses as well as chairman and CEO Greg Hayes's annual letters to shareholders. I noticed most of the company's materials discussed megatrends that drove their strategy—urbanization and the emergence of a global middle class.

So at a cocktail party the evening before my talk, I pulled Greg aside and asked him if he had ever considered entering the agriculture business. He looked suspiciously at me and asked why I would think a technology-intensive manufacturing company would want to do that. (Separately, I suspect at that point he also questioned the decision to have me as an external speaker at his meeting!) I discussed how urbanization and a rising global middle class would drive demand for protein. He indicated that no one had ever suggested that they enter agriculture, and that they probably wouldn't do so, but thanked me for the idea before walking away to mingle with others.

Over the next year or so, Greg and I would get together from time to time to discuss global dynamics and how they might affect United Technologies. And then he asked me to help with a very interesting decision that he and the board of the company were about to make. They were going to propose a breakup of United Technologies. Greg explained that he and the board wanted an honest broker to independently think through why they shouldn't pursue the breakup, given that most of the company's formal advisors had incentives to encourage the spin-offs. I was honored to be asked to play the role of devil's advocate (regardless of my personal views) and developed an argument against the breakup.

Ultimately, Greg and the board decided to break up the business into three companies, but I like to believe they did so with greater conviction having had at least one person tasked with telling them why not to do it. In fact, Greg later asked me to help him think through why he shouldn't pursue a merger with Raytheon. Again, despite my best efforts (separate from my personal views) to convince him and the board not to do it, they went forward with the transaction. And again, I believe they did so with confidence that a serious effort had been made to consider alternative actions.

One of the reasons that Greg and the United Technologies board have been successful in very volatile environments over long periods of time, I believe, is that they are not just open-minded, they actually go out to seek the disagreement that Sloan and Drucker have mentioned is so critical to sound decision making and effective leadership.

One tool I used in my analyses for Greg was a prospective hindsight exercise, more colloquially described as a premortem analysis. Research conducted by Deborah Mitchell, Jay Russo, and Nancy Pennington found that the exercise of thinking about how projects may fail in advance increased the ability of correctly identifying possible trajectories by around 30 percent.[14] A premortem analysis considers how decisions made today might end up being seen as foolish in the future. The idea is to imagine future failure and then think through what might have caused it. The exercise is one that can complement the engagement of a devil's advocate and, as eloquently summarized by Gary Klein in a 2007 *Harvard Business Review* piece, "in the end, a premortem may be the best way to circumvent the need for a painful postmortem."[15]

. . .

Every perspective is biased and incomplete. So why settle for adopting your natural default perspective as the only one you utilize to make decisions? Rather, it would make sense to seek out, appreciate, and develop multiple perspectives to help you shed light on the topic of interest. The key is to triangulate a version of reality from multiple perspectives. Just think about my mortgage mayhem. First Republic Bank earned my business and loyalty by taking what my admittedly biased perspective suggested was a no-brainer risk. And Bob Woodward built a career out of treating the world's most powerful people as seriously as they take themselves—by diving deep in data and stories to recreate their perspectives. Or recall the approach taken by Jim and Gerald Timmerman, using every opportunity to learn from anyone and everyone, wherever and whenever possible.

We can all generate insight from seeking alternatives to our own perspectives. For hundreds of years, the Roman Catholic Church utilized the position of a devil's advocate to argue why a person was not worthy of sainthood, despite the evidence being presented. Perhaps we should all employ a devil's advocate to help us navigate life's tough calls.

Thinking for ourselves in the twenty-first century is quite difficult in a world that is surrounded by experts, technologies, and overwhelming quantities of data and information. One way to retain autonomy amidst the deluge is to adopt multiple perspectives in a quest to triangulate insights. There are plenty of dots in the world today—and all of us are generating more each day. The real, sustainable know-how we must all develop is the ability to connect them. To lift our heads up and notice the context. And to constantly question underlying assumptions, thinking for ourselves independently and not blindly relying on the opinions of others.

Questions to Ask Yourself

- **What would those with different perspectives think about your decision?** Understanding that every perspective is biased and incomplete, imagine how workers, customers, suppliers, spouses, or friends might think about your chosen action. Use every opportunity to learn from those with different backgrounds.

- **Are you thinking about problems broadly enough? Have you defined the problem correctly?** Many experts live in silos and develop a deep focus on their chosen domain. But perhaps the problem at hand calls for an attention to the connections between various expert insights. There are plenty of dots, value may be found in connecting them.

- **What would a devil's advocate say is wrong with your approach?** Employ a structural naysayer to rigorously develop an argument that the decision you are going to pursue is wrong. Doing so provides the psychological safety to enable a rigorous discussion about the downsides of a big decision, without the naysayer fearing punitive politics.

- **How might your decision lead to a massive failure in the future?** Conduct an exercise in prospective hindsight, something also known as a premortem analysis. Think through how future commentators might describe the path that led to a bad outcome.

CHAPTER 10

Keep Experts on Tap,
Not on Top

Among the many qualities that distinguish successful leaders from millions of less-successful executives in the world is an awareness of the limits of their knowledge. They know what they know, they appreciate what they don't know, and they have a healthy respect for what they don't know they don't know. In short, they have great *metaknowledge*.

Metaknowledge can be thought of as a lack of hubris, an intellectual humility of sorts. Those who see the world probabilistically seem to better navigate volatile environments because they are wired to embrace uncertainty. They understand that they don't know anything with 100 percent certainty, and are therefore open to ideas very different than their own.

Psychologists Kahneman and Tversky, whom we met earlier in the book, demonstrated quite convincingly that we human beings are not the model-optimizing rational actors that many economists historically believed we are. One of their key findings was that humans are consistently overconfident, suggesting that we generally have poor metaknowledge. The findings are robust and have been validated and confirmed in dozens of studies.[1] The unfortunate reality is that we tend to think we know more than we actually know. A corollary of this result is that we also tend not to know what we do not know.

In my experience, experts are among the least successful predictors in times of massive uncertainty. They often think they know more than they actually do and therefore exhibit more confidence than is warranted. Hubris tends to affect their objectivity, particularly when they become the go-to thinkers to help others who by definition are admittedly confused. The result: a significant number of very visible expert predictions have gone embarrassingly wrong.

Many of these experts adopted single-discipline approaches to developing insights; they were specialists truly knowledgeable within their domain. But it was often developments outside of their domain that derailed their predictions. By focusing on their areas of expertise, they allowed depth to trump breadth. And herein lies the fundamental difficulty of working with experts. There are times when it is critical that we have an expert to help us; there are other times when an expert is exactly the wrong antidote to our woes. Which leads me to, drumroll please, an obvious and critically important question: *How the heck can we tell when we should seek the input of experts and when we should not?* As luck would have it, it turns out that the context in which you're operating (and that incidentally is something only you can fully appreciate) holds the key to how and when to seek the input of expertise.

Cynefin: Who and When

Fortunately, consultants David Snowden and Mary Boone, along with some others, developed a framework that can help us answer this critical question. By using insights from the field of complexity science, they suggest that an absolutely essential factor is *context*. In a November 2007 *Harvard Business Review* article titled "A Leader's Framework for Decision Making," Snowden and Boone suggest that different conditions require different approaches. A very important variable for us to consider is the environment in which we face a decision.[2]

The Cynefin framework they developed differentiates four different contexts in which we may find ourselves: (1) simple, (2) complicated, (3) complex, and (4) chaotic.[3]

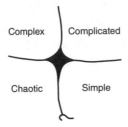

Simple contexts are characterized by stability, clear cause-and-effect relationships, and straightforward management and monitoring. Disagreement about what needs to be done is rare. This is a domain in which automation, adherence to rules, and best practices tend to work well. Process-oriented decision making is best. For instance, how much interest should be charged to a customer's credit card account? Sure, you can have a person calculate the average daily balance and then multiply it by the rate and charge the account. But you could also have a basic rule embedded in software to do the math and calculate the amounts. Regardless of who makes the decision, the situation is stable and a correct answer exists.

Complicated contexts, by contrast, may contain multiple right answers. There is usually a clear relationship between cause and effect, but it's very difficult for most of us to see or understand the nuances or mechanisms of various connections. An example of a complicated topic can be found in the functioning of highly interconnected technologies—such as a car. If your car is malfunctioning or breaks down, there is probably a correct answer to the question of "What is broken and needs to be fixed?" The problem is it's not obvious to a nonspecialist. It requires an expert to help identify the problem and propose a solution. The answer exists, but it is buried in interwoven layers that obscure it. Complicated environments are where experts thrive.

Complex contexts are ambiguous, poorly defined, and characterized by emergence. They are hard to predict due to constant flux and dynamic, shifting relationships. Complex environments are best thought of as probabilistic and cannot be solved. Answers don't exist. The best one can hope for in a complex situation is to understand some of the dynamics, monitor the situation closely, and adjust course as new information surfaces. This is the domain of anything that is highly interactive with feedback loops. Think of trying to understand a society after a new technology is introduced. How rapidly will it be adopted? Will it displace others? Will social relationships shift? What happens to the economy, jobs, or alternative technologies? The number of possible interactions to consider is overwhelming, making predictions effectively speculations. The correct approach to navigating complexity, the authors argue, is to allow the path forward to reveal itself. Probing, sensing, and responding are key activities. It's a dot-connecting exercise, not a dot-generating one.

In chaotic contexts, searching for right answers is futile. Relationships between cause and effect are shifting constantly, with no manageable patterns, thereby creating rigorous analysis useless. Snowden and Boone suggest these environments are rare, usually temporary, and can be effectively approached by trying to establish order and regain stability however possible—even if only in certain subdomains.[4] Here's a good example of a chaotic context:

It's Saturday morning around 8 a.m. My two kids are watching TV with our dog laying in front of the couch they're sitting on. The temporary calm is intoxicating enough for me and Kristen to actually talk about current affairs, our workweeks, or even upcoming holidays. But then, out of nowhere, with no explanation, and with no logical cause, all hell breaks loose. There is screaming, the dog is barking, and tears are flowing. For good measure, throw in a neighbor ringing the doorbell and the Amazon Echo device starting to play horror movie music. I suspect the correct approach to take is try to install some stability—separate the kids, take the dog outside, thank the neighbor for stopping by but suggest they return in five years when things might be more in control, or ask Alexa to play happy music. Then, and only then, can I try to move forward. The key for me is to turn the three-ring circus into something I can engage with on a somewhat rational basis, and the blunt reality is that it's impossible to understand cause and effect with everything happening at the same time! That's the advice I imagine Snowden and Boone would give me and my wife.

But let's stop for a moment and think about how the Cynefin framework can help us decide when to seek the help of a focused, narrow, deep expert and when we might be better with a generalist. I think it has to do with the nature of the issue we have and the topic with which we might need help. If there is a clear cause-and-effect relationship, we could benefit from an expert. So, there's water flowing out of the ceiling directly below the upstairs bathroom. This might be a simple context (toilet is leaking, so stop the leak), but it also may be complicated (perhaps the shower pan has a crack and the water is flowing along a beam and then flowing through the floor). In either case, an expert will be useful in solving the issue.

Now suppose instead that you are facing a more problematic, emergent phenomenon that constantly takes place in the domain of investing or medicine. Sure, there are simple and complicated problems that arise in investing (I want to express a bullish bet on a security and have a target price I've already determined and want help figuring out how to best execute the trade) and medicine (I broke a bone and need a cast), but these domains also have lots of complex problems as well.

Own Your Decisions

Put yourself in my situation. The year is 2011 and I hadn't been feeling well for weeks; I was groggy, exhausted, and sleeping poorly . . . at least at night. Between 2 and 5 p.m., yeah, that was a different story. I could sleep like a baby then. Something was off. I wasn't myself. And so after almost three weeks of involuntary napping, I went to see my doctor.

After a battery of tests, I was told all were negative. "Drink fluids and get lots of rest" was the prescription I received. It might have been a simple problem (for example, lack of sleep), but it wasn't. It might have been a complicated problem (Lyme disease, low iron, mononucleosis, etc.), but it wasn't. I fundamentally faced a complex problem that could only be handled via a systems approach, one that included looking at my whole body and the connections within it. And so, I took control and found myself eventually in the office of Mark Hyman, a doctor who adopted a systems approach to medicine known as functional medicine.

At the time, the tagline Dr. Mark Hyman used on his website was "Causes, not Conditions." The basic underlying philosophy of functional medicine is that symptoms can be generated by many causes. So don't focus on symptoms. Instead focus on how the body is functioning. Fix the malfunctions and many of the symptoms will go away. The key was to address root causes, not the conditions they produce.

The battery of tests that Mark then subjected me to was overwhelming. But they weren't the normal types of tests that my prior doctor had ordered. Sure, he checked cholesterol, but he cared more about particle size than levels. He also checked the level of toxic elements in my body like mercury and lead. And he looked for vitamin deficiencies and hormonal imbalances. And it wasn't just blood tests. My stool, urine, saliva, and hair were also evaluated. The ecology of my gut was explored. He tested, and tested, and then tested again.

After a couple of weeks, the results came in. We then had an hour-long phone call to discuss them. The findings were stunning—everything from the identification of higher-than-expected mercury and aluminum to a severe vitamin D deficiency. And the tests on food sensitivities and allergies returned a plethora of findings that indicated diet was contributing heavily to my fatigue and general health. I was blown away. Why hadn't my other doctor seen these? It seemed almost obvious. Yet he didn't pay attention to these possibilities. He was focused elsewhere.

Over the next month or so, I worked closely with Mark and a nutritionist to design a program of medications, supplements, and a modified diet to help fix the parts of my body that were malfunctioning. Mark was focused on fixing causes; he only tangentially monitored my symptoms.

To make a very long story short, the process I followed—led by Mark and supported by a nutritionist—changed my life. I began eating differently to accommodate the undiagnosed allergies that this process had

The Night's Watch

During the height of the 2017 missile testing standoff between US president Donald Trump and North Korean leader Kim Jung Un, I was invited to join a group of senior executives on a three-day trip to visit US Air Force facilities in Colorado. The trip was led by Barbara Faulkenberry, a friend and retired US Air Force general who at one point had run a major portion of US Air Force logistics. Unsurprisingly, the trip was extremely well organized and efficiently run.

While it was thrilling to visit Cheyenne Mountain and spend time with the leadership of the Air Force Academy, the biggest surprise of the trip took place in a remote parking lot on a hot August afternoon. Just as I caught a glimpse of the main entrance to US Northern Command (US-NORTHCOM) and the North American Aerospace Defense Command (NORAD) in the distance, several hundred yards away, the bus came to a stop. Upon disembarking, I was greeted by General Lori Robinson, who was bus-side in the sweltering August heat.

To appreciate why this was so unusual, let me share a bit about General Robinson. She is one of the most accomplished women in the US military—ever. She is one of a handful of women who rose to become a four-star general, the first female commander of NORAD (reporting to both the US president and Canadian prime minister), and the first female combatant commander (head of USNORTHCOM) in American military history. Leaders like General Robinson generally don't wait in parking lots for guests to arrive, especially not on a hot August day. But as I learned, she's not like most leaders.

I've spent some time talking with and meeting with General Robinson since my visit to her offices in Colorado, and while her accomplishments are impressive, it's her approach to managing that struck me as truly special. A defining moment of her career, as she recalled to me, was the death of her stepdaughter Taryn Ashley Robinson. Taryn was a 2005 graduate of the Air Force Academy and an aspiring fighter pilot. During routine training, Taryn's plane crashed in Texas and she died months later.

From that moment forward, General Robinson found gratitude in "the opportunity and ability to wake up every morning," as she told me in one conversation. Petty bureaucratic battles became less important, allowing her to focus on the mission of serving her country. From that point forward, her career skyrocketed, with stars being pinned onto her uniform every three to four years.

While the hit HBO series *Game of Thrones* showed how the Night's Watch military order protected the Seven Kingdoms from the wildlings and White Walkers, General Robinson and her team at NORAD had the watch over North America during a time of frequent rocket launches by a rogue North Korean regime. One can only imagine the pressure of having mere minutes to decide a course of action once US satellites or sensors identified a missile launch.

"I simply had to rely upon others," said General Robinson. But she did so mindfully, always retaining ownership of the decision while proactively seeking input from others: "I sought everyone's thoughts, ideas and values, including those that push back on my thinking . . . because over the years, I've learned they help me make smarter decisions."

This does not come naturally, particularly in a hierarchical organization like the US military. General Robinson commented that the key was to develop a situation in which everyone felt comfortable and safe in sharing their views, even if they differed with hers: "Any good leader will create the environment for people to bring their voices and thoughts to the table so the decision maker can make an informed decision."

When making tough decisions that affect our health, wealth, or happiness, we can all lead like General Robinson. First, it is critical to create the context in which advisors can offer their best advice; then, take a step back to see the big picture and our objectives; and finally, make an informed choice with the benefit of expert input. But throughout, we need to mindfully keep experts on tap, not on top.

unveiled. I took vitamins and other supplements. I began using the sauna at the gym regularly. I even switched from an antiperspirant (since most contain aluminum) to a deodorant.

I am an entirely different person today than I was before seeing Mark. This is not an exaggeration. I lost over seventy pounds over eighteen months, my hair stopped receding and even grew darker, my energy levels jumped and have stayed high, I sleep better, and I feel great. I think I am smarter and funnier as well, but my friends tell me that's wishful thinking. Oh well.

The point of this story is that my health issues at the time were not simple or even complicated; they were complex, with a slew of interacting and overlapping problems that defied a reductionist approach that merely looked at the parts. Mark helped me get better by looking at how my body was functioning rather than focusing solely on how it was malfunctioning. As a generalist, he was able to triangulate through multiple lenses to turn the complex problem into a collection of complicated ones that we then methodically addressed.

Miraculous Maneuvers

To make successful decisions, we must understand the environment we face. This ability to match context with an approach to working with advisors is what Joseph Nye calls "contextual intelligence" and is an essential skill for leaders of all stripes.[5] When we appreciate the context and can quickly determine whether we face a simple, complicated, complex, or chaotic environment, we are better suited to tap into experts as needed. But we also need to demand that the experts we rely upon understand the context we face. What are their limits? What do they not know about what's happening outside of their silos? For an example of an expert who understood his role, retained his mission orientation, and thought for himself, let's turn to a situation in which the mindful management of expertise helped avoid the publication of more than 150 obituaries.

Imagine you're on board a plane that loses thrust in all engines during the critical takeoff stage of a flight. Who do you want in the cockpit? My guess is that you'd want a graduate of the Air Force Academy, an experienced pilot with thousands and thousands of flight hours, a leader who isn't paralyzed by stress, a thoughtful expert who understands the risks and rewards of various actions, and someone who doesn't blindly outsource his thinking to checklists or technology. You'd want a pilot with a range of vision that appreciates not only the likely outcome but also those that are probable, possible, and remote.

Fortunately for the 150 passengers and five crew members aboard US Airways Flight #1549, that's exactly who they had in the cockpit on the morning of January 15, 2009, when their flight encountered a flock of geese upon departure from New York's LaGuardia Airport.[6] Four minutes after both engines failed, Captain Chesley Sullenberger (Sully) ditched the plane on the Hudson River. Every soul aboard survived. Sullenberger's book, *Highest Duty*, and *Sully*, the Clint Eastwood film about his miraculous maneuver, illustrate how his approach to managing focus and retaining control saved lives.[7]

As someone who had been flying jets for his entire adult life and had logged around 20,000 hours of experience in numerous types of aircraft, Sully was more than qualified from an experience perspective.[8] He had flown gliders, understood the practical nuances of aerodynamics, and taught courses on leadership and decision making to fellow pilots. His wife, Lorrie, called him a "pilot's pilot,"[9] and she noted that Sully didn't just fly, "he wore the airplane; it was as if he put it on. It wasn't like he went and just flew the machine. It became a part of him."[10]

Jeff Skiles, Sully's copilot on that January morning, noted that "Sully is a man who likes to plan." A documentary about him stated, "For Sully Sullenberger, preparation is everything. . . . He has a distinct dislike for surprises."[11] To illustrate just how Sully's mind works, here's a story his wife shared about a trip when the two of them were flying privately for a hike in a remote location:

I'm not fond of flying in smaller airplanes and I didn't want to go, so I said to him, "Oh my gosh they're never going to find our bodies out here," and he said, "No, I've had an emergency landing site in sight the entire trip. . . . Everywhere we went, I knew where I could ditch the airplane." In the back of his head, he's always planning.[12]

But experience and expertise are necessary but not sufficient capabilities. The expertise would prove useful if the situation was complicated . . . but it wasn't merely complicated. It was complex. The situation was unprecedented and emerging in real time. On that fateful January day, Sully described the developments as "shocking, more than anything I'd experienced in forty-two years of flying and twenty thousand hours in the air." In fact, Sully later recalled vividly remembering his first three thoughts after losing thrust: "'This can't be happening,' and that was followed immediately by 'this doesn't happen to me,' and my third thought was a realization that unlike every other flight I've had, this one probably would not end on a runway with the aircraft undamaged."[13]

In fact, the dialogue that Sully had with the control tower captures the essence of how he and Skiles kept the distant advisors on tap, not on top. He didn't blindly cede control. Soon after both engines failed, Sully and Skiles relayed their status to an air traffic controller who offered an emergency landing option at LaGuardia.[14] Sully responded that the plane may not make it and might land on the Hudson. He then inquired about New Jersey's Teterboro Airport, where the controller quickly secured him a runway. Throughout this conversation, Sully noted, the controller did not try to steer him in a particular direction: his "choice of phrasing was helpful to me. Rather than telling me what airport I had to aim for, he asked me what airport I wanted. His words let me know that he understood that these hard choices were mine to make, and it wasn't going to help if he tried to dictate a plan to me."[15]

Twenty-two seconds after Sullenberger proposed Teterboro, he abandoned the possible destination, quickly concluding a landing on the Hudson was the best course of action. Even after Sully's decision, the controller kept offering suggestions, unable to stomach the thought of a water landing. Ditching a plane on water is a risky maneuver, one best avoided if possible. In fact, the controller later noted he worried the plane would be cartwheeling in the Hudson River, like the images he had seen of Ethiopian Airlines Flight 961.[16]

As the movie *Sully* dramatically illustrates, Sullenberger then tuned out the controller: "I knew that he had offered me all the assistance that he could, but at that point, I had to focus on the task at hand. I wouldn't be answering him."[17] Rather than let technology or experts take the wheel, abdicating his responsibility as leader, Sully took control, thought for himself, and utilized the inputs of others as just that—inputs into *his* thinking. Sullenberger succeeded in part because he leveraged the air traffic advisors without ceding control.

Let's contrast Sully with the pilots of Air France Flight 447, which we encountered earlier in the book. Their routine eleven-hour flight from Rio de Janeiro to Paris belly-flopped into the Atlantic Ocean on the evening of May 31, 2009. A simple airspeed indicator had briefly malfunctioned, transforming a mere technological blip into a death sentence for the 228 passengers. Actually, the real cause was not a technological failure but the narrow focus the technology encouraged.

Langewiesche's article about AF447 clearly described the pilots' inability to look away from the screens.[18] Unlike Sully, who was had experience in gliders and seemed to have a deep feel for the aircraft, the AF447 pilots were dedicated to the instruments. They outsourced their thinking, knowledge, and responsibility for the 228 passengers to a system that temporarily stopped working, setting off a sequence of fatal events. How might the fate of those aboard AF447 been different if the pilots understood indicators fail but do not necessitate dramatic corrective action? What if they kept technology on tap, not on top? It wasn't a question of competence, as they had been rigorously trained by a world-class national airline. The problem was a lack of thinking; they might have thought about their speed and pitch, realizing that lowering the nose might help the aircraft regain adequate speed to avoid crashing.

And then there's the issue of outsourcing to rules and checklists. Checklists are an important tool in a pilot's arsenal. And with good reason:

they help to reduce human error in aviation, just as they do in medicine. Sully himself is a checklist advocate. They help mitigate the disastrous potential of complacency from repeated success to generate sloppiness and risky corner-cutting. But checklists only contemplate small slivers of the situations in which we may find ourselves.

Sully and his copilot Skiles made careful use of checklists when things began deteriorating. But the situation was unprecedented, making strict adherence to the checklist's script a liability. In fact, Skiles explained that "the checklist for this particular emergency was four pages long; it was really designed to be done at 30,000 feet; it wasn't designed to be done at 3,000 feet in three minutes' time."[19] Clearly, following the checklist wouldn't help. As Sully wrote, "Not every situation can be foreseen or anticipated. There isn't a checklist for everything."[20]

In the movie, we see investigators interrogating Sully and his copilot about the steps they took. They have to explain why they did not follow the standard emergency protocol, which, while useful in the abstract, was not appropriate for the situation at hand. So while standard protocols can be useful, they should not be rules that leaders blindly follow in all cases; context matters. As Sully eloquently summarizes: "These days, there are virtually no cowboys in the skies, ignoring items on their checklists. At the same time, however, I am concerned that compliance alone is not sufficient. Judgment . . . is paramount."[21]

The differences between US1549 and AF447 could not be more extreme. Sully and Skiles were experts *with an appreciation for the context.* They had common sense. They understood the importance of the task and were not technologically dependent. They knew how to fly a plane without cheat-sheets. They tapped into assistance from the air traffic experts as needed. Bonin, the pilot who was flying AF447, on the other hand, was a *relative* amateur. Sure, he was appropriately trained and met all the certifications required, but much of his hours flown had been via highly automated cockpits on primarily long-haul, uneventful flights.

The value of Sully's perspective is that he understood not just the system he was working with but exactly what it was propping up, and thus what to do when it failed. He knew when to dismiss air traffic guidance and when to consider their inputs. We need experts like Sully who can contextualize the individual metrics, switches, and protocols while retaining a strong grasp of his ultimate mission. Otherwise, you end up with pilots who understand the dashboard but not the plane.

Ask, Ask, and Ask

We may not all have the experience and conviction to handle radical uncertainty with the quiet confidence that Sully did; in fact, it would be rare if anyone could. But that does not mean we need to abandon our efforts to combat the domineering and controlling nature of expert power. We need to retain control, and one way to do so is to ask questions. In fact, asking questions is a critical capability and skill that each of us should refine and further develop.

Let's return for a minute to the movie *Sully*. The drama of the story (as portrayed on the big screen) revolves around the National Transportation Safety Board's investigation of the incident. Initially, investigators believed that the plane's engine could have restarted and pilot error was to blame. And computer simulations suggested that Sullenberger could have made it to LaGuardia or Teterboro, thereby preventing millions of dollars in damages and costs. To convince the NTSB that he made the right decision, Sully arranges for human-operated simulations of these scenarios to be streamed live at the hearings. When those don't go his way, he argues—convincingly—that neither the computer nor human simulations are using realistic assumptions.

In the movie, it is a question that leads the NTSB panel to ultimately dismiss the charges of pilot error. Sully asks how many times the pilots in the simulator had practiced. The answer, which is met with a great gasp from the room of investigators, bureaucrats, executives, reporters, and others: "Seventeen." Sully and Skiles hadn't practiced once. The pilots in the simulator had been demonstrating actions in a complicated context. They knew what was happening and what they needed to do. They had lots of practice. Sully and Skiles thought for themselves while facing an emerging, complex problem.

The lead investigator from the NTSB then asked for new human simulations under more realistic assumptions. This time, the pilots waited thirty-five seconds after the simulated bird strikes before turning back to LaGuardia or toward Teterboro. Under these more realistic conditions, their efforts result in the simulated flight crashing, vindicating Sully and Skiles.

Today, we seem all too ready to trust the apparent conclusions of computer simulations or controlled social-scientific experiments without questioning how valid their application is to the real world. While *Sully* may have exaggerated the antagonism between the investigators and the pilots, the film is a useful parable about the creeping propensity to trust models over human testimony. Let's not forget the models themselves are irreducibly human as well, usually written and coded by humans.

Questions can also be useful in highlighting the limits of an expert's knowledge. One of my favorite questions to ask when seeking help on a matter of judgment is: Do you know or think this to be true? The question opens the door to a nonantagonistic discussion of the how the expert has generated her judgment. It also helps us, as nonexperts, retain control by realizing the gaps in knowledge that may exist, gaps that we can fill through the insights of other, complementary experts. It enables us to generate a mosaic of reality using the tiles of individual specialist insights.

One of the world's best questioners is Frank Sesno. A former news anchor, White House correspondent, and Washington Bureau Chief for CNN, Sesno has had the chance to interview many of the world's most accomplished leaders and experts. He's asked questions of US presidents and other heads of state and currently serves as the director of the School of Media and Public Affairs at George Washington University in Washington, DC.

And it's not just because I had to endure being questioned by him in front of hundreds of people at a conference that I know he's a great questioner, it's also because he's literally written a book on the power of questions. And don't ask if the book is worth reading . . . that's a dumb question—of course it is! There's a section of *Ask More* that is extremely relevant. I'll just repeat verbatim what he says in a section called "Challenge the Expert":

> The expert you're dealing with could be a doctor or a roofer, a high-priced consultant or a friend down the street. But even if they have far more experience than you'll ever have, be prepared to ask them about their diagnosis. How did they reach it? What is it based on and what is the prognosis? Ask about their process, their experiences in similar situations, and your options, risks and next steps. Questioning an expert can be daunting and difficult. But often it's necessary.[22]

It's necessary because it helps us retain control. In fact, questioning and challenging experts is one of the primary strategies suggested by Noreena Hertz, author of *Eyes Wide Open: How to Make Smart Decisions in a Confusing World*. In a talk she gave about managing experts, she explicitly stated that, "we've got to be ready and willing to take experts on . . . persisting in the face of their inevitable annoyance when, for example, we want them to explain things to us in language that we can actually understand." She went on to describe how her doctor had, after she had an operation, warned her to be on the lookout for hyperpyrexia: "He could have just as easily said 'watch out for a high fever.'"[23]

Noreena suggests asking questions is the key to taking on experts, noting we must be "willing to dig behind their graphs, their equations, their forecasts, their prophecies, and being armed with the questions to do that— questions like 'What are the assumptions that underpin this? What is the evidence upon which this is based? . . . and what has it ignored?'"[24]

And Noreena and Frank are in good company with their emphasis on asking questions. Peter Drucker put it bluntly: "The important and difficult job is never to find the right answer. It is to find the right questions."[25]

Another set of questions that can be awkward to ask has to do with the incentives experts have to recommend a particular course of action or a specific product. I know this can be very difficult to ask, but why not bluntly inquire if the expert has any financial incentive that may skew his or her objective counsel? For instance, do you, Mr. Financial Advisor, earn any additional compensation from the investment managers of the funds that you are recommending? Or do you, Dr. Cardiologist, have any "horse in the race" when you are suggesting I opt for one medicine over another? Or if you're having surgery, it may be worth asking the doctor recommending the procedure if she will actually be performing it or if there will be others involved. You might also ask your surgeon how many surgeries he does at the same time. (If this sounds odd to you, I'd encourage you to read the *Boston Globe* Spotlight report titled "Clash in the Name of Care."[26])

Tony Robbins is even more blunt than I am. In his book *Unshakeable: Your Financial Freedom Playbook*, Robbins has a section about financial advisors that he titles "You Can Trust Me . . . to Take Advantage of You!"[27] He talks about the more than two hundred different names that people use to indicate that they are supposedly in the business of helping—including "financial advisors," "wealth advisors," "financial consultants," and so on. And the bottom line, notes Robbins, is that 90 percent or so of the financial advisors in America are actually just brokers trying to sell financial products in return for a fee: "If calling themselves a wizard, a pixie, or an elf helped them make more commissions," he goes on, they'd be fine with that. Robbins then eloquently summarizes the issue at hand:

> Warren Buffett jokes that you never want to ask a barber
> whether you need a haircut. Well, brokers are the barbers of
> the financial world. They're trained and incentivized to sell,
> regardless of whether you need what they're selling! That's not
> a criticism. It's just a fact.[28]

Robbins offers blunt advice on how to unveil these conflicts of interest. He proposes asking questions, such as "Are you a registered investment advisor?" and "Are you affiliated with a broker-dealer?" as well as questions about how the advisor makes money.[29] Fundamentally, it's about peeling back what's known in academic circles as a principal-agent problem. Agents are often motivated by different objectives than their clients because they tend not to have skin in the game. If an advisor makes money by getting you to buy and sell, they are not aligned with your objective of generating investment returns. As a principal, you care about returns. In this case, your agent cares about commissions and transaction activity. Obviously, such conflicts can lead to suboptimal performance for the principal.

Sitting, Standing, and Obvious Positions

While it's useful to expose the potential conflicts of interest that may exist with an advisor's recommendations, there is a far more insidious conflict that often lies under the surface. Namely that an advisor is structurally unable to provide sound advice because of their position, company, or status. People with hammers, unsurprisingly, tend to see nails. Joseph Nye, an accomplished policymaker who has served as dean of the Harvard Kennedy School and with whom I'm lucky to have had numerous conversations, said that, "In policy circles, the old adage is that where you stand depends on where you sit."[30] Nye's statement is about how most people are structurally unable to look beyond the silos in which they live.

He goes on: "In intelligence, what you foresee is often affected by where you work. The primary duty of departmental analysts is to respond to the needs of their organizations." But Nye drives his point home, noting "Diplomats are supposed to negotiate solutions . . . [and] Generals are supposed to win battles."[31] This means that even in desperate and only remotely hopeful situations, analysts from the State Department tend to suggest diplomacy. Sit in the State Department, recommend diplomacy. In the Pentagon? Recommend military action. Treasury? Sanctions. And so on.

Imagine how that might apply in a nongovernmental domain. While getting seen by a cardiologist, you have to be aware of the fact she's got loyalty to the cardiology department, not the gastrointestinal or gynecology departments. Career incentives and departmental (i.e., silo) loyalty run rampant, and they sometimes even run roughshod over objective advice.

But the worst part of this latter hidden conflict is that it's not malicious or for that matter, even intentional. It's structural and as such, it's often hard to see. The departmental analysts Nye mentions genuinely believe in the advice they're giving. They are usually good people with good intentions, but alas, their position living in a silo has the potential to lead to bad advice. And sometimes, the best course of action may be to do nothing. What?! No action? Which department or silo is organized to support the lack of action? Sadly, none.

To Do or Not to Do

Now consider the following scenario, faced by my friend and Harvard colleague Esko Aho, former prime minister of Finland. As one of the youngest prime ministers of a developed nation—ever—Esko was faced with an inordinate number of challenges during his tenure in the early 1990s: (1) he was welcomed into office during a nasty recession, (2) he was asked to help determine the future relationship between Finland and the European Union, and (3) he had to manage the risks emanating from the implosion of a global superpower that shared a several-hundred-mile border with the country he was now leading.

Esko was kind enough to visit my class and spend a few hours with my students. During our discussion, he recalled getting a call at 2 a.m. from one of his top advisors informing him that "shots were being fired in Moscow." The advisor feared a coup was underway and Finland would need to handle an influx of refugees, possible military defections, and instability on its more than 1,300 kilometer border with Russia. The situation was presented as dire, necessitating immediate action and planning to handle what would likely turn into a messy situation.

Esko then asked my students what they would have done if they were in his shoes. Everyone agreed it was important to gather top military commanders and begin planning. Some suggested calling Moscow to offer support. Many other ideas surfaced of what could be done to prepare for the likely chaos. After listening carefully to every suggestion, Esko shared what he did: "I hung up the phone and went back to sleep."

He knew he needed to be rested and alert in the morning because he would likely awake to enormous pressures. He also knew that his advisors would call back if the matter grew more urgent . . . and he feared that by staying up and acting, he may act unnecessarily. And he understood his advisors all had a limited perspective. They lived in silos—silos that structurally limited their perspective. So he did nothing. By the morning, the situation had grown less urgent and he was able to calmly and thoroughly plan for various scenarios with his team.

Esko's advice about choosing to do nothing resonated with many of my students, many of whom had some experience working in finance. Several noted the relevance of Esko's insight to investing. Investment management is an uncertain endeavor in which risk and reward must be constantly gauged as part of a never-ending quest to generate returns. Because of the unpredictable nature of market movements, every investor is destined to make mistakes.

But an investor can choose what type of mistake to make, and in times of lofty valuations or bubbly conditions, it's better to make errors of omission rather than errors of commission. When the potential rewards appear limited and risks elevated, it's better to do nothing and miss gains than to do something and capture losses. As noted by Warren Buffett, "frequently, the best decision is to do nothing."[32]

Most experts, when presented with a problem, recommend an action of some sort. After all, most of us seek out experts precisely to figure out what to do. How satisfied would you be with an advisor who answered your concerns with, "I don't recommend you do anything"?

A friend of mine was diagnosed as having prostate cancer about ten years ago. The diagnosis hit him and his wife like a ton of bricks. A week after he found out, I happened to run into him. He wasn't his usual upbeat self. I asked, and that's when I learned of his situation. We spent hours chatting over coffee how he might move forward with a treatment plan and what this all meant for his life, his wife, his marriage, his kids, and the unfulfilled dreams he still wanted to pursue. I offered to help him think through the choices.

When I dug into the research findings, what I found stunned me. I won't repeat it here, given I discussed it earlier in this book, but it's worth reiterating the bottom-line findings of the medical literature: many men will die with prostate cancer, very few will die because of it. I helped my friend design a list of questions to ask when he returned to his urologist. At the very top of the list: What if I chose to do nothing?

Ultimately, that's what he chose to do. He opted for what is now seen as a medically acceptable process of watchful waiting. And fortunately, he seems to have, in the language used earlier in the book, a turtle cancer that doesn't seem problematic. Aside from the mental anxiety produced by the diagnosis, and regular visits to the doctor for monitoring, his life hasn't really changed at all.

. . .

We can and should retain control and ownership of our problems and decisions, tapping experts for help as needed. And experts need to understand that they only see a portion of the entire picture, meaning their incomplete perspective should allow for a collaborative relationship with their clients rather than one in which they dictate a process.

We need to think of ourselves as an artist preparing a mosaic. Experts provide fragments of tiles that vary in color and size. But forming the image is our responsibility, taking insights on an as-needed basis from those best suited to provide information and analysis.

Questions to Ask Yourself

- **Is the type of decision you need to make one in which an expert can be helpful?** Think through the Cynefin framework of simple, complicated, complex, and chaotic contexts. If the situation is complicated, an expert can help. If it's complex, however, you need to own the problem and tap into expertise that can help you understand how to move forward.

- **What are the assumptions behind the advice?** Taking advice from experts is often very useful, but you should not hesitate to ask them to explain their logic and evidence to you in language you understand. Don't be intimidated by their status.

- **What incentives may be impacting the guidance received from advisors?** Remember that the principal-agent problem can generate substantial conflicts of interest that materially impact progress toward your objective.

- **What if I do nothing?** Sometimes it's best to do nothing. Exploring this possibility with those that are recommending action may be difficult to do, but the upside of doing so may be enormous.

PART FOUR

A PATH FORWARD

As we cope with a world of overwhelming information, we must develop the tools to reclaim control. Self-reliance in the twenty-first century is not about doing everything by yourself; it's about staying in charge and tapping into expertise as and when needed, always mindful of the limitations of the guidance you receive. But it's also about learning to navigate the omnipresent uncertainty by imagining multiple futures and balancing breadth with depth. Embracing ambiguity and ignorance as positives, it turns out, can help us identify unique opportunities. Ultimately, restoring common sense requires we think for ourselves.

CHAPTER 11

Navigating Uncertainty

The learned dependency and blind obedience described earlier in the book has been amplified by the increasingly obvious uncertainty that plagues our daily lives. Given our deep discomfort with uncertainty and the promise of expert-led optimal decision making (even in the face of such ambiguity), we are increasingly drawn to experts. Noreena Hertz, the woman who earlier encouraged us to push back against experts and ask questions, described the current predicament of expert dependency in a TED talk:

> In a world of data deluge and extreme complexity . . . in an age that is sometimes nowadays frightening or confusing, we feel reassured by the almost parental-like authority of experts who tell us so clearly what it is we can and cannot do. But I believe that this is a big problem, a problem with potentially dangerous consequences for us as a society, as a culture and as individuals. It's not that experts have not massively contributed to our world, they have. The problem lies with us. We've become addicted to experts. We've become addicted to their certainty, their assuredness, their definitiveness, and in the process, we've ceded our responsibility, substituting our intellect and our intelligence for their supposed words of wisdom. We've

surrendered our power, trading off our discomfort with uncertainty for the illusion of certainty that they provide.[1]

Rather than fear uncertainty, we should learn to embrace it and develop the skills to navigate through it. And in this regard, it's worth looking to the work of futurologists and scenario planners. Just as Bob Woodward wonders what the bad guys are doing right now, we can and should consider alternative future possibilities for how the world may unfold. Doing so can help us navigate the overwhelming complexity and uncertainty we all face in virtually every segment of our lives. But it's important to note that scenarios are not predictions or extrapolations of trends.

The Futility of Predictions

Morgen Robertson was a former cabin boy in the merchant marine, had tired of sea life, spent a decade as a diamond setter, and eventually turned to writing stories about life at sea. He never made much money and died at the age of fifty-three from an overdose.[2]

Before he died, Robertson wrote a novel about "the largest craft afloat the greatest of the works of men," a novel he titled *Futility*. The vessel was the embodiment of "every science, profession, and trade known to civilization" and was a modern-day technological marvel.[3] The boat was deemed unsinkable, and it attracted famous people from around the world to journey across the Atlantic in unrivaled comfort and style. Nineteen water-tight compartments assured the boat's buoyancy, as she could continue to sail with nine of them flooded. And because the vessel was deemed indestructible, it carried an inadequate number of lifeboats—enough to only handle one-sixth of the passengers aboard. The name of the ship was the *Titan*.

In Robertson's tale, on a voyage through the North Atlantic one April, the ship struck an iceberg and sank. The story goes on to describe the drama associated with a disgraced naval officer who worked as a deckhand on the *Titan*, John Rowland. Rowland ends up rescuing a young girl but is later accused by the girl's mother (who happens to have been his former lover) of kidnapping her. A true Hollywood-esque drama, for sure! And given that authors often look to historical events for inspiration, you might dismiss Robertson's novel as being in the same vein as James Cameron's blockbuster 1997 movie *Titanic*.

Don't!

Why's that? Because *Futility* was written fourteen years **before** the actual *Titanic* sank. Aside from the similarities of name and method of demise, consider the facts in the following table:

TABLE 11-1

The *Titan* versus the *Titanic*

	Futility (1898)	*Titanic* (1912)
Vessel name	Titan	Titanic
Ship length	800 ft	882 ft
Ship displacement	45,000 tons	46,000 tons
Ship speed	22.5 knots	25 knots
Popular description	"Unsinkable"	"Unsinkable"
Lifeboats	24	16
Passengers and crew	2,500	2,200
Cause of accident	Iceberg impact	Iceberg impact
Location	North Atlantic	North Atlantic
Precise location	400 nm from Newfoundland	400 nm from Newfoundland
Date	"April"	April 14, 1912
Survivors	13	705
Propellers	3	3

After the sinking of the actual *Titanic*, Robertson was celebrated by many as a clairvoyant, as possessing extraordinary skills of precognition. He dismissed these claims, suggesting it was his knowledge of maritime matters that gave him the ability to write about ships with detail. Yet the world refused to give up on the possibility that he had in fact seen the future.

It's such an intriguing story that the 1990s American TV series *Beyond Belief: Fact or Fiction* featured the *Titan-Titanic* story in an episode, highlighting during the short segment that "the only difference between fiction and nonfiction is that fiction hasn't happened yet." Host Jonathan Frakes (yes, the one of *Star Trek* fame) tells the story from the perspective of a struggling author, and ends the story by asking viewers if the coincidence was "another example of art foreshadowing life? The same way Jules Verne wrote of submarines long before their invention? Or DaVinci sketched flying machines centuries before the Wright brothers?" At the end of the episode, he reveals the story was in fact true.[4]

Coincidences happen, for sure. And anyone prognosticating on the future has likely heard the clichés, "even a broken clock is right twice a day" or "every now and then a blind squirrel will find a nut," statements that might suggest mere luck as the reason for Robertson's supposed ability to see the future. In fact, Robertson's title hints at the primary criticism regularly hurled at those thinking about the future—it's an act of futility. And as the common saying goes, "It's dangerous to make predictions, especially about the future."

One need only look to expert predictions to see just how inaccurate predictions can be. Consider *The Great Depression of 1990* by Southern Methodist University economist Ravi Batra (which stayed on the bestseller list for ten months in hardcover and over nineteen months as a paperback). It totally missed the technological developments that made the 1990s among the most productive decades ever.[5] Numerous other examples exist of similarly mistimed or wrong predictions. Yet despite this mixed (at best) track record of those in the predictions business, we humans seem to have an insatiable appetite to consume their prognostications about the future. Nobel Laureate Ken Arrow captured the desire for predictions quite eloquently in recalling his work for the US Army Air Force. Despite concluding that the weather predictions upon which the superiors relied were entirely useless (i.e., statically random, no better than a guess), he was rebuffed, told that "The Commanding General is well aware that the forecasts are no good; however, he needs them for planning purposes."[6]

As comical as that statement sounds, I find it quite useful—and helpful. *The blunt reality is that accuracy cannot and should not be the criteria upon which to evaluate thinking about the future. Usefulness, I propose, is a far better standard.* Just as it's impossible to evaluate the quality of a decision process by its outcome, so too is it unproductive to evaluate the quality of a prediction by its accuracy. Good processes sometimes result in bad outcomes, something known colloquially as a bad break. Likewise, bad processes sometimes result in good outcomes, also known as dumb luck. But over time, good processes should result in a higher probability of good outcomes and bad processes should result in a higher probability of bad outcomes.

If we apply this logic to predictions about the future, we quickly learn to appreciate the value they may provide in helping us to think differently. They can help nudge us away from our default position and widen our view of the possibilities ahead.

Think in Futures

Mechanical as it may be, thinking about various scenarios of how the future may unfold may be the most useful way to support decision making in the face of radical uncertainty. Scenarios are stories of possible futures. They may be high or low probabilities associated with each scenario, but the act of articulating scenarios can help us appreciate our assumptions about the future and give us a map of the terrain that we may encounter.

There is a long and storied history behind the use of scenarios as a means to navigate uncertainty. The practice really began with Herman Kahn, who took military scenario planning from the US Air Force and tried to adapt it to the business context. A systems thinker, Kahn founded the Hudson Institute and gained prominence as a strategist at the RAND Corporation thinking about nuclear war. In 1967, he and colleague Andrew Wiener penned *The Year 2000: A Framework for Speculation on the*

Next Thirty-Three Years. In 1976, he and some colleagues wrote a book entitled *The Next 200 Years: A Scenario for America and The World.*

One of the stories Kahn painted, which at the time might have seemed a bit far-fetched, was that South Korea—one of the poorest countries in the world in the 1970s—would emerge as an economic powerhouse by the turn of the century. Kahn was an optimist, and in 1983 as the United States was emerging from an economic contraction, wrote *The Coming Boom* which suggested Ronald Regan's reform agenda would unlock tremendous economic, political, and social progress.

If Kahn is the father of modern scenario planning, Pierre Wack is the son who took its usefulness to new heights in the business community. Wack and his colleagues in the group planning department at Royal Dutch/Shell understood the price of oil was critical for their business, but because the price had been relatively steady for long periods of time, few worried about it. The planners thought this was a flawed way to think about the future and in the early 1970s began developing stories of possible scenarios that might affect the oil price. One scenario involved the newly formed Organization of Petroleum Exporting Countries (OPEC) flexing its muscles, with huge ramifications for the oil price. And after the Yom Kippur War led to an oil price shock, Shell was more prepared than most because its managers had already thought through how to act in such a world. Peter Schwartz, who also served in the group planning department at Shell, summarized the value of the scenarios used by Shell in *The Art of the Long View,* "The end result . . . [was] not an accurate picture of tomorrow, but better decisions about the future."[7]

We can all learn from the success of Shell navigating the 1970s oil shocks. The world is uncertain; we all know that. But we need not be surprised by developments within it. In fact, by hiding from the uncertainty rather than embracing it, we might miss obvious risks and forego tremendous opportunities. After all, we're all capable of imagining scenarios that may or may not transpire. It's a skill that children exercise regularly. Author, educator, and creativity expert Ken Robinson gave one of the most eloquent stories illustrating this natural power of imagination during his TED talk titled "Do Schools Kill Creativity?" He tells a story of a little girl in a drawing lesson:

> She was six, and she was at the back, drawing, and the teacher said this girl hardly ever paid attention, and in this drawing lesson, she did. The teacher was fascinated. She went over to her, and she said, "What are you drawing?" And the girl said, "I'm drawing a picture of God." And the teacher said, "But nobody knows what God looks like." And the girl said, "They will, in a minute."[8]

This creativity and open-mindedness is natural to the young. Children tend to speak their minds, free and clear of filters. In fact, the Robinson story reminds me of a Thanksgiving celebration years ago. Over the course of the prior year, I had lost a noticeable amount of weight. When we finally all sat down to eat, the topic of conversation somehow drifted to my waistline. "Wow . . . you've lost so much weight. . . . How did you lose the weight? I'd like to lose that much weight!" and so on. In the midst of this casual banter, one of my children (to protect the innocent, I won't say which) decided to interject a bit of commentary during a lull in the conversation: "Haha! Daddy lost a lot of weight. Mommy found it."

Oops! Sure, my wife Kristen had gained a little weight . . . but nothing noteworthy. After the initial giggles, the silence that followed was deafening and both my and Kristen's faces turned bright red. We were both embarrassed. But it kinda serves her right, because years earlier (before I had lost the weight), I had announced I was going to be doing a triathlon . . . and when my family asked, "Which race?" I replied, "A sprint distance race, maybe the Wells Kennebunk triathlon or the Pumpkinman race in New Hampshire." Kristen's reaction: "Pumpkinman? Sounds about right. Definitely not an Ironman."

Hmmm . . . come to think about it, maybe some filters are useful.

But back to the point about natural creativity. This imagination tends to get slowly trained out of us over time . . . but it need not happen. We can and should regularly think about possible futures. Not doing so can be tragic. The 9/11 Commission, chaired by former governor of New Jersey Thomas Keane, concluded in its final report that the terrorist attacks of 9/11 on the United States were a "failure of imagination."[9] (Relatedly, no one has suggested that Pearl Harbor was a failure of imagination, because thirty-six years earlier the Japanese had conducted an almost identical surprise attack on the Russian Pacific Fleet based in Port Arthur.)

Consider the (Seemingly) Irrelevant

There are lots of examples where a broad perspective that connects the seemingly irrelevant yields surprising and powerful insights. In my work as a roving global generalist, I've managed to find a plethora of surprising and powerful connections between ideas and topics that might not naturally be linked. In fact, for two years, I wrote a weekly piece (posted to my LinkedIn account and also on my personal website) in which I connected seemingly irrelevant topics and then discussed the implications of what is meant.

In one piece, I considered how the American obsession with guacamole could be linked with marginal impacts on climate change and organized crime in Mexico.[10] After all, when one looks at the data, you can see that around 80 percent of the Haas avocadoes consumed in the United States come from the Michoacan state in Mexico, home to some of the most intense gang warfare in the country. The connection of economic incentives to deforestation is also clear when you empathize with local landowners as they make decisions about what to plant and why.

In another piece, I explored how the weather may have affected the outcomes of polls and elections in both Colombia and the United Kingdom.[11] In 2016, the people of Colombia rejected a proposed peace agreement that would have ended more than fifty years of fighting. Likewise, the referendum regarding whether Britain should remain in or leave the European Union resulted in a surprising victory for the Leave camp. Could these two outcomes be related? Well it does turn out that the weather may have played a role in both referendums. In Colombia, Hurricane Matthew barreled through many "yes" strongholds on the day of voting, resulting in low turnouts. Similar dynamics transpired in the United Kingdom, where very heavy rains (a typical month's worth) fell in areas that were overwhelmingly polling in favor of Remain. Could it be that seemingly irrelevant factors like weather could be playing a big role in major policy decisions? Might our focus on surface explanations obscure underlying dynamics?

Or what about the domain of financial bubbles? Might it be possible to glean insights on the nature of likely bubbles by looking at architecture? It turns out that the world's tallest skyscrapers tend to telegraph financial bubbles because they are literal embodiments of hubris, easy money conditions, and speculative tendencies. After all, we've been around long enough that we don't need to have the world's tallest anything. It's not rational! Secondly, because skyscrapers are rarely built without borrowed money, banks and money conditions need to be easy (or the buildings wouldn't be built). And lastly, the world's tallest skyscrapers are usually built by a developer adopting a speculative philosophy of "build it, and the tenants will come."

The skyscraper indicator seems to work. In 1929, three NYC buildings competed for the status of the world's tallest tower—40 Wall Street, the Chrysler Building, and the Empire State Building. The Great Depression followed. In 1973 and 1974, NYC's World Trade Center and Chicago's Sears Towers took the titles, as the economy entered a decade of stagflation and suffered multiple oil price shocks. In 1997, the tallest tower status moved to Malaysia, where the Petronas Tower claimed the title just as the region succumbed to the Asian Financial Crisis. Likewise, Taipei 101 (Taiwan was the home of the hardware/semiconductor side of the tech boom) foretold the story of the internet/technology bubble, and the Burj Dubai (later renamed Burj Khalifa) took the title of the world's tallest freestanding structure in 2007, shortly before the global financial crisis.

So what are we to make of the fact that Saudi Arabia had plans to build a 1-kilometer-high tower, one that would claim the title of world's tallest building? Or that Dubai does not want to be outdone by their Arabian peer and has since proposed the 1.3-kilometer-tall Dubai Creek

Tower? These plans may never come to fruition, but the mere announcements are enough to catch my attention! For those wanting to read more specifically about the Skyscraper Indicator and its theoretical logic, I'd encourage you to read *The Skyscraper Curse* by Mark Thornton.

Imagine Alternatives

If not thinking about possible developments is risky, might doing so reveal opportunities? Unadulterated imagination will produce some whacky thoughts, for sure, but some of them may prove to be revolutionary. After finishing school, my job dominated my life and I had very little time to read. With the time I did read, I always felt the pressure to read the latest nonfiction books about topics related to investing, business, or economics. But in the past decade, I've taken to regularly reading fiction to help me imagine different worlds, possible scenarios, and alternative futures. I highly recommend it. And in fact, whereas I once felt guilty about watching movies in the middle of the day, I've done so (without remorse!) a couple of times when I find my thinking in a rut. Stories tend to help us get out of our own heads and to think about scenarios that may not naturally enter our frame of view. For as Jessamyn West once said, "fiction reveals truths that reality obscures."[12]

One of the more powerful novels I've read was *One Second After,* published in 2009. The book, written by military historian William Forstchen, explores the possibility of the United States being crippled by an electromagnetic pulse (EMP) attack that knocks out the electrical power infrastructure. In the foreword, former speaker of the house Newt Gingrich describes the book as a 'future history' that might come true."[13] I've even used the book in the class I teach on systems thinking to illustrate the dependency we have on critical infrastructure and how many of our social, cultural, economic, and political systems might break down. The book paints such a visceral image of what life might be like in the event of an EMP attack that I would never have understood or imagined the full impact without reading the detailed scenario as presented in the novel.

Another novel that left me with an indelible image of a possible future was *Oryx and Crake*, written by Margaret Atwood, acclaimed author of the *Handmaid's Tale*. It's a story of how large corporations unleash bioengineered innovations that ultimately overcome their creators. The story describes how pigoons, genetically engineered pigs, are used to grow bespoke organs for humans, but they ultimately come to think for themselves and eventually come to hunt humans. What I find fascinating about the story is that Atwood refuses to call her novel science fiction because, as she wrote in 2004, the "label denotes books with things in them we can't yet do or begin to do." In essence, the scary world she describes is not one that needs future technological innovations to transpire, because it's based on currently possible developments. By describing her work as "speculative fiction," Atwood is forcing us to think differently about the trends emanating from today's world of existing technologies.[14] If that's not the essence of getting someone to adopt a different perspective, I'm not sure what is!

I've also enjoyed watching movies to help me envision worlds and perspectives different than my own. Just think about how the opening lines of the movie *Armageddon* fundamentally force the viewer to think differently. It begins with an image of the earth from afar, and the voiceover begins: "This is the Earth at a time when the dinosaurs roamed a lush and fertile planet . . ." and the scene then shows an asteroid heading toward it. The voice continues, "A piece of rock just six miles wide changed all that."[15]

After showing the asteroid colliding with Earth, the narration explained: "It hit with a force of 10,000 nuclear weapons . . . a trillion tons of dirt and rock hurled into the atmosphere, creating a suffocating blanket of dust the sun was powerless to penetrate for a thousand years." As the image shows the entire Earth covered from the blast generated by the asteroid impact, the music turns ominous and the voice warns: "It happened before. It will happen again. It's just a question of when."[16]

If you think this is just Hollywood dreaming up fantastic stories to help us escape the reality of life, consider the fact that the *Economist* on August 1, 2015, proposed a scenario for consideration entitled "What If an Asteroid Heads for Earth?"[17] Published as part of the magazine's annual set of scenarios called *The World If*, the collection is meant to accompany their heavily read "The World in XXXX" set of predictions. Yet the scenarios have enormous standalone value in forcing readers to think. As you can probably tell, I'm a fan and read them religiously.

Other topics explored in their 2015 edition of *The World If* included the possibility of Russia breaking up, India's monsoon failing, and the building of a canal in Nicaragua that rivals the Panama Canal. The following year's scenarios, published in July 2016, led with a story that many dismissed as highly unlikely: "What if Donald Trump Was President?"[18] The story they wrote, fictionally dated April 2017, reads as eerily predictive and foreshadows much of what actually transpired during the first one hundred days of the Trump administration. Other 2016 scenarios include the collapse of the North Korean regime and a mass hacking of the financial system. And the 2017 *The World If* raised the prospect of an EMP attack on the United States (uh-oh, *One Second After* doesn't seem so fictional anymore) that brings down the entire electricity grid, the emergence of a true fiduciary standard, and drumroll please . . . that Donald Trump's popularity surges, leading to his reelection in 2020.[19]

And it's not just reading scenarios that helps jar us from the normal rhythm of our thoughts, it's also seeing them. Hollywood is great at the storytelling business, and stories tend to be more effective at having a lasting impact on thoughts than does text. So let's consider another scenario: the possibility of California disconnecting from the mainland of the United States. Probably sounds as far-fetched as an asteroid hitting the Earth, right? What if I told you there were serious thinkers focused on this exact possibility?

Just watch the movie *San Andreas*. Yes, the human drama was an emotional hook around which the story is told, but the part that struck me as really jarring was the scene of boats driving through downtown San Francisco. Is this a possibility? How real is it? Aren't we just wasting precious brain-processing power and limited attention on a very remote possibility? Maybe, but maybe not.

Kathryn Schulz is a writer for *The New Yorker* and author of a book called *Being Wrong: Adventures in the Margin of Error.* In addition to penning a fabulous book about handling error (a book that Drew Faust, president of Harvard University, recommended every freshman read before they begin classes), she also wrote an article about the possibility of an earthquake that completely transforms the Pacific Northwest. The subheading for her June 2015 *New Yorker* piece titled "The Really Big One" was "An earthquake will destroy a sizable portion of the coastal Northwest. The question is when."[20] Sure resembles the opening of *Armageddon* to me!

A word of caution. While it's easy to dismiss *San Andreas* and *Armageddon* as mere movies about low-probability natural disasters, doing so would miss their real value. By forcing us to think about radical scenarios, they're expanding our imaginations about what our future might look like. And because good movies need to be realistic enough for us to believe them (else we wouldn't get lost in them), seemingly irrelevant details must be carefully considered.

One movie that I think is particularly good at painting a scenario with realistic details in adjacent areas is *Contagion*, the 2011 story about a pandemic that creates fear and chaos in much of America. It's such a wonderful example of a scenario that creates feedback loops and throws off an entire system that I've required my students to watch it. We usually spend an entire class discussing it. The movie begins *in media res* when a woman who returns home from a trip to Hong Kong and develops unexplainable symptoms and dies. Soon others with whom she physically interacted are sick with similar symptoms. As we watch the epidemic unfold, we watch the disturbing breakdowns in political, social, economic, and moral behavior that barrels the society toward chaos. Every time I watch the movie I'm disturbed at these second-order effects—after all, it's bad enough to have a devastating illness spreading rapidly through a population. But the impact of the fear, the breakdown of society's order, the closing of borders, the involvement of the military in containing and controlling the movement of people, and the conflicts of interest which rear their ugly head are downright disturbing. But it's useful to think of these impacts. How might you act if you were militarily contained because your neighbor had been infected with a deadly disease and society determined it necessary to quarantine you with her?

Without ruining the movie for those who haven't watched it, we ultimately learn the cause of the disease is zoonoses, the jumping of a pathogen from an animal to a human. To some extent, the movie's a warning against urbanization and globalization because without development in former jungles, it's unlikely problematic human infringement on animal habitats would have occurred . . . and without the interaction, the pandemic might not have started.

So given that urbanization is marching forward virtually unabated, what can we learn from this scenario? Should the CDC begin stockpiling treatments for rare diseases on the off chance that they may spread through populations so rapidly that manufacturing treatments at that point would be too slow? What about developing contingent coordination plans with multinational organizations like the World Health Organization? Surely such preparedness might prove useful, right? Maybe just-in-time strategies need to be replaced with just-in-case logic?

Because the value of scenario planning can be so high, we need to be careful not to overly define the various situations we're prepping to occur. We need to allow a certain amount of fuzziness when preparing for contingencies. If we're too focused in our preparation, we may not be able to respond well. We want to focus on planning not on the plans, just as famous boxer Mike Tyson has noted, "Everyone has a plan until they get hit."[21] We need to retain the ability to adjust dynamically to accommodate conditions as they emerge.

In April 2017, for instance, after months of training, I boarded a bus in Boston that was taking me to Hopkinton. I was about to run my first marathon, as a charity runner supporting John Hancock and the Torit Foundation. I had a great plan, had prepared to execute on it, and was ready to go. But then, after seventeen miles of running, my legs somehow turned into bricks. I literally had to stop and stretch for minutes as I tried to restore my ability to move. My plan was great, but more important was my ability to adjust based on the dynamics that emerged as the world unfolded. I'm pleased to say I finished, albeit in more than double the time it took the elite runners to complete the same distance. Oh well!

Four years earlier, the ability to dynamically adjust to shifting conditions proved critical on April 15, 2013, at 2:49 p.m. when an improvised explosive device (IED) detonated near the finish line of the Boston Marathon, killing three and hospitalizing more than 260. The Boston Athletic Association, organizers of the race, had planned on addressing emergencies as they evolved, and was in close coordination with local medical and emergency personnel. But no one had anticipated the set of events that unfolded on that terrible afternoon. Instead, what we witnessed was an amazing and seemingly uncoordinated response that proved effective at assisting the injured to secure appropriate medical attention. All victims needing medical help had left the scene within twenty-two minutes. The immediate response was a success, and the subsequent mission-oriented coordination proved effective at tracking down the Tsarnaev brothers who had planned and executed the marathon bombing.[22]

It turns out that Boston responded so well to the marathon bombing precisely because they planned for and practiced disaster response, but without getting bogged down in specific plans. They generically played through several scenarios of scenarios demanding an emergency response. In fact, it's part of their normal preparation for big events like the Boston Marathon.[23]

Embrace Ambiguity

It should not come as a surprise that many of the lessons learned in this chapter could easily have appeared in other chapters. That's true because of the highly interconnected society in which we live; it's also why systems thinking is so valuable in understanding the relationship in a dynamic situation. To navigate uncertainty, it's useful to think like a systems thinker and study how feedback loops matter. And systems thinking is more about connecting dots than generating them. How does one variable affect another one? It also forces a big-picture perspective, one in which the normal narrowness is replaced with a zoomed-out overview.

Former Secretary of State Dean Acheson described strategic planning as looking ahead, "not into the distant future, but beyond the vision of the operating officers caught in the smoke and crisis of current battle; far enough ahead to see the emerging form of things to come and outline what should be done to meet or anticipate them."[24] Sounds a lot like adjusting your focus. Strategic planning "can also be about reinterpreting past and current actions through a new analytical lens."[25] Also, speaking of filtering through information and deliberately establishing your area of focus, Secretary of State George Marshall, who led the State Department when the policy planning staff was founded, gave George Kennan, its first director, a concise directive: "Avoid trivia."[26]

If that's not the most eloquent expression of the dot connecting, uncertainty navigating, scenario appreciating approach presented in this chapter, I'm not sure anything is! Trivia is, of course, random tidbits of information removed from the context in which they might normally appear. And like I finally did with the 1980s board game Trivial Pursuit, it's best to shelve random disconnected thoughts (i.e., trivia) and replace them with zoomed out, big-picture thinking that connects to things you care about. Doing so allows us to break out of our thinking and consider how developments in one domain might inspire and drive progress in another.

Scatter Your Mind

Many busy professionals feel guilty about having a creative passion, yet they may be doing themselves a professional and personal disservice by constraining their interest. In addition to the personal satisfaction and enjoyment from its pursuit, artistic endeavors may spur the imagination and enable breakthrough thinking. There is evidence to support this claim; some of the most accomplished folks in their fields do exactly that. For instance, research shows that Nobel laureates are much more likely to have been engaged in arts and crafts than other scientists.[27] Likewise, people who have started businesses and contributed to successful patents are more likely to be engaged in the arts.[28]

But it also means that we should be open-minded to nonlinear thinking and activities in our personal and professional lives. We need to scatter our thinking with lots of experiences so that we have them to draw upon when needed. One great way to think more broadly and to imagine more creatively is to read fiction and watch movies. But another, perhaps more practical way to scatter your mind is to pursue professional opportunities in different functions or geographies. I suspect we'd all be better off thinking of career progress as playing on jungle gyms rather than climbing ladders. Sometimes the fastest way to get from A to B is to go horizontally; or climb down first, then clamber to a different part of the structure before again going up. Who knows, you might even get a different view of the playground!

When facing massive uncertainty it is essential to appreciate both what one does know as well as what one does not know. Such logic is not shocking, but it has significant ramifications for how one should manage his or her career and how organizations should manage their human resources. Specifically, those who possess above-average skepticism and intellectual humility and can think about the possible without being wedded to the supposedly likely are better able to navigate uncertainty. Individuals should therefore seek career paths that constantly put them in unfamiliar roles and through which they can learn what they don't know. The feedback one receives through these roles will likely improve one's intellectual self-awareness and ability to navigate unknown terrains.

Key Takeaways

- **When navigating uncertainty, it's best to think in terms of multiple possible futures.** Prediction can be productive, even if it isn't accurate. The key is whether the predictions helped you think more deeply about the present and how to make decisions in the face of an ambiguous future.

- **Fiction encourages imagination and helps expand the universe of potential considerations that affect our decisions.** Often, busy professionals prioritize nonfiction and documentaries over novels, science fiction, or dramatic movies. But fiction and imaginative stories can help us think more broadly and differently about the future.

- **Rather than shunning ambiguity, embrace it.** Thinking through possible futures enables one to spot possible opportunities buried in the uncertainty as well as to identify lurking risks. Uncertainty and ambiguity enable both innovative breakthroughs and spectacular failures. Engage deeply with possible scenarios while retaining broad perspectives. Employ systems logics to connect dots and consider feedback loops.

CHAPTER 12

Self-Reliance in the Twenty-First Century

We need to reclaim our lives from experts and technologies, a challenge that requires faith in ourselves and trust in our instincts—in short, a twenty-first-century self-reliance. We need to restore our faith in our own common sense and overcome our love affair with technology—it's a tool to supplement, not replace, our thinking. We should keep experts on tap, not on top. We all have the ability and responsibility to see the big picture and connect the dots, because not doing so is likely to create more problems than it solves. But most importantly, we need to come up with a new way to engage experts. To do so requires that we abandon our devotion to depth and reintroduce a greater focus on breadth. It's the only way we can reclaim the control we've mindlessly handed over to the various focus managers discussed in this book.

Fundamentally, self-reliance in the twenty-first century is about thinking for yourself. And even though it was written in 1841, Ralph Waldo Emerson's words ring as true today as they did then. He basically urged us to think for ourselves: "a man should learn to detect and watch that gleam of light which flashes across his mind from within, more than the lustre of the firmament of bards and sages."[1] We could easily replace "bards and sages" with "experts and technology" and it would feel relevant.

Just think about the fact that Steve Jobs, product developer extraordinaire, attributed the success of Apple's beautiful typefaces to a calligraphy class he took at Reed College (after he dropped out). He had been taking classes out of pure interest, not because it would count toward a degree. Jobs later noted that, "10 years later, when we were designing the first Macintosh computer, it all came back to me . . . and we designed it into the Mac . . . it was the first computer with beautiful typography. If I had never dropped in on that single course in college, the Mac would never have had multiple typefaces or proportionally spaced fonts. And since Windows just copied the Mac, it's likely that no personal computer would have them." But when Jobs took the calligraphy class, he had no idea it would prove useful. He was pursuing his interests, and as he said, "It was impossible to connect the dots looking forward when I was in college . . . but it was very very clear looking backwards."[2]

The lesson Jobs articulates is that overly planned and focused thinking today can impair your ability to connect dots tomorrow. Because we don't know which dots may prove useful to connect, it's useful to have a bunch of them in our repertoire. But specialization minimizes our appreciation of the number, type, and range of dots that exist; it limits our awareness of the context. And as society has marched onwards toward ever increasing degrees of specialization, we've come to look down on breadth. The scales of focus currently overweight depth; it's time to rebalance and acknowledge the value of breadth.

Learn from the Feeble-Minded

"Profession" is a fabulous short story written by Isaac Asimov in 1957 and illustrates, perhaps better than more modern anecdotes, the fundamental shortcomings of deep specialization and skills-based education.[3] The story, set in the distant future, is about the educational path toward various professions. Although set on Earth, the story includes characters from distant planets known as Outworlds and is about the main character, George Platen, and his quest to become a registered computer programmer.

The development trajectory of humans in this future setting is punctuated with three key days: Reading Day, Education Day, and the Olympics. Reading Day is a day during which eight-year-old boys and girls report to a doctor, who puts wires on their foreheads that are connected to a machine. After several procedures, every child leaves with the ability to read. Education Day take place approximately ten years after Reading Day, and was the be-all, end-all event for parents and children alike, because that's the day that determined what specialization would be installed, not unlike software on a computer, into a child's brain, thereby enabling the individual to have a profession. (Incidentally, Education Day is a bit like the day in South Korea during which students take their university entrance exams, leading the *Economist* to refer to Korea as "The One-Shot Society."[4]) And the Olympics is a day of competition to establish the most capable person within each profession.

George is the son of a registered pipefitter on Earth who desperately wants to be a registered computer programmer so he can potentially find a home on a desirable planet in the Outworlds. During Reading Day, we learn that the doctor who installs George's ability to read notices anomalies in the process . . . the cause of which is unveiled during his Education Day experience.

On Education Day, George fails to be educated and is sent to meet Sam Ellenford, who states: "To begin with, you can't be a Computer Programmer, George. You've guessed that I think."

After acknowledging this bitter reality, he asks "What will I be, then?"

"That's the hard part to explain, George," Ellenford answers. "Nothing. . . . Every once in a while, George, we come up against a young man whose mind is not suited to receiving a superimposed knowledge of any sort."

"You mean I can't be Educated?" George asks.

"That is what I mean." Ellenford then describes to George how he is now a ward of the planet and will be protected. George inquires, "You mean, I'm going to be in a prison?"

"Of course not; You will simply be with others of your kind . . . you need special treatment."

A dejected George asks questions about the shame that will flow to his family. He is assured that they've been told he's been sent away on a special assignment. Eventually, George is paired with another "uneducable" roommate. The property at which he finds himself is called "A House for the Feeble-Minded." Furious to have been placed there, George remains convinced that a grave mistake has taken place. He escapes and tries to convince others of his capability, refusing to accept that he cannot be educated. Through what appears to be dumb luck, George meets a historian who tries to help him.

In the course of their discussions, the historian answers George's questions about why Education works the way it does:

> The turning point came when the mechanics of the storage of knowledge within the brain was worked out. Once that had been done, it became possible to devise Educational tapes that would modify the mechanics in such a way as to place within the mind a body of knowledge ready-made, so to speak. Earth exports Education tapes for low-specialized positions and that keeps the Galactic culture unified . . . and Earth exports high-specialized professionals. . . . Furthermore, tapes and men are paid for in material which we much need and on which our economy depends. Now do you understand why our Education is the best way?

The historian, a self-described social scientist, asks to study George. George refuses, unless the historian can help him. George asks for an interview with an Outworld official, and soon finds himself communicating with one. He tries to convince the official that he's worthy of hiring, telling a story of a friend who failed to learn because of insufficient access to tapes.

George describes: "Tapes are actually bad. They teach too much; they're too painless. A man who learns that way doesn't know how to learn any other way. He's frozen into whatever position he's been taped. Now if a person weren't given tapes but were forced to learn by hand, so to speak, from the start; why, then he'd get the habit of learning and continue to learn." He goes on to suggest that by disrupting the cycle of learning via tapes, it would be possible to break the dependency upon Earth.

The official then asks, "And where does everyone get knowledge without tapes? From interstellar vacuum?"

"From books," George responds. "By studying the instruments themselves. By thinking."

The Outworld official remains skeptical, suggesting the time needed to acquire proficiency was too great, and that even if proficiency was eventually acquired, it wouldn't be as good as a competitor who had learned from tapes. He tells George that the self-educated person would not be as capable as a tape-educated one. George attempts to respond: "Wait, let me finish. Even if he doesn't know something well, it's the ability to learn further that's important. He may be able to think up things, new things that no tape-Educated man would. You'll have a reservoir of original thinkers."

Although amused by George's ideas, the official dismisses them as random banter of a wayward human. After the communication screen goes blank, a depressed George drifts off . . . only to awake back in the House . . . where his roommate greets him as his eyes open, informing him the historian was actually sent to help him adjust to his un-educated status.

And the light bulb goes off for George, "Now I see it . . . who makes Education tapes? Special tape-making technicians? Then who makes tapes to train them? More advanced technicians? Then who make their tapes— You see what I mean. Somewhere there has to be an end. Somewhere there must be men and women with capacity for original thought."

His roommate notes, "The Institute of Higher Studies is the correct name for places like this."

"Why wasn't I told this at the beginning?" George asks.

His roommate then reveals that approximately one in ten thousand people show signs of some propensity for original thought during Reading Day, but because there is no known way to detect such a capacity, they are again checked during Education Day. "Those who remain are sent to places like this," the roommate notes, going on to say that the creative original thinkers are never revealed publicly because "we can't have all those [Educated] people considering themselves failures. They aim at the professions and one way or another they all make it. Everyone can place after his or her name: Registered something-or-other."

He continues, "Nine out of ten of those who come here are not quite the material of creative genius, and there's no way we can distinguish those nine from the tenth that we want by any form of machinery. . . . We bring you here to a House for the Feeble-Minded and the man who won't accept that is the man we want. . . . There are ten thousand men like you, George, who support the advancing technology of fifteen hundred worlds."

Balance Breadth with Depth

Here on Earth, nowhere is the current debate over depth and breadth more active than in the domain of education. For years, policymakers have bemoaned the lack of skills-oriented education, often belittling those who pursue a liberal arts education. Consider President Barack Obama's 2014 comments while visiting Wisconsin to promote skills-based training to help revitalize US manufacturing: "I promise you folks can make a lot more . . . with skilled manufacturing . . . than they can with an art history degree."[5] Or what about Florida governor Rick Scott's comments about anthropology: after noting that education takes public resources from other uses, he asked, "Is it a vital interest of the state to have more anthropologists? I don't think so."[6] And lastly, there were the comments of North Carolina governor Patrick McCrory, who advised those interested in gender studies to attend a private school, because he didn't "want to subsidize that if it's not going to get someone a job."[7]

I could go on and on . . . but the point is straightforward: the post-2008 economic environment has put a premium on practical training and education. In fact, this usefulness orientation has become so fashionable that politicians and pundits regularly praise vocational and technical education over the liberal arts. It's best, according to this logic, to become a Registered something or other.

Perhaps this recent debate over the instrumentality of education is due to recent technological advancements that are creating ever-escalating skills requirements for desirable jobs? Or perhaps twenty-first century globalization is forcing young professionals everywhere to compete with the best minds from everywhere else? Both of these are very logical-seeming explanations for why American pundits and politicians emphatically demand usefulness as a key criteria by which to measure education success.

Consider the following quote, taken from the *Atlantic*: "What can I do with my boy? I can afford, and am glad, to give him the best training to be had. . . . I want to give him a practical education; one that will prepare him, better than I was prepared, to follow my business or any other active calling."[8] An excellent sense of the current anxiety felt by every parent today, right? Most parents instantly identify with the angst.

Would it surprise you to learn that the article from which this quote was taken was written in February 1869 by Charles Eliot, a future president of Harvard University? Bottom line: the issue of the practicality of education is simply not new. It's been around for hundreds (if not thousands) of years, and although it seems a worthy topic of debate, there is ample material to understand how prior debates have gone.

The modern debate on the philosophy of education can be traced back to the "Reports on the Course of Instruction in Yale College" written by a Committee of the Corporation and the Academical Faculty in 1828. Known today as the 1828 Yale Report, the authors suggest that a classical liberal education should focus on "two great points to be gained" from student efforts while at college—namely the development of "the *discipline* and the *furniture* of the mind; expanding its powers and storing it with knowledge." And for decades after the report was written, those two objectives—teaching students how to think as well as filling their mind with information—dominated the logic of liberal education. Notice the absence of any practicality component to the report. In fact, it even went so far as to say that the point of good liberal arts education was "not to teach that which is peculiar to any one of the professions; but to lay the foundation which is common to them all."[9]

Looking at the highly practical and research-oriented European polytechnic institutes, Charles Eliot went on to propose in his 1869 piece that

American colleges supplement their classic teaching orientation with a research effort.[10] He felt that the colleges needed to migrate toward universities in which the undergraduate focus remained on teaching and students, and the graduate focus was upon research and the practical benefits of specialization. And for better or worse, that blend of research-focused graduate schools and teaching-oriented undergraduate efforts has remained intact since Eliot's time as Harvard president.

Fareed Zakaria eloquently summarized the Eliot piece in his book *In Defense of Liberal Education* and also went on to highlight an innovative attempt to redesign education for the twenty-first century. The program Zakaria describes as perhaps "the most interesting and ambitious" attempt to redesign a liberal arts education is something I was fortunate enough to participate in during the summer of 2016.[11] About as far away from New Haven, CT as possible, a joint venture between Yale and the National University of Singapore (NUS) is seeking to reinvent liberal arts education. Yale-NUS College is an attempt by two of the world's leading universities to design, from the ground-up and free and clear of historical baggage, a residential liberal arts education for the twenty-first century.

After reading the Yale-NUS curriculum report once it was published in April 2013, I immediately reached out to the new college's president, Pericles Lewis, and offered to help however possible . . . and unlike most American universities where they struggle to find a departmental home for me given the variety of my interests, Yale-NUS had no such problem. Why's that? Because Yale-NUS has no departments, viewing them instead as barriers to interdisciplinary and multidisciplinary teaching and learning.

As a result, you won't find a professor of economics at Yale-NUS. Instead, you'll find a professor of social science who happens to spend most of her time focused on economics topics. She may end up coteaching a class on climate change along with a professor of science who happens to focus on environmental topics as well as others. The result, which I was able to witness first hand when I co-taught a class on inequality with my friend Paul Solman at Yale-NUS during 2016, was a more collaborative faculty that brought integrated teaching into each classroom.

It's unclear if Yale-NUS will succeed. Fareed Zakaria, who served as a member of the Yale Corporation, the governing body of the university, when the decision was made to move forward with Yale-NUS, is explicit about the risks: "It may not be able to implement all of its ideas . . . [and] the tensions between freedom of inquiry and the still-closed political system in Singapore might undermine the project."[12] Regardless, Yale-NUS is an ambitious attempt to modernize liberal arts education by delicately tipping the balance (ever so slightly) back in the direction of breadth; as noted by founding president Pericles Lewis, "Especially in an age of commodified information, an important part of our task is furnishing young minds with stories, histories, and patterns of thought from a *variety* of cultures."[13] Bottom line: Yale-NUS is helping install global furniture in the minds of tomorrow's global leaders while also developing the discipline to think across subjects of inquiry.

But even as the Yale-NUS experiment progresses, further education innovations continue. A September 2017 piece in *The Chronicle of Higher Education* titled "A New Liberal Art" suggests that systems-oriented education may prove to be the future of liberal education. It defines systems thinking as "a discipline that examines the relationships between essential parts of an organization or a problem, and determines how to manage those relationships to get better outcomes."[14] While linear thinkers believe that problems have direct causes and you can optimize the whole by optimizing each of the parts, systems thinkers know that problems can have hidden, indirect causes, and it's the relationship among the parts that matters most.

The article highlights a few practical, career-oriented institutions that ground students in a systems-thinking approach: the California State University Maritime Academy (also known as Cal Maritime), where students learn to keep boats' mechanical elements running and interacting within a chain of command; the Culinary Institute of America, where students learn to confront unexpected problems, try their hand at leadership, and see the interlocking human and technical systems.

And of course, there are many new virtual education efforts aimed at balancing breadth and depth, the most prominent of which is the

Minerva School at Keck Graduate Institute. Minerva's founding dean, Stephen Kosslyn, had previously spent thirty years at Harvard University in positions ranging from professor of psychology to department chair to dean of social sciences.

The Atlantic magazine, in a story titled "The Future of College?" noted the effort is stripping college "down to its essence, eliminating lectures and tenure along with football games, ivy-covered buildings, and research libraries."[15] The model is pretty easy to describe: online education that is supplemented with a global residential living experience. In 2017, it was reported that Minerva Schools accepted a mere 2 percent of the applicants that applied, making it the most selective school in the United States.

But the most interesting part of the Minerva story, in my eyes, is how they are positioning the school. Here is the lead tagline that was on its website in November 2017: "Preparing to succeed in an era of global uncertainty requires developing your intellect, building your character, and learning practical capabilities." The emphasis on practicality is noteworthy, from the very get go, and is supplemented with a strong emphasis on breadth: The school highlights the need for both "broad knowledge and practical skills."[16] Part of this practicality is a global awareness, which Minerva hopes to infuse graduates with through a network of seven residential locations around the world (San Francisco, Seoul, Hyderabad, Berlin, Buenos Aires, London, Taipei). And each concentration listed on the website also had an accompanying list of possible careers that might flow from it. Again, it's too early to tell if this more practically oriented but broad education will be the appropriate balance, but it's worth watching.

Recognize Water

In 2005, MacArthur Fellow, English professor, and writer David Foster Wallace delivered the Kenyon College commencement speech. After welcoming the graduating students and their guests, he dove into a simple yet powerful parable: "There are these two young fish swimming along and they happen to meet an older fish swimming the other way, who nods at them and says 'Morning, boys. How's the water?' And the two young fish swim on for a bit, and then eventually one of them looks over at the other and asks, 'What the hell is water?'" The point of the fish story, Wallace noted, is to highlight that "the most obvious, important realities are often the ones that are hardest to see."[17]

Downplaying the importance for furniture of the mind, Wallace went on to note "a liberal arts education is not so much about filling you up with knowledge as it is about quote teaching you how to think . . . this isn't really about the capacity to think, but rather about the choice of what to think about." Wallace's ultimate message was that we all have the capacity to interpret realities in different ways, and the choice of how we do is up to us. We need not default to looking only where the spotlight is shining.

Wallace noted: "The point here is that I think this is one part of what teaching me how to think is really supposed to mean. To be just a little less arrogant, to have just a little critical awareness about myself and my certainties." He went on to highlight the natural and literal self-centeredness native to all humans: "everything in my own immediate experience supports my deep belief that I am the absolute center of the universe; the realist most vivid and important person in existence. . . . Think about it, there is no experience you have had that you are not the absolute center of. . . . The world as you experience it is there in front of you or behind you, to the left or right of you on your TV or your monitor."

To illustrate the point, he used a seemingly trivial example to illustrate the power of how we choose to think about what's happening in front of us:

> I can spend time in the end–of–the–day traffic being disgusted about all the huge, stupid, lane-blocking SUV's and Hummers and V-12 pickup trucks, burning their wasteful, selfish, forty-gallon tanks of gas, and I can dwell on the fact that the patriotic or religious bumper-stickers always seem to be on the biggest, most disgustingly selfish vehicles, driven by the ugliest, most inconsiderate and aggressive drivers.

And while choosing to think these thoughts doesn't seem to bother Wallace, doing so mindlessly does. An automatic, subconscious default setting about how all events affect us as individuals needs to be broken, because it may not be true. We need to entertain other possibilities, because as Wallace observed, there are lots of other, very different, ways to think about or understand such situations. It's possible that "the Hummer that just cut me off is maybe being driven by a father whose little child is hurt or sick in the seat next to him, and he's trying to get this kid to the hospital, and he's in a bigger, more legitimate hurry than I am, and it is actually I who am in his way."

Wallace encouraged us to empathize, considering what another person may be going through before forming our conclusions. "If you're aware enough to give yourself a choice, you can choose to look differently at this fat, dead-eyed, over-made-up lady who just screamed at her kid in the checkout line. . . . Maybe she's not usually like this. . . . Maybe she's been up three straight nights holding the hand of a husband who's dying of bone cancer."

Fundamentally, Wallace wanted us to retake control of our thinking, to not allow our default assumptions and natural self-centeredness to run roughshod over alternative interpretations and to empathize with others. As he concluded his powerful speech, he stated, "The really important kind of freedom involves attention and awareness and discipline. . . . The alternative is unconsciousness, the default setting, the rat race, the constant gnawing sense of having had, and lost, some infinite thing." We must, Wallace noted, be aware of "what is so real and essential, so hidden in plain sight all around us, all the time, that we have to keep reminding ourselves over and over: this is water . . . this is water."

One of the most "water-aware" people I know is Bruce Grewcock, chairman and former chief executive officer of Kiewit Corporation. Kiewit is one of the country's leading construction firms and also happens to be an employee-owned company. As the company has prospered over the past few decades, so too have the employee shareholders benefited.

When I was teaching my seminar on business ethics at Yale, I invited Bruce and a few of his colleagues to join my class for a discussion of whether Kiewit should be a public company. The facts presented were compelling—Kiewit shareholders would likely see the value of their shares double, the company would obtain a lower cost of funding, and the extra money would enable more competitive bidding for large projects. Further, having publicly traded equity would probably allow the company to acquire other companies on advantageous terms if it chose to do so.

After allowing the students to debate the topic and a variety of views to surface, I turned to Bruce. "So what do you actually think?" I asked. What he revealed in the brief discussion that followed indicated a deep awareness of how he and the current shareholders fit into the storied history of an amazingly successful business. He first indicated that he doubted any Kiewit employee would ever suggest the company go public because everyone realized it would change the company's culture. . . . They all understood it was their money at risk and made decisions differently than they would if they were just employees and not owners.

Then Bruce reached into his battered briefcase and pulled out a page he had clearly ripped from a magazine. The page was crumpled, faded, and frayed; it had clearly been with him for a long time. I also assumed he would keep digging for something else. But he didn't. He lifted the page for all to see.

It was an advertisement for Patek Philippe, the iconic Swiss watch. The picture had a father and a son with a caption that Bruce read: "You never actually own a Patek Philippe. You merely look after it for the next generation." He indicated that was how he felt about Kiewit. Sure, he was the company's chairman, chief executive officer, and its largest shareholder at the time, but he felt he was merely looking after it for the next generation. Unlike lots of other successful executives, Bruce understood the company's ownership structure and the historical context played a role in his and the company's success. He was also unlike others in that the default self-centeredness that Wallace highlighted was absent. He and the dozens of other Kiewit leaders I've met have a deep appreciation that they are part of something bigger than themselves. They recognize the water around them, and I suspect that such awareness is one of the main reasons Kiewit has outperformed most of its peers.

He might as well have said, "This is Kiewit. . . . This is Kiewit."

See Specialness Everywhere

David Foster Wallace's speech was intended to knock Kenyon's graduates out of their default position of self-centered interpretations of events transpiring all around them. A few years later, in wealthy Boston suburb, David McCullough Jr. attempted to deliver a similar message to the graduates of Wellesley High School.

Over the course of an approximately twelve-minute speech, McCullough observed to the graduates: "Your ceremonial costume . . . shapeless, uniform, one-size-fits-all. Whether male or female, tall or short, scholar or slacker, spray-tanned prom queen or intergalactic Xbox assassin, each of you is dressed, you'll notice, exactly the same. And your diploma . . . but for your name, exactly the same. All of this is as it should be, because none of you is special. You're not special. . . . You're not exceptional." He went on to note the empirical evidence. Three point two million high school graduates across the United States from around 37,000 high schools: "That's 37,000 valedictorians . . . 37,000 class presidents . . . 92,000 harmonizing altos . . . 340,000 swaggering jocks . . . 2,185,967 pairs of UGGs."[18]

As the audience nervously laughed during his speech, McCullough continued, noting that even being one in a million meant there were thousands of others of comparable uniqueness. And he noted that in a world where everyone is special, no one is. "If everyone gets a trophy, trophies become meaningless."

Realizing this was a far greater phenomenon than one exclusive to Wellesley, McCullough went on to say that "We have of late, we Americans, to our detriment, come to love accolades more than genuine achievement. We have come to see them as the point—and we're happy to compromise standards, or ignore reality, if we suspect that's the quickest way, or only way, to have something to put on the mantelpiece, something to pose with, crow about, something with which to leverage ourselves into a better spot on the social totem pole." And in the résumé wars typical of college-bound students, "building a Guatemalan medical clinic becomes more about the application to Bowdoin than the well-being of Guatemalans." Worthy endeavors, McCullough noted, get cheapened by the epidemic of ubiquitous specialness.

His ultimate advice is to change our focus. To look inward for motivation, to think for ourselves, to not allow the sentiment of others drive our behavior: "Climb the mountain not to plant your flag but to embrace the challenge, enjoy the air, and behold the view. Climb it so you can see the world, not so the world can see you. Go to Paris to be in Paris, not to cross it off your list and congratulate yourself for being worldly. . . . The sweetest joys in life, then come only with the recognition that you're not special . . . because everyone is."

McCullough's message is about shifting our focus. It's about trying to minimize the Wallace-described default assumptions, natural self-centeredness, and to see the world with different eyes. See the specialness everywhere.

Embrace Fresh Eyes

No self-respecting book these days, it seems, can be written without a witty quote from Mark Twain . . . and so I'm thrilled that I can fulfill that obligation while also providing a truly insightful comment. Twain said, "It ain't so much the things that people don't know that makes trouble in this world, as it is the things that people know that ain't so."[19] This is the main reason that an outsider's or a novice's perspective can be so valuable, a concept widely accepted among philosophers. Zen master Shunryu Suzuki notes that "the mind of the beginner is empty, free of the habits of the expert, ready to accept, to doubt and open to all possibilities."[20] Experience and expertise close our mind to certain possibilities, thereby creating unwarranted confidence in what we think we know.

This problem, I suggest, is one of the most pressing challenges in our current quest to restore common sense, achieve a twenty-first-century self-reliance, and reclaim our lives from the ubiquitous focus filters that hold us hostage. While we believe we are free, our existences may be more managed than any of us fully appreciates. This is not to suggest that we should not outsource our attention to others. If we do so mindfully, so be it. But the kind of unquestioning, blind obedience to focus filters is antithetical to any vision of freedom, self-reliance, or restored autonomy. It's what David Foster Wallace called "an imprisonment so total that the prisoner doesn't even know he's locked up."[21]

Don't Squander Ignorance

The key to breaking free is to somehow get out of your entrenched patterns and begin questioning what you know for sure. A fresh perspective is almost always difficult to proactively obtain, because it requires a meta-awareness and mindfulness that breaks the rigid routines that tend to dominate our lives. This is why it's important to step back and recognize that it's possible to get fresh perspectives by changing your field of attention, even within your area of focus. Is your job focused on equities? Consider debt, maybe even in other countries. Are you a cardiothoracic surgeon? Read a bit about dermatology, nutrition, or even diseases affecting nonhumans. Simple attention shifts like these increase the potential to generate fresh eyes to address problems. Only after taking such detours might we be able to revisit existing challenges with an open-mindedness that may generate a much-needed breakthrough.

To illustrate the power of ignorance and fresh eyes, let's go back in time to the ancient Egyptian city of Thonis-Heracleion. Supposedly a key religious center and trade hub for the ancient world (as well as the place where the Trojan prince Paris brought the kidnapped Helen of Troy), archaeologists and experts found little evidence of the city where it supposedly at one point had existed.[22] Now it's one thing to not find evidence of a specific artifact, or a specific building, but of an entire city? Some surmised the city disappeared through a set of natural disasters including rising sea levels and a series of earthquakes. Others doubted it ever existed.

Enter Franck Goddio, a financial and economic consultant who had conducted numerous missions for the United Nations in Laos, Cambodia, and Vietnam. He even assisted the French Foreign Ministry and served as a financial advisor to the Kingdom of Saudi Arabia, among other nations. But Goddio was fascinated by underwater archaeology and had been involved in finding shipwrecks in the Philippines and other locations.[23]

When Goddio had heard of an apparently undiscovered city supposedly near Alexandria, Egypt, he couldn't resist the challenge. So he took his mathematical mind and applied it to a problem that had puzzled professionals for hundreds, if not thousands, of years. He began with a review of ancient texts referencing the city to help guide his instincts on probable locations. Goddio then mathematically and systematically, over a period of approximately five years, mapped an area of the sea the size of Paris off the coast of Alexandria. His early findings nudged him in a direction that professionals had dismissed as unlikely. He conducted dozens of samples via minor excavations, and used the data acquired to refine his mathematically guided exploration.[24]

Then in 2000, he discovered the lost city of Thonis–Heracleion, an archaeological find that has been called the greatest discovery, perhaps ever.[25] The treasure trove he found is gigantic and will likely take decades to fully uncover. And all of this from a mathematically inclined financial consultant. Is it possible that it's precisely because Goddio was not trained as an archaeologist that he was able to find the lost ancient city? Might the experiences of professional archaeologists have created glaring blind spots that prevented them from achieving what Goddio did?

How we might celebrate ignorance and the idea that an absence of knowledge may in fact be better than knowledge based on questionable assumptions. Consider the case of PayPal, where cofounder Peter Thiel noticed that the more experience someone had in banking, the more certain they were that PayPal could never succeed. The intellectual freedom that emerges from ignorance is an amazing untapped resource, one historically stumbled upon rather than conscientiously developed or embraced.

So if unadulterated vision can help us navigate uncertainties by identifying risks and spotting opportunities, how can we go about freshening our eyes? The first is to embrace and seriously consider professional opportunities that may not seem consistent with your existing career trajectory. It's like Suzuki stated: "In the beginner's mind there are many possibilities, in the expert's mind there are few."[26]

Think about the story I shared earlier about David Swensen, who arrived at Yale University to run the endowment with exactly . . . drumroll please . . . zero days of experience as a professional money manager. In fact, David has told me multiple times that he originally thought it was a joke that they had hired him, made more believable by the fact that his first day on the job was April 1, 1985. But his academic advisors at Yale (where he had completed his PhD a few years earlier) convinced him to take an 80 percent pay cut and move from NYC to New Haven. His fresh perspective was, in all likelihood, responsible for his return to first principles and independent thinking—both of which were critical to the development of what has since become the Yale model of long-term investing.

It's worth noting that the professional world can sometimes be less hospitable than the academic, with a more cutthroat approach to employment decisions. But that doesn't mean fresh perspectives aren't possible—they are. Every hiring (and firing) is an opportunity to change the embedded default assumptions of a leader. Think about Steve Jobs, who was fired from Apple at the age of thirty. Although he was devastated at the time, he later commented that "getting fired from Apple was the best thing that could have ever happened to me." How's that? Freed from the spotlight of senior corporate leadership, Jobs noted that "the heaviness of being successful was replaced by the lightness of being a beginner again, less sure about everything."[27] Less sure about everything? Sure sounds like the medicine that Dr. Twain would prescribe for successfully navigating uncertain times!

The fresh perspective obtained from having his assumptions shaken, Jobs said, "freed me to enter one of the most creative periods of my life; during the next five years, I started a company called NeXT, another company named Pixar, and fell in love with an amazing woman who would become my wife."[28] Pixar went on to become the world's most successful animation studio, and NeXT (which was bought by Apple, enabling Jobs's return to the company) is believed to have been behind the revival of Apple's products and technologies. The fresh perspective, decluttered from day to day burdens of managing Apple, that Jobs obtained by being fired likely contributed to his breakthrough thinking.

When you think about the approach that most people adopt when thrown into a role for which they don't have a deep background, it usually begins with studying up on the issues of relevance. But let's look at how Nikki Haley, a governor who had limited experience in foreign affairs, prepared for her new role as US ambassador to the United Nations: "I was a foreign policy novice, who faced a learning curve when I became Ambassador. I studied a lot before coming to New York . . . but I purposely didn't study the United Nations itself . . . and here's why: I wanted to preserve my ability to see the UN through new eyes with a fresh perspective."[29]

Fresh perspectives on old challenges can also identify opportunities in business as well. Consider the case of Herb Kelleher, the maverick lawyer turned entrepreneur who founded Southwest Airlines. Airline executive Rollin King was having a drink with Kelleher when they devised the idea for Southwest Airlines. It all began with a sketch of a triangle on the back of a cocktail napkin. The points of the triangle represented Houston, Dallas, and San Antonio. They believed that the hassles of travel between these three cities were annoying enough that customers would opt to fly over driving if given an inexpensive option.[30]

The swashbuckling, chain-smoking, Wild Turkey–drinking Kelleher had a different focus than others in the industry.[31] While most analysts and industry insiders thought about dividing the existing pie of air passengers into smaller and smaller pieces, Kelleher and King believed their low-cost offering could compete with those who might otherwise drive. They focused on potential customers, looking to grow the pie; it was wrong to assume, they believed, that the market for travel between these cities was limited to those who currently flew between them. Southwest decided to compete against buses and drivers as well as other airlines. In some ways, Kelleher was like Sheldon Adelson, thinking about potential customers rather than relying on dividing the pie of existing customers. Their offering would grow the pie by attracting new flyers. And like Swensen, Kelleher didn't turn to HBS case studies or existing models to form his business model; he thought for himself. And with little experience in the airline industry, he and King frankly didn't know any better. They had fresh eyes.

So what happened? Wherever Southwest goes, three things tend to occur rapidly and simultaneously. First, airfares for the routes they enter plunge immediately. Second, traffic spikes dramatically as the pie of travelers expands. And third, the airline develops a loyal fan base. The success is so consistent that it's become common for cities to petition Southwest Airlines to service their airports. All of it made possible by fresh thinking.[32]

Let's now turn to a situation where one with absolutely no experience in the field was given a seemingly impossible task. Not knowing any better, he went after a solution with dogmatic persistence. The result was hailed as a modern-day miracle, but for those who think through the dynamics, it was really a fresh perspective that saved the lives of thirty-three men who had been buried alive.

The Guillotine of Granite

People have been mining for gold and copper in the San José Mine since 1889. The mine produces around the clock, situated deep inside a lifeless mountain in Chile's Atacama Desert. The only noticeable living presence in the desert is the flow of miners in trucks and buses headed to the mines. (I've been to the Atacama Desert, and despite the striking beauty of the place, it definitely feels lifeless and extremely remote.)

In contrast to the vast expanse of the dessert, life in the mine is restricted to a series of tunnels and ramps that descend from the surface for several hundred meters. And on August 5, 2010, a block of stone weighing seven hundred thousand tons broke loose, leading to a mining disaster as the mountain collapsed upon itself. Thirty-three miners were buried alive.[33]

Hundreds of miles away, the newly appointed minister of mines, Laurence Golborne, received a text at 11 p.m. that evening: "Mine cave-in Copiapó; 33 victims."[34] A former business executive with no mining experience, Golborne decided to travel to the disaster site, despite his chief of staff advising him against it. Her research showed no mining minister had ever visited the site of an ongoing crisis; further, the political risks were incalculably high.

"Mining is my subject in the government," Golborne later explained. "Although I do not come from the mining world and was questioning myself what I could do in the mine—how I could help in the rescue given the magnitude of the problem?—I understood I had to be there."[35]

On August 7, the day of his arrival, one of the rescue crewmembers privately shared his thoughts with Golborne: "They must be dead . . . and if they are not dead, they will die."[36] The rescue crew found that a fresh cave-in had blocked any direct access to the miners and further, continued geologic instability made it unsafe for rescuers to reenter the mine. Despite the grim prognosis, Golborne refused to give up.[37]

After an emotional, rollercoaster experience of promise and failure, one of the multiple rescue drilling efforts managed to penetrate the refuge area where the miners would likely be. When the drill was raised, a newly painted red mark was found near the bit—along with a few scraps of paper. One of the scraps read: "We are all well in the refuge, the 33 miners."[38]

But Golborne didn't stop there. He now shifted his focus from finding the miners to saving the miners. He consulted with America's NASA and the Chilean Navy to learn about the psychology and physiology of living in cramped quarters and to plan for an extraction tube to lift the miners to safety. Nutritionists considered vitamin D deficiencies, and doctors recommended regular sleep schedules to help manage moods.[39] Golborne employed multiple drilling contractors from around the world, creating a *de facto* race among them. And sixty-nine days after the mine collapse, as more than a billion people globally watched their ascent from the newly drilled shaft, all thirty-three miners returned to the surface of the planet.[40] Golborne's star skyrocketed, and he was briefly a presidential candidate, with 95 percent popularity rankings. ("Even the communists supported me!" he noted during a phone call I had with him in 2017.[41])

The rescue was celebrated, books were written, movies made. It was a miracle, and fundamentally one that was due to the fresh, unadulterated perspective that Golborne brought to the task. In fact, it's possible to suggest that it's precisely Golborne's lack of mining knowledge that led him to be so successful. Given most mining rescue efforts fail, what if Golborne had had decades of experience in mining and even participated in multiple mining disasters from which there were no survivors? Or what if he had the mining industry experience to think he knew how to coordinate the effort rather than to tap into a wide variety of experts that had specialized knowledge?

Golborne was, in many ways, not well prepared to lead the rescue. While he had studied civil engineering at one of Chile's top universities, he was a businessman. Before joining the government a mere months prior to the mining disaster, he had been chief executive of Cencosud, Chile's largest retail chain.[42] When Golborne stepped down as CEO in 2009, the company employed more than 100,000 people and reported revenue of more than $10 billion. Impressive to be sure, but running a retail company is a far cry from trying to save thirty-three men who were buried alive. But might his ignorance of mining have formed his open-minded approach?

During one of my conversations with Golborne, I asked him to reflect on some of the key learnings from the experience, noting the value of some distance from the events. One of his answers captures the essence of his calibrated, open-minded approach. "I let the experts talk." He then described an instinct of his that enabled him to retain control while tapping into the expertise he needed and lacked: "I have this ability to tell when people understand what they're talking about, and when they're bluffing."[43] Bottom line: he shifted his focus from the content to the people.

Golborne noted his sister was a Communist who hastily burned her Marxist literature after the 1973 coup that brought Augusto Pinochet to power. His brother was a right-wing extremist with ties to the paramilitary group *Patria y Libertad* (Fatherland and Freedom). Golborne said he considers himself lucky to have come from a discordant background: "It teaches you how to live with different points of view. I think that as a result I have a very well-developed sense of tolerance. I'm open to different ideas."[44]

His childhood experience with strikingly different viewpoints may have primed Golborne to entertain ideas that others would have dismissed straight away, like consulting psychics or attaching panic buttons to rats before sending them into the mine.[45] He received emails with many ideas, some good, some . . . less good. He read all of them. Golborne's open-minded approach, due in large part to the fresh perspective of being a nonminer facing a mining challenge, was clearly instrumental in saving the lives of the buried men.

Druck's Luck

In 1977, a disgruntled graduate student studying economics found his course of study "overly quantitative and theoretical, with little emphasis on real-life applications."[46] He dropped out and took a position as a management trainee at the Pittsburgh National Bank. After several months on the job, he received a call from the manager in the trust department. He was asked if he had an MBA and the trainee answered that he didn't. The manager responded: "That's even better! Come on up; you're hired."[47]

And so our the management trainee got offered a position as a stock analyst, with responsibility for bank and chemical stocks, an offer he rapidly accepted because because the head of the loan department told him he didn't have what it took to be a loan officer. And so Speros Drelles, the director of investments at Pittsburgh National Bank, had a new analyst, Stanley Druckenmiller.

A year after starting as an analyst, Drelles summoned Druckenmiller to this office and told him that he was getting a promotion. At the age of twenty-five, the young analyst became the head of equity research for the bank. As Druckenmiller later explained, "This was quite a bizarre move, since my boss was about fifty years old and had been with the bank for over twenty-five years . . . moreover, all the other analysts had MBAs and had been in the department longer than I had."[48] The rationale, as recounted by Druckenmiller to Jack Schwager, in *The New Market Wizards: Conversations with America's Top Traders*:

> "You know why I'm doing this, don't you?" he asked.
>
> "No," I replied.
>
> "For the same reason they send eighteen-year olds off to war."
>
> "Why is that?" I asked.
>
> "Because they're too dumb to know not to change." Drelles continued. "The small cap stocks have been in a bear market for ten years and I think there's going to be a huge, liquidity-driven bull market sometime in the next decade. Frankly, I have a lot of scars from the past ten years, while you don't. I think we'll make a great team because you'll be too stupid and inexperienced to know not to try to buy everything. That other guy out there," he said, referring to my boss, the existing director of equity research, "is just as stale as I am."[49]

A year later, when Drelles left the bank, the young director of research was surrounded by more experienced and older executives seeking to fill the hole. It was widely assumed that Druckenmiller would be lucky to even keep his job, let alone get promoted. But as Druckenmiller noted, good luck combined with his inexperience to generate the perfect conditions for his star to rise further. Shortly after Drelles left, Iran bubbled over. The shah was overthrown. As he recalls, "Here's where my inexperience really paid off. . . . I decided that we should put 70% of our money in oil stocks and the rest in defense stocks; the course of action seemed so logical to me that I didn't consider doing anything else. At the time, I didn't yet understand diversification."[50] Within a year, Druckenmiller was given the title of director of investments.

After being mentored by Drelles, Druckenmiller went on to work with George Soros. After doing careful analysis of the British pound's value relative to the German deutsche mark, Druckenmiller decided it was time to make a big bet. As he recalled during a speech in 2015, Druckenmiller's conversation with Soros about increasing the bet did not go as expected. After explaining to Soros the rationale and indicating that he was going to sell $5.5 billion worth of pounds that night and buy marks, meaning 100 percent of the fund would be in this one trade, Soros responded: "This is the most ridiculous use of money management I ever heard. What you described is an incredible one-way bet. We should have 200 percent of our net worth in this trade, not 100%. Do you know how often something like this comes along? Like once in twenty years. What's wrong with you?"[51] So much for learning about diversification!

Eventually, Soros told Druckenmiller, as recounted in Sebastian Mallaby's book *More Money Than God*, that he "should go for the jugular" and short $15 billion.[52] The trade went on to break the British pound, netting the fund a gain of over a billion dollars.

Since that trade Druckenmiller has continued to post an unrivaled investment record through 2010, when he stopped managing money for others. According to those that know him well and have seen his performance reports, money invested with "Druck" would have outperformed money invested with Warren Buffett or virtually any other money manager between 1980 and 2010. So what accounts for this repeated series of success? I suspect one of the main reasons that Druckenmiller has been so successful is that he is constantly refreshing his perspective. And he's learned to trust his insights, rather than rely on others, enabling a greater authenticity in behavior than most people achieve. But if it weren't for his initial luck (or was it ignorance?) in getting promoted, or his inexperience in money management, might he have turned out to be a loan officer at the Pittsburgh National Bank instead of one of America's most respected financiers (and most charitable people)? Perhaps we can all learn from his experience and do our best, as Peter Thiel urges, to not squander our precious ignorance.[53]

Might Breadth Trump Depth?

When it comes to someone who's made a career out of figuring out what matters to who and when, Matthew Winker is one of the most accomplished and well-informed people I know. As the founding editor in chief of Bloomberg News, Matt made a conscious effort to cater to those with the most at stake. And his approach is worth understanding because I believe it has broad relevance for all of us in many scenarios.

I've had the pleasure of getting to know Matt over the course of almost ten years in numerous situations. He's joined me and students for discussions at both Yale and Harvard, we've had numerous meals and coffees, and have spent time debating market dynamics and economics. But what I've enjoyed most about my interactions with Matt is his breadth of perspective and knowledge. It's truly stunning. We've talked about functional medicine and the potential of injectable vitamins to help individuals overcome chronic health conditions, we've debated the prospects for a large Indian middle class (and its corresponding implications for emerging markets investors), and he's shared lessons learned from building a news organization from scratch. He even titled a talk he gave to a seminar I was running at the Harvard Kennedy School "Truth in an Age of Twitter," a fabulous session in which he carefully disentangled the cross currents of accuracy and the need for speed in today's hyper-connected global economy.

He is such a clear thinker on the business of journalism that his manifesto, *The Bloomberg Way: A Guide for Reporters and Editors*, has been reprinted and updated more than a dozen time since 1990 when he first put thoughts to paper.[54] Matt has won lots of awards for his impact on the fields of business and financial journalism, including the New York Financial Writers Association's Elliot V. Well Award for providing a "significant long-term contribution to the profession of financial journalism,"[55] the National Academy of Television Arts and Sciences "Emmy" Lifetime Achievement Award for business and financial reporting, the Gerald Loeb Foundation Lifetime Achievement Award for "exceptional career achievements in business, financial and economic news writing," and a list of other honors too numerous to mention here.[56]

The key, I believe, to Matt's success, is that he's been a generalist. Generalists are those who have broad knowledge but do not claim to be a deep expert at anything, making them psychologically more receptive to ideas distant or different from their own. Instead, they tap into those with knowledge in areas that they may need to learn more about. They are, it seems, more aware of what they do not know and understand that there is a large body of information that they do not know they do not know.

Matt put it best in one of our 2019 conversations about the relative value of breadth and depth in navigating uncertainty. He said, "If the news business essentially is harvesting and bringing perspective to myriad surprises, generalists are advantaged by the self-awareness of never knowing enough about anything. This makes them perpetually curious and willing to challenge prevailing assumptions."[57] Not only is Matt someone who balances breadth with depth while habitually connecting dots that many others dismiss as irrelevant, he's also helped thousands of others do the same. And by doing so, he is responsible for growing Bloomberg News from an idea in Michael Bloomberg's head into what some would call the most powerful economic, business, and financial news organization the world has ever encountered.

We can all learn from Matt. The idea of being broad enough to contextualize information is critical; it helps generate awareness that there are those who know more than we do and allows us to place the inputs of experts and specialists in perspective. Such intellectual humility also leaves us open-minded to surprises and new information, spurring the supposedly naïve inquiries that question basic assumptions. As the world gets increasingly interconnected and complex, might breadth soon trump depth?

Key Takeaways

- **In an age of experts and artificial intelligence, depth of expertise must be balanced with breadth of perspective.** In educating future leaders, this means we must focus on developing critical thinking capabilities that allow us to evaluate our default operating assumptions. Liberal general education must retain a role and must not be sidelined by today's short-term infatuation with skills-based training.

- **Use empathy to remain humble.** As noted by Wallace and McCullough, the blunt reality is that we are definitionally self-centered in how we experience the world. Others have different perspectives and trying to consider them can help us calibrate our thinking. Recall the example of Kiewit.

- **Celebrate ignorance and fresh eyes.** Independent, unbiased thinking that is free from the baggage of historical experience need not be dismissed as useless. In fact, some of the most impressive individuals in numerous walks of life were successful precisely because they lacked the experience that might otherwise have prevented their differentiated thoughts.

Restoring Common Sense

Many of the pressures discussed in these pages show no signs of dissipating. Information, data, and choice continue to expand in exponential ways leading to a constant and never-ending sense of drowning. If there was too much to know yesterday, there's more today, and tomorrow will have yet more. There is no way to catch up.

And yet the promise of optimized decision making in the face of overwhelming choice is as alluring as ever. All indicators suggest the availability of a perfect selection, one that does more than merely providing a good outcome. We live in constant fear of missing out on ideal choices. But because we cannot optimize every decision, we turn (with high hopes) to those who know more than we do about the domains in which we must decide.

The experts and technologies that offer salvation, however, are fundamentally constrained and in certain circumstances, may be structurally flawed. The problem stems from the deep and narrow focus that tends to accompany specialized expertise—it inhibits an understanding of the whole situation or the context in which decisions are being made. By turning to experts, technologies, and rules, we end up ceding control of our focus and our thinking to those who are unable to appreciate our specific situation. As our self-reliance skills atrophy, we become dependent and blindly follow expert guidance. The result is often suboptimal outcomes driven by dynamics transpiring in the shadows of an expert's spotlight.

To combat this mindless outsourcing, we must learn to proactively manage our focus. This begins with awareness of the filters and focus managers that we utilize to screen out the supposed noise. Shifting our attention by looking at problems differently (zooming out, investigating lateral dynamics, etc.) is one way to mindfully reclaim control of our focus. We need to question the decision frames set by focus managers.

And since experts and technologies cannot appreciate the entirety of our decision domain or our ultimate objectives, they optimize tasks. They help us win battles. But great tasks and victorious battles are no solace for failed missions or lost wars. We need to remain goal-oriented and not allow advisors to divert us from keeping an eye on the prize we seek.

The other dynamic that tends to plague our thinking is a devotion to convention and historical precedent. Truly independent thinking is risky and we therefore tend to do less of it. As we noticed with David Swensen and Trisha Torrey, doing so can both minimize risks and generate opportunities.

But because each and every perspective (including our own) is biased and incomplete, it makes a great deal of sense to employ multiple perspectives and to triangulate insights from several lenses. We need to empathize with those around us and constantly role-play for different functions over different time frames. Installing a dedicated devil's advocate, conducting premortem analyses, and flipping perspectives are some strategies that can help.

Ultimately, however, we must restore our autonomy. We need to retake control, which means we must learn to lead. Expert and technological input is essential, even if not sufficient. But we must always keep experts on tap, not on top. We are the artist, with full contextual knowledge, preparing our mosaic. Experts provide tiles. We should utilize these tiles as needed in the process of forming our map of how to proceed.

It's time to rethink many of society's embedded assumptions. We prize depth, perhaps too much so. Might we also value breadth? We revere those with deep expertise. Might we raise the status of those with broad perspective? Further, the nature of omnipresent uncertainty is that we must learn to embrace ambiguity and to learn how to navigate through probabilistic scenarios. We have to think in terms of multiple futures and to nurture the creative imagination that can minimize the negative impact from the inevitable surprises. Fundamentally, we need to (re)learn to think for ourselves.

The stakes of doing so have never been higher. Consider the following comment from Stephan Paternot, an entrepreneur who founded theglobe.com and has been an astute observer of social technology trends for decades: "There has been the emergence of a very few concentrated players controlling the tech world, which has led to the loss of transparency, the harvesting of data, and the weaponizing of our highly personal information against our own interests."[1]

And if you think Stephan is a conspiracist, please think about the following. Google has billions of Android users. Each one of those devices constantly sends data back to Google. What kind of data? Well, it turns out that most devices have a barometric pressure sensor, a gyroscope, an accelerometer, and a magnetic field detector. So, in addition to all the data relating to your use of the device, Google can calculate your heart rate, how fast you're moving, and so on. In fact, as noted in a recent *New Yorker* article, "This constant flow of information allows your phone to track whether you're sleeping or awake; whether you're driving, walking, jogging or biking; whether you're in the Starbucks on the ground floor or the lawyer's office on the tenth."[2]

This is the basis of what Harvard Business School professor Shoshana Zuboff calls surveillance capitalism, in which these big companies use the information they gather about us to determine what we do now, soon, or later. As she explained in an interview with the *Guardian*, the power these companies wield "usurps decision rights and erodes the processes of individual autonomy."[3] Fundamentally, big tech appears to be in the game of trying to do your thinking for you, and worse, trying to get you to act on those thoughts.

Because of the algorithms used, companies like Google, Facebook, and Amazon are de facto able to influence your decisions in ways that may not be obvious. They manage your focus and do your filtering. They set your decision frames. Zuboff describes the problem in more stark terms, highlighting the potential of surveillance capitalism to undermine humanity: "What is abrogated here is our right to the future tense, which is the essence of free will . . . without autonomy in action and in thought, we have little capacity for the moral judgment and critical thinking necessary for a democratic society."[4]

We are at a serious inflection point. In an age of experts and artificial intelligence, critical thinking skills and the expression of moral judgments are more important than ever. Thinking for ourselves can inoculate us from many ills and may even help us defend against big tech's attempts to rob us of our autonomy.

There's a scene in the movie *The Iron Lady* in which an aging Margaret Thatcher is with her doctor, who asks how she is feeling. She responds with "People don't think anymore; they feel. . . . One of the great problems of our age is that we are governed by people who care more about feelings than they do about thoughts and ideas. Now thoughts and ideas, that interests me. . . . Ask me what I'm thinking!"

So the doctor asks, "What are you thinking, Margaret?"

She responds with what was, in Lady Thatcher's actual life, one of her most memorable quotes: "Watch your thoughts for they become words; watch your words for they become actions; watch your actions for they become habits; watch your habits for they become your character. And watch your character for it becomes your destiny. *What we think, we become.*"[5]

Given the criticality of thinking for ourselves, we need to protect ourselves from the excessive influence of experts and technologies. We must manage them. And when thinking about how to manage them, we might benefit from looking at the approach taken by one of the world's most accomplished orchestra conductors. In addition to being the subject of executive leadership courses, Wolfgang Heinzel, former conductor of the Deutsche Philharmonie Merck (the Merck Orchestra) has decades of experience in bringing together the capabilities of various specialists to produce inspired music. He explains that "A maestro cannot play all the instruments," and therefore needs to rely on his string, woodwind, brass, and percussions performers. But in speaking of his team, Heinzel notes, "They know their instruments, they know how to play their parts . . . but now I have to bring it all together."[6]

Sure sounds like life in the twenty-first century! Everyone knows their parts, but we have to bring it all together. If you stop and think about the role of the conductor, I think it really is all about conscientiously leading a group of specialists to *integrate* their inputs into something neither conductors nor players could produce on their own. Shouldn't we too be trying to become the conductors of our lives by integrating the inputs of experts and technologies to fulfill our potential?

Dots are everywhere. The real, sustainable know-how we must all develop is the ability to connect them. To lift our heads up and notice the context. And to constantly question the underlying assumptions that we retain as "true," thinking for ourselves independently and not blindly relying on the opinions of others. Doing so, in my opinion, is modern day common sense. For as E. O. Wilson, the legendary biologist has said: "We are drowning in information, while starving for wisdom. The world henceforth will be run by synthesizers, people able to put together the right information at the right time, think critically about it, and make important choices wisely."[7]

The future, it seems, belongs to those who think for themselves.

ACKNOWLEDGMENTS

Anyone who's ever written a book understands it is rarely an individual endeavor. This book is no exception. The number of people who have contributed to the ideas described herein are too numerous to mention. Despite the difficulty of naming everyone, some individuals deserve special mention for having had a disproportionate influence on my thinking and this project.

At the top of the list is my family, for having tolerated the multiyear endeavor and for having taught me a great deal about life. I want to specifically thank my ever-patient wife Kristen, my always-encouraging daughter Tori, and my constantly cheerful and supportive son Kai.

I also want to thank the leadership team at Kiewit Corporation (specifically Bruce Grewcock, Rick Lanoha, and Scott Schmidt) for always stimulating debates about business, economics, and the power of crossing silos. Senior leaders at United Technologies, LVW Advisors, Timmerman & Sons, and Tenaska were also instrumental in helping me form many of my ideas.

I also owe a debt of gratitude to the educational institutions at which I've worked. At Harvard, the Mossavar-Rahmani Center for Business & Government at the Harvard Kennedy School and the Harvard John A. Paulson School of Engineering provided supportive environments in which I could interact with bright students and even brighter colleagues. Special thanks to Richard Zeckhauser, Lawrence Summers, John Haigh, Rakesh Khurana, Fawwaz Habbal, Cherry Murray, Frank Doyle, Ash Carter, and Dana Born. Howard Stevenson deserves special mention for his encouragement to pursue this project and to work with Harvard

Business Review Press. At Yale, I want to thank the program in ethics, politics, and economics and the department of political science for giving me a home within a fabulous academic institution. Special thanks to Peter Salovey, Sam Chauncey, David Swensen, and Charley Ellis. The students at both schools have been a real joy to teach, and it is debatable whether they or I learned more.

This book also benefited immensely from the efforts of several research assistants. Nick Levine and Nina Russell dedicated themselves selflessly to the book for months on end, while Tobias Peter, Jared Middelman, Allan Wang, and Lily Jampol-Auerbach all contributed at various times. Lindsay Day's efforts to keep me organized during the project's early stages were also noteworthy.

Many of my ideas benefited from feedback received in the course of delivering talks over the past few years. I want to explicitly thank Tony D'Amelio and his team for their support and faith that my unconventional ideas were worth sharing. I also want to thank the team at HBR Press, especially Jeff Kehoe. From our very first meeting, he understood my message and has tirelessly helped to craft it. I cannot thank him enough for his support in nudging the book to its current form.

And lastly, I would be remiss if I did not thank the numerous experts, agents, and advisors to whom I have blindly outsourced my own thinking—they've all taught me a great deal about why I need to retain control and not let them take over.

NOTES

Preface

1. Vikram Mansharamani, "All Hail the Generalist," *Harvard Business Review*, June 4, 2012, https://hbr.org/2012/06/all-hail-the-generalist.

2. Jill Rosenfeld, "CDU to Gretzky: The Puck Stops Here!" *Fast Company*, June 30, 2000, https://www.fastcompany.com/40565/cdu-gretzky-puck-stops-here.

Introduction

1. Comments made by Irving Fisher at a meeting of the Purchasing Agents Association, October 15, 1929, as reported in "Fisher Sees Stocks Permanently High," *New York Times*, October 16, 1929.

2. Paul Ehrlich, *The Population Bomb* (Cutchogue, NY: Buccaneer Books, 1968), xi.

3. William Deresiewicz, *Excellent Sheep: The Miseducation of the American Elite and the Way to a Meaningful Life* (New York: Free Press, 2014).

4. Isaiah Berlin, *The Hedgehog and the Fox: An Essay on Tolstoy's View of History* (Chicago: Elephant Paperbacks, 1953), 3.

5. Berlin, *Hedgehog and the Fox,* 3.

6. Yogi Berra, *The Yogi Book* (New York: Workman Publishing, 1998), 118–119.

7. Edmund Andrews, "Greenspan Concedes Error on Regulation," *New York Times*, October 23, 2008, http://nytimes.com/2008/10/24/business/economy/24panel.html.

8. Philip Tetlock, *Expert Political Judgment: How Good Is It? How Can We Know?* (Princeton, NJ: Princeton University Press, 2005), 2.

9. Baba Shiv, "Sometimes It's Good to Give up the Driver's Seat," *TEDx Stanford*, May 2012, 9:32, https://www.ted.com/talks/baba_shiv_sometimes_it_s_good_to_give_up_the_driver_s_seat.

10. Thomas Paine, *"Common Sense"* (Washington, DC: National Humanities Center, 2014), http://americainclass.org/wp-content/uploads/2014/07/Common-Sense-_-Full-Text.pdf.

Chapter 1

1. Roma Panganiban, "How Many Books Have Ever Been Published?" *Mental Floss*, September 9, 2016, http://mentalfloss.com/article/85305/how-many-books-have-ever-been-published.

2. Arif Jinha, "Article 50 Million: An Estimate of the Number of Scholarly Articles in Existence," *Learned Publishing* 23, no. 3 (July 2010): 258–263.

3. "Anxiety UK Study Finds Technology Can Increase Anxiety," Anxiety UK (website), July 9, 2012, http://www.anxietyuk.org.uk/for-some-with-anxiety-technology-can-increase-anxiety/.

4. Andrew Robinson, *The Last Man Who Knew Everything* (New York: PI Press, 2005), 3.

5. Robinson, *The Last Man*, ix.

6. Edward Carr, "The Last Days of the Polymath," *1843*, Autumn 2009, https://www.1843magazine.com/content/edward-carr/last-days-polymath.

7. Benjamin Jones, "Age and Great Invention," *Review of Economics and Statistics* 92, no. 1 (February 2010): 1–14.

8. Benjamin Jones, E. J. Reedy, and Bruce Weinberg, "Age and Scientific Genius," in *The Wiley Handbook of Genius*, ed. Dean Simonton (Hoboken, NJ: Wiley-Blackwell, 2014), 422–450.

9. Benjamin Jones. "The Burden of Knowledge and the 'Death of Renaissance Man': Is Innovation Getting Harder?" NBER Working Paper 11360 (Cambridge, May 2005), https://www.nber.org/papers/w11360.pdf.

10. Stefan Wuchty, Benjamin Jones, and Brian Uzzi, "The Increasing Dominance of Teams in Production of Knowledge," *Sciencexpress,* April 12, 2007, http://www.kellogg.northwestern.edu/faculty/jones-ben/htm/Teams.ScienceExpress.pdf.

11. Marc Levsky et al., "A Descriptive Analysis of Authorship within Medical Journals, 1995–2005," *Southern Medical Journal* 100, no. 4 (April 2007): 371–375, https://www.ncbi.nlm.nih.gov/pubmed/17458396.

12. Dennis Overbye, "The Particle That Wasn't," *New York Times*, August 5, 2016, http://www.nytimes.com/2016/08/05/science/cern-large-hadron-collider-particle.html.

13. G. Aad et al., "Combined Measurement of the Higgs Boson Mass in pp Collisions at $\sqrt{} =7$ and 8 TeV with the ATLAS and CMS Experiments," *Physical Review Letters* 114 (May 15, 2015): https://journals.aps.org/prl/pdf/10.1103/PhysRevLett.114.191803.

14. Osamu Shimomura, Toshio Goto, and Yoshimasa Hirata, "Crystalline Cypridina Luciferin," *Bulletin of the Chemical Society of Japan* 30, no. 8 (November 1957): 929–933.

15. Osamu Shimomura, "Interview with Osamu Shimomura," interview by Adam Smith, Nobel Prize (website), October 8, 2008, https://www.nobelprize.org/prizes/chemistry/2008/shimomura/25936-interview-with-osamu-shimomura/.

16. Måns Ehrenberg, "The Green Fluorescent Protein: Discovery, Expression, Development," Royal Swedish Academy of Sciences/Nobel Prize (website), September 30, 2008, http://nobelprize.org/uploads/2018/06/advanced-chemistryprize2008-1.pdf.

17. Ehrenberg, "Green Fluorescent Protein."

18. Ehrenberg, "Green Fluorescent Protein."

19. Shimomura, "Interview with Osamu Shimomura."

20. Adam Smith, *The Wealth of Nations* (London: William Strahan, 1776).

21. Robert L. Heilbroner, *The Worldly Philosophers: The Lives, Times, and Ideas of the Great Economic Thinkers* (New York: Simon and Schuster, 2011), 173.

22. Sheena Iyengar and Mark Lepper, "When Choice Is Demotivating: Can One Desire Too Much of a Good Thing?" *Journal of Personality and Social Psychology* 79, no. 6 (2000): 995–1006.

23. Sheena S. Iyengar, Wei Jiang, and Gur Huberman, "How Much Choice Is Too Much? Contributions to 401(K) Retirement Plans," in *Pension Design and Structure*, ed. Olivia Mitchell and Stephen Utkus (Oxford: Oxford University Press, 2004), 83–94.

24. Barry Schwartz, *The Paradox of Choice: Why More Is Less* (New York: Harper-Collins, 2003), 3.

25. Schwartz, *Paradox of Choice*, 2. Bold added.

26. Turkle, *Reclaiming Conversation: The Power of Talk in a Digital Age* (New York: Penguin, 2015), 145.

27. Turkle, *Reclaiming Conversation*, 146.

28. Kelly Wallace, "Teen 'Like' and 'FOMO' Anxiety," CNN, December 6, 2016, https://www.cnn.com/2016/12/06/health/teens-on-social-media-like-and-fomo -anxiety-digital/index.html.

29. See http://i.huffpost.com/gen/1660901/original.jpg.

30. Peter Singer and Emerson Brooking, *LikeWar: The Weaponization of Social Media* (New York: Houghton Mifflin, 2018), 59–60.

31. Matt Keeley, "More People Die Taking Selfies Than by Shark Attacks," *Newsweek*, June 27, 2019, http://www.newsweek.com/selfies-deadlier-shark-attacks -1446363.

32. John Patrick Pullen, "6 Times People Died While Taking Selfies," *Time*, March 14, 2016, http://time.com/4257429/selfie-deaths/.

33. Justin Worland, "German Tourist Dies Posing for Photo at Machu Picchu," *Time*, July 1, 2016, https://time.com/4392100/machu-picchu-tourist-death/.

34. Michael Miller, "German Tourist Falls to His Death While Posing for Photo Atop Machu Picchu," *Washington Post*, July 1, 2016, https://www.washingtonpost.com /news/morning-mix/wp/2016/07/01/german-tourist-falls-to-his-death-while-trying -to-take-photo-atop-machu-picchu/.

35. Harriet Torry, "Please Like My Vacation Photo. I Hired a Professional," *Wall Street Journal*, November 20, 2019, http://www.wsj.com/articles/please-like-my -vacation-photo-i-hired-a-professional-11574268729.

36. Maura Kelly, "How We Meet Our Spouses," *Wall Street Journal*, March 27, 2014, https://www.wsj.com/articles-how-we-meet-our-spouses-1395859838.

37. Michael Rosenfeld and Reuben Thomas, "Searching for a Mate: The Rise of the Internet as a Social Intermediary," *American Sociological Review* 77, no. 4 (2012): 523–547.

38. Tim Urban, "How to Pick Your Life Partner—Part 1," *Wait but Why* (blog), February 12, 2014, http://www.waitbutwhy.com/2014/02/pick-life-partner.html; and Tim Urban, "How to Pick Your Life Partner—Part 2," *Wait but Why* (blog), February 13, 2014, http://www.waitbutwhy.com/2014/02/pick-life-partner-part-2-html.

39. Urban, "How to Pick Your Life Partner—Part 1."

40. Ellie Krupnick, "Is Too Much Choice Ruining Dating? Science Might Have the Answer," *Mic*, January 23, 2015, http://mic.com/articles/107210/is-too-much-choice -ruining-dating-science-might-have-the-answer.

41. Sarah Knapton, "Couples Who Met Online Three Times More Likely to Divorce," *Telegraph*, September 26, 2014, http://www.telegraph.co.uk/news/science /science-news/11124140/Couples-who-met-online-three-times-more-likely-to -divorce.html.

42. Jenna Birch, "I Quit Online Dating. Should You, Too?" Yahoo Lifestyle, November 9, 2015, https://www.yahoo.com/health/i-quit-online-dating-should -1292905613991990.html; Aziz Ansari, *Modern Romance* (New York: Penguin, 2016); Aziz Ansari and Eric Klineberg, "How to Make Online Dating Work," *New York Times*, June 13, 2015, http://www.nytimes.com/2015/06/14/opinion/sunday/how-to -make-online-dating-work.html?_r=0; Krupnick, "Is Too Much Choice Ruining Dating?"

43. Maldlen Davies, "Rise of Smartphone Injuries," *Daily Mail*, November 9, 2015, https://www.dailymail.co.uk/health/article-3310195/Rise-smartphone-injuries-43 -people-walked-glued-screen-60-dropped-phone-face-reading.html.

44. Adario Strange, "Japanese Ad Uses Samurai and Ninjas to Stop Smartphone Use While Walking," *Mashable*, December 7, 2015, http://mashable.com/2015/12/07/japan -smartphone-ad/#W5hIS25AEkq9.

45. Kathleen Lane, "You Might Be Putting First Responders at Risk," National Safety Council (website), April 15, 2019, http://www.nsc.org/safety-first-blog/you -might-be-putting-first-responders-at-risk.

46. See Evgeny Morozov, *The Net Delusion: The Dark Side of the Internet* (New York: Hachette, 2012); and Evgeny Morozov, *To Save Everything, Click Here: The Folly of Technological Solutionism* (New York: Hachette, 2013).

47. Cal Newport, *Deep Work: Rules for Focused Success in a Distracted World* (New York: Grand Central Publishing, 2016).

48. Kiely Kuligowski, "Distracted Workers Are Costing You Money," *Business News Daily*, May 7, 2019, https://www.businessnewsdaily.com/267-distracted -workforce-costs-businesses-billions.html; see also "You Waste a Lot of Time at Work," infographic produced by Atlassian, https://www.atlassian.com/time-wasting-at-work -infographic.

49. Joshua Rothman, "A New Theory of Distraction," *New Yorker*, June 16, 2015.

50. Erin Anderssen, "Digital Overload: How We Are Seduced by Distraction," *Globe and Mail*, March 29, 2014.

51. Daniel Kahneman, *Thinking: Fast and Slow* (New York: Farrar Straus & Giroux, 2013).

52. Deborah Cohen and Susan Babey, "Contextual Influences on Eating Behaviors: Heuristic Processing and Dietary Choices," *Obesity Review* 13, no. 9 (2012): 766–779, http://www.ncbi.nlm.nih.gov/pmc/articles/PMC3667220/#R115.

53. Eric Johnson and Daniel Goldstein, "Do Defaults Save Lives?" *Science* 302 (November 21, 2003): 1338–1339, https://ssrn.com/absract=1324774.

54. Barbara McNeil et al., "On the Elicitation of Preferences for Alternative Therapies," *New England Journal of Medicine* (May 27, 1982): 1259–1262.

55. Kahneman, *Thinking*, 441.

56. Amos Tversky and Daniel Kahneman, "Judgment under Uncertainty: Heuristics and Biases," *Science* 185, no. 4157 (September 27, 1974): 1124–1131.

57. Daniel Kahneman, Jack Knetsch, and Richard Thaler, "Anomalies: The Endowment Effect, Loss Aversion, and the Status Quo Bias," *Journal of Economic Perspectives* 5, no. 1 (Winter 1991): 193–206.

58. Bryan D. Jones, "Bounded Rationality," *Annual Review of Political Science* 2 (1999): 297–321.

59. Herbert Simon, "Rational Choice and the Structure of the Environment," *Psychological Review* 63, no. 2 (1956): 129–138, https://uk.sagepub.com/sites/default/files /upm-binaries/25239_Chater~Vol_1~Ch_03.pdf.

Chapter 2

1. "NFL Combine Drills 101: What Each Drill Measures," NFL Combine Results (website), April 23, 2016, http://www.nflcombineresults.com/nfl-combine-drills-101 -what-each-drill-measures/.

2. "NFL Combine Results, 2000," NFL Combine Results (website), accessed January 26, 2020, http://nflcombineresults.com/nflcombinedata_expanded.php?year =2000&pos=QB&college=.

3. "Tom Brady NFL Combine Scores," NFL Combine Results (website), accessed January 26, 2020, http://www.nflcombineresults.com/playerpage.php?f=Tom&l =Brady&i=4732.

4. Aren Wilborn, "5 Hilarious Reasons Publishers Rejected Classic Bestsellers," *Cracked*, February 13, 2013, https://www.cracked.com/article_20285_5-hilarious -reasons-publishers-rejected-classic-best-sellers.html.

5. Eric Sharp, "The First Page of Google by the Numbers," Protofuse (website), April 30, 2014, http://www.protofuse.com/blog/first-page-of-google-by-the-numbers/.

6. Jennifer Langston, "GPS Routed Bus under Bridge, Company Says," *Seattlepi*, April 17, 2008, http://www.seattlepi.com/local/article/GPS-routed-bus-under-bridge -company-says-1270598.php.

7. Dave Smith, "Apple Maps Fails Again: Alaska Drivers Directed onto Airport Taxiway, No Fix in Sight," *International Business Times,* September 25, 2013, https:// www.ibtimes.com/apple-maps-fails-again-alaska-drivers-directed-airport-taxiway-no -fix-sight-1410830.

8. Casey Chan, "This Is What Happens When the GPS Is Wrong," *Gizmodo*, October 2, 2010, http://gizmodo.com/5654044/this-is-what-happens-when-the-gps-is -wrong.

9. Cailey Rizzo, "Italian Town Bans Google Maps after Bad Directions Lead to 144 Rescue Missions," *Travel + Leisure*, October 15, 2019, https://www.travelandleisure.com /travel-news/baunei-sardinia-italy-bans-google-maps-after-tourists-drive-wrong -directions.

10. Julia Buckley, "Mountain Village Begs Tourists Not to Follow Google Maps and Get Stuck," CNN, October 15, 2019, https://www.cnn.com/travel/article/sardinia -google-maps-tourists-lost-baunei/index.html.

11. Angela Giuffrida, "Mayor of Sardinian Village Blames Google Maps for Lost Tourists," *Guardian*, October 15, 2019, https://www.theguardian.com/world/2019/oct /15/sardinian-village-blames-google-maps-lost-tourists.

12. William Langewiesche, "The Human Factor," *Vanity Fair*, September 17, 2014, https://www.vanityfair.com/news/business/2014/10/air-france-flight-447-crash.

13. Langewiesche, "The Human Factor."

14. Freddy "Tavarish" Hernandez, "Here Are Some of the Most Bizarre DMV Horror Stories Ever," *Jalopnik*, June 17, 2015, http://thegarage.jalopnik.com/here-are-the-some-of-the-most-bizarre-dmv-horror-storie-1711970247.

15. Hernandez, "Here Are Some of the Most Bizarre DMV Horror Stories Ever."

16. "Timeline: How Ebola Made Its Way to the U.S.," NBC News, October 2, 2014, https://www.nbcnews.com/storyline/ebola-virus-outbreak/timeline-how-ebola-made-its-way-u-s-n216831.

17. Michael Winter, "Timeline Details Missteps with Ebola Patient Who Died," *USA Today*, October 17, 2014, https://www.usatoday.com/story/news/nation/2014/10/17/ebola-duncan-congress-timeline/17456825/.

18. *Testimony provided to the US House Energy and Commerce Committee, Subcommittee on Oversight and Investigations* 113th Congress, 2nd Session (October 16, 2014) ("Examining the US Public Health Response to the Ebola Outbreak," Daniel Varga, Chief Clinical Officer and Senior Executive Vice President, Texas Health Resources), https://www.govinfo.gov/content/pkg/CHRG-113hhrg93903/html/CHRG-113hhrg93903.htm.

19. Divvy Upadhyay, Dean F. Sittig, and Hardeep Singh, "Ebola US Patient Zero: Lessons on Misdiagnosis and Effective Use of Electronic Health Records," *Diagnosis* 1, no. 4 (October 23, 2014): 283, https://www.ncbi.nlm.nih.gov/pmc/articles/PMC4687403/.

20. Abigail Stevenson, "The Market and Fear of Ebola: Cramer Weighs In," CNBC, October 13, 2014, https://www.cnbc.com/2014/10/13/the-market-and-fear-of-ebola-cramer-weighs-in.html.

21. Jason Sickles, "Nina Pham Identified as Dallas Nurse Diagnosed with Ebola," Yahoo! News, October 13, 2014, https://news.yahoo.com/nina-pham-identified-as-dallas-nurse-with-ebola-165521689.html.

22. Amy Davidson Sorkin, "Amber Vinson's Flight: An Ebola Nurse and the CDC," *New Yorker*, October 16, 2014, https://www.newyorker.com/news/amy-davidson/amber-vinson-ebola.

23. John Maynard Keynes, *The General Theory of Employment, Interest and Money* (New Delhi: Atlantic Publishers & Distributors, 2008), 141.

Chapter 3

1. Eviatar Zerubavel, *Hidden in Plain Sight: The Social Structure of Irrelevance* (Oxford: Oxford University Press, 2015).

2. Daniel Simons and Christopher Chabris, "Selective Attention Test," YouTube, 1999, 1:21, https://www.youtube.com/watch?v=vJG698U2Mvo.

3. Emile Durkheim, *Sociology and Philosophy* (New York: Routledge, 2010), 21.

4. Gijsbert Stoet, Daryl B. O'Connor, Mark Conner, and Keith R. Laws, "Are Women Better than Men at Multi-Tasking?" *BMC Psychology* 1 (October 24, 2013), https://bmcpsychology.biomedcentral.com/articles/10.1186/2050-7283-1-18.

5. Garth Sundem, "This is Your Brain on Multitasking" *Psychology Today*, February 24, 2012, https://www.psychologytoday.com/us/blog/brain-trust/201202/is-your -brain-multitasking.

6. H. Gilbert Welch, Lisa Schwartz, and Steven Woloshin, *Overdiagnosed: Making People Sick in the Pursuit of Health* (Boston: Beacon Press, 2011).

7. Welch, Schwartz, and Woloshin, *Overdiagnosed*, 47.

8. H. Gilbert Welch, *Less Medicine, More Health: 7 Assumptions That Drive Too Much Healthcare* (Boston: Beacon Press, 2015).

9. Welch, Schwartz, and Woloshin, *Overdiagnosed*, 47.

10. Wael Sakr et al., "Age and Racial Distribution of Prostatic Intraepithelial Neoplasia," *European Urology* 30 (1996): 138–144.

11. Welch, Schwartz, and Woloshin, *Overdiagnosed*.

12. Welch, Schwartz, and Woloshin, *Overdiagnosed*, 59–60.

13. Richard Ablin, "The Great Prostate Mistake," *New York Times*, March 9, 2010, https://www.nytimes.com/2010/03/10/opinion/10Ablin.html.

14. Ablin, "The Great Prostate Mistake."

15. Richard Ablin, *The Great Prostate Hoax: How Big Medicine Hijacked the PSA Test and Caused a Public Health Disaster* (New York: St. Martin's Press, 2014).

16. Welch, Schwartz, and Woloshin, *Overdiagnosed*, 59–60.

17. Laurence J. Peter and Raymond Hull, *The Peter Principle: Why Things Always Go Wrong* (New York: Harper Business, 2009).

18. Vikram Mansharamani, "Scale and Differentiation in Services: Using Information Technology to Manage Customer Experiences at Harrah's Entertainment and Other Companies" (PhD diss., MIT, February 2007), https://dspace.mit.edu/handle/1721.1/39479.

19. Philip Tetlock, *Expert Political Judgment: How Good Is It? How Can We Know?* (Princeton, NJ: Princeton University Press, 2005).

20. Peter and Hull, *Peter Principle*, 57.

21. Christopher Cerf and Victor Navasky, *The Experts Speak: The Definitive Compendium of Authoritative Misinformation* (New York: Pantheon, 1984).

22. "A Historical Perspective of Businessweek, Sold to Bloomberg," *Talking Biz News*, October 13, 2009, https://talkingbiznews.com/they-talk-biz-news/a-historical -perspective-of-businessweek-sold-to-bloomberg/.

23. Ken Olsen, Comments to the 1977 Boston meeting of the World Future Society, as cited by David Mark, "Digital Equipment Corporation—PCs," http://www .maynardlifeoutdoors.com/2020/01/digital-equipment-corporation-pcs.html.

24. Jeff Jacoby, "The Gurus Got It Wrong Last Year. They'll Get It Wrong This Year, Too," *Boston Globe*, December 29, 2016, https://www.bostonglobe.com/opinion /2016/12/29/the-gurus-got-wrong-last-year-they-get-wrong-this-year-too /UWvC5rsO8jriZnwShwe01L/story.html.

25. Sander Duivestein, "Steve Ballmer Laughs at the iPhone," YouTube, July 6, 2011, 0:44, https://www.youtube.com/watch?v=qycUOENFIBs.

26. Scott Anthony and Evan I. Schwartz, "What the Best Transformational Leaders Do," *Harvard Business Review*, May 8, 2017, https://hbr.org/2017/05/what-the-best -transformational-leaders-do.

27. William N. Thorndike, *The Outsiders* (Boston: Harvard Business Review Press, 2012), 109.

28. Thorndike, *The Outsiders*, 112.

29. Thorndike, *The Outsiders*, 112.

30. Julian Sonny, "The 10 Most Successful People with ADHD," *Elite Daily*, April 1, 2013, https://www.elitedaily.com/money/10-successful-people-adhd; and Joseph Maddia, "20 Public Figures with ADHD," RXwiki (website), July 1, 2014, https://www.rxwiki.com/slideshow/20-public-figures-adhd.

31. Kendra Cherry, "Why Does Attention Blink Happen?" *VeryWell*, October 6, 2019, https://www.verywell.com/what-is-attentional-blink-2795017.

32. Jeremy Hsu, "People Choose News That Fits Their Views," *LiveScience*, June 7, 2009; https://www.livescience.com/3640-people-choose-news-fits-views.html.

Chapter 4

1. Greg Ip, *Foolproof: Why Safety Can Be Dangerous and Danger Makes Us Safe* (New York: Little Brown, 2015).

2. Hyman Minsky, "The Financial Instability Hypothesis" (working paper, Jerome Levy Economics Institute of Bard College, Annandale-on-Hudson, NY, May 1992).

3. Quoted in Tom Schardin, "Would Football Be Safer with No Helmets, Pads?" swnewsmedia, August 30, 2018, https://www.swnewsmedia.com/prior_lake_american /news/sports/would-football-be-safer-with-no-helmets-pads/article_d2e0bf7d-5a86 -5eec-bcf2-79c4792ddd82.html.

4. California, Connecticut, Delaware, Hawaii, Illinois, Maryland, Nevada, New Hampshire, New Jersey, New Mexico, New York, Oregon, Vermont, Washington, West Virginia, as well as Washington, D.C., Puerto Rico, Guam, and the US Virgin Islands.

5. Alice Foster, "Phone Driving Laws 2017: New Rules Explained and How Much YOU Could Be Fined," *Daily Express*, March 3, 2017, http://www.express.co.uk/life -style/cars/774549/phone-driving-laws-2017-new-rules-explained-how-you-could-be -fined-lose-points-penalties.

6. Jonathan Zittrain, *The Future of the Internet and How to Stop It* (New Haven, CT: Yale University Press, 2009), 127.

7. Jonna McKone, "'Naked Streets' without Traffic Lights Improve Flow and Safety," City Fix, October 8, 2010, http://thecityfix.com/blog/naked-streets-without -traffic-lights-improve-flow-and-safety/.

8. Stephen Markley, "Can Turning Off Traffic Lights Reduce Congestion?" Cars .com (website), September 3, 2009, https://www.cars.com/articles/2009/09/can -turning-off-traffic-lights-reduce-congestion/.

9. Gerald Wilde, *Target Risk: Dealing with the Danger of Death, Disease and Damage in Everyday Decisions* (Toronto: PDE Publications, 1994).

10. H. Gilbert Welch, Lisa Schwartz, and Steven Woloshin, *Overdiagnosed: Making People Sick in the Pursuit of Health* (Boston: Beacon Press, 2011), 15–16.

11. Welch, Schwartz, and Woloshin, *Overdiagnosed*, 35.

12. Welch, Schwartz, and Woloshin, *Overdiagnosed*.

13. Mark Hyman, "The Harm of Statins and Right Diet for Cancer Prevention," Dr. Hyman (blog), accessed January 26, 2020, https://drhyman.com/blog/2017/03/05 /harm-statins-right-diet-cancer-prevention/.

14. Wendy Wolfson, "Playing the Odds with Statins: Heart Disease or Diabetes?" National Public Radio, March 10, 2015, https://www.npr.org/sections/health-shots /2015/03/10/390944811/playing-the-odds-with-statins-heart-disease-or-diabetes.

15. See Framingham Heart Study (website), accessed January 26, 2020, https:// www.framinghamheartstudy.org.

16. Marion Nestle, "Did the Low-Fat Era Make Us Fat?" *Frontline*, PBS, December 10, 2003, https://www.pbs.org/wgbh/pages/frontline/shows/diet/themes/lowfat .html.

17. Jonny Bowden and Stephen Sinatra, *The Great Cholesterol Myth* (Beverly, MA: Fair Winds Press, 2012), back cover text.

18. "Heart Disease Facts," Centers for Disease Control and Prevention, last updated December 2, 2019, https://www.cdc.gov/heartdisease/facts.htm.

19. Christie Aschwanden, "Lipitor Rage," *Slate*, November 2, 2011, https://slate .com/technology/2011/11/lipitor-side-effects-statins-and-mental-health.html.

20. Trisha Torrey, phone interview with the author, January 6, 2016.

21. Trisha Torrey, "Trisha's Misdiagnosis Story," Trisha Torrey (blog), accessed January 27, 2020, https://trishatorrey.com/who-is-trisha/misdiagnosis/.

22. Torrey, "Trisha's Misdiagnosis Story."

23. Torrey, "Trisha's Misdiagnosis Story."

24. Torrey, interview.

25. Torrey, interview.

26. Torrey, "Trisha's Misdiagnosis Story."

27. Michael van Straten and Barbara Griggs, *Superfoods* (New York: Dorling Kindersley, 1990).

28. "Superfoods You Need Now," *Health*, October 27, 2009, https://www.health .com/food/superfoods-you-need-now.

29. Lindsey Funston, "Stress Eating Helps, When They're These Superfoods," CNN, April 13, 2015, https://www.cnn.com/2015/04/13/health/superfoods-stress -relief/index.html.

30. "What Did the Incas Eat?" Eat Peru (website), June 12, 2019, https://www .eatperu.com/what-did-the-incas-eat-foods-of-the-ancient-peruvian-empire/.

31. Devin Windelspecht, "Cacao: Mayan 'Food of the Gods,'" Ricochet Science (website), April 12, 2016, http://ricochetscience.com/cacao-mayan-food-gods/; "Chocolate Use in Early Aztec Cultures," International Cocoa Organization, last updated January 8, 2011, https://www.icco.org/faq/54-cocoa-origins/133-chocolate-use -in-early-aztec-cultures.html.

32. Marion Nestle, "The Latest in Food-Industry Sponsored Research: Pears!" *Food Politics*, July 12, 2016, https://www.foodpolitics.com/2016/07/the-latest-in-food -industry-sponsored-research-pears/.

33. Jo Abi, "What Happens When You Only Eat 'Superfoods' for Three Weeks?" *MamaMia*, December 12, 2015, https://www.mamamia.com.au/only-eating -superfoods/.

34. Abi, "What Happens When You Only Eat 'Superfoods' for Three Weeks?"

35. Alastair Jamieson, "Too Many Superfoods Could Be Harmful," *Telegraph*, January 28, 2010, https://www.telegraph.co.uk/foodanddrink/foodanddrinknews/7091143 /Too-many-superfoods-could-be-harmful.html.

36. Annalee Newitz, "James Watson Says Antioxidants May Actually Be Causing Cancer," *Gizmodo*, January 10, 2013, https://io9.gizmodo.com/james-watson-says -antioxidants-may-actually-be-causing-5975002.

37. Caitlin White, "That Kale Sweatshirt from Beyonce's '7/11' Video Is Cropping up Everywhere," MTV News, January 10, 2015, http://www.mtv.com/news/2043813 /beyonce-kale-sweatshirt-celebs/.

38. Ross Bridgeford, "The Truth about Oxalate (Is Kale Bad after All?)," *LiveEnergized*, accessed January 27, 2020, http://liveenergized.com/live-energized-tv/truth -about-oxalate/.

39. Anna Hodgekiss, "Why So-Called 'Superfoods' Could Be Bad for You," *Daily Mail*, April 7, 2014, https://www.dailymail.co.uk/health/article-2598694/Why-called -superfoods-BAD-Nutritionist-says-kale-send-thyroid-haywire-quinoa-irritates-gut .html.

40. Hodgekiss, "Why So-Called 'Superfoods' Could Be Bad for You."

41. Petronella Ravenshear, "Lifting the Lid on Superfoods," *Vogue*, April 8, 2014, https://www.vogue.co.uk/gallery/foods-of-the-gods.

42. Michael Specter, "Against the Grain: Should You Go Gluten Free?" *New Yorker*, October 27, 2014, https://www.newyorker.com/magazine/2014/11/03/grain.

43. David Perlmutter, *Grain Brain* (New York: Hachette, 2013); and William David, *Wheat Belly* (New York: Rodale, 2011).

44. Rita Rubin, "The Gluten Debate Continues," WebMD, December 12, 2013, https://www.webmd.com/digestive-disorders/news/20131212/celiac-disease-gluten -sensitive#1; and Elaine Watson, "30% of Americans Trying to Cut down on Gluten, NPD Group Claims," FoodNavigator (website), March 8, 2013, https://www .foodnavigator-usa.com/Article/2013/03/08/30-of-US-adults-trying-to-cut-down-on -gluten-claims-NPD-Group.

45. Vikram Mansharamani, "We're in a Gluten-Free Bubble That's about to Burst," *Fortune*, May 5, 2015, https://fortune.com/2015/05/05/gluten-free-foods/.

46. "Arsenic in Your Food," *Consumer Reports*, November 2012, https://www .consumerreports.org/cro/magazine/2012/11/arsenic-in-your-food/index.htm.

47. Donna Berry, "Special Report: Glute-Free Enters the Mainstream," *Food Business News*, July 13, 2017, https://www.foodbusinessnews.net/articles/9612-special -report-gluten-free-enters-the-mainstream.

48. Louise Foxcroft, *Calories and Corsets: A History of Dieting over 2000 Years* (London: Profile Books, 2011), 15.

49. Dan Buettner, "The Island Where People Forget to Die," *New York Times Magazine*, October 24, 2012, https://www.nytimes.com/2012/10/28/magazine/the-island -where-people-forget-to-die.html.

50. Jason Fung, *The Complete Guide to Fasting* (Las Vegas: Victory Belt Publishing, 2016), 8, 9.

Chapter 5

1. Philip Zimbardo, "When Good People Do Evil," *Yale Alumni Magazine*, January/February 2007, http://archives.yalealumnimagazine.com/issues/2007_01/milgram.html.

2. Stanley Milgram, *Obedience to Authority* (New York: Harper, 2009); see also Mitri Shanab and Khawla Yahya, "A Cross Cultural Study of Obedience," *Bulletin of the Psychonomic Society* 11, no. 4 (1978): 267–269, https://link.springer.com/content/pdf/10.3758%2FBF03336827.pdf.

3. Zimbardo, "When Good People Do Evil."

4. Atul Gawande, *The Checklist Manifesto* (New York: Metropolitan Books, 2009).

5. Brian Gage et al., "Selecting Patients with Atrial Fibrillation for Anticoagulation," *Circulation* 110, no. 16 (October 19, 2004), https://www.ahajournals.org/doi/full/10.1161/01.CIR.0000145172.55640.93.

6. Anupam Jena, Vinay Prasad, Dana P. Goldman, and John Romley, "Mortality and Treatment Patterns among Patients Hospitalized with Acute Cardiovascular Conditions during Dates of National Cardiology Meetings," *JAMA Internal Medicine* 175, no. 2 (February 2015): 237–244, https://jamanetwork.com/journals/jamainternalmedicine/fullarticle/2038979.

7. National Academy of Sciences, *Lessons Learned from the Fukushima Nuclear Accident for Improving Safety of U.S. Nuclear Plants* (Washington, DC: National Academies Press, 2014), https://www.ncbi.nlm.nih.gov/books/NBK253939/.

8. *Frontline*, season 30, episode 7, "Inside Japan's Nuclear Meltdown," written, produced, and directed by Dan Edge, aired February 28, 2012, on PBS, https://www.pbs.org/wgbh/frontline/film/japans-nuclear-meltdown/.

9. *Frontline*, season 30, episode 7, "Inside Japan's Nuclear Meltdown."

10. Carl Pillitteri, "None of You Are Getting out of Here," *Salon*, March 9, 2012, https://www.salon.com/2012/03/09/none_of_you_are_getting_out_of_here/.

11. Pillitteri, "None of You."

12. *Frontline*, season 30, episode 7, "Inside Japan's Nuclear Meltdown."

13. *Frontline*, season 30, episode 7, "Inside Japan's Nuclear Meltdown."

14. *Frontline*, season 30, episode 7, "Inside Japan's Nuclear Meltdown."

15. *Frontline*, season 30, episode 7, "Inside Japan's Nuclear Meltdown."

16. *Frontline*, season 30, episode 7, "Inside Japan's Nuclear Meltdown."

17. *Frontline*, season 30, episode 7, "Inside Japan's Nuclear Meltdown."

18. Justin McCurry, "Fukushima Boss Hailed as Hero Dies," *Guardian*, July 10, 2013, https://www.theguardian.com/world/2013/jul/10/fukushima-plant-boss-hero-dies.

19. Norimitsu Onishi and Martin Fackler, "In Nuclear Crisis, Crippling Mistrust," *New York Times*, June 12, 2011, https://www.nytimes.com/2011/06/13/world/asia/13japan.html.

20. Onishi and Fackler, "In Nuclear Crisis, Crippling Mistrust."

21. Onishi and Fackler, "In Nuclear Crisis, Crippling Mistrust."

22. Onishi and Fackler, "In Nuclear Crisis, Crippling Mistrust."

23. McCurry, "Fukushima Boss Hailed as Hero Dies."

24. "Fukushima Nuclear Accident 'Man-Made,' Not Natural Disaster," *Sydney Morning Herald*, July 5, 2012, https://www.smh.com.au/world/fukushima-nuclear -accident--manmade-not-natural--disaster-20120705-21jrl.html.

25. *Official Report of The Fukushima Nuclear Accident Independent Investigation Commission, July 2012* (Tokyo: National Diet of Japan, 2012), http://japan311disaster.com/wp -content/uploads/2013/05/Kurokawa-Commission-Report-7-5-12-English.pdf.

26. Kiyoshi Kurokawa, "Message from the Chairman," in *Official Report of the Fukushima Nuclear Accident Independent Investigation Commission, July 2012* (Tokyo: National Diet of Japan, 2012), 9, http://japan311disaster.com/wp-content/uploads/2013/05 /Kurokawa-Commission-Report-7-5-12-English.pdf.

27. Kiyoshi Kurokawa, "Message from the Chairman," 9.

28. Ranjay Gulati, Charles Casto, and Charlotte Krontiris, "How the Other Fukushima Plant Survived," *Harvard Business Review*, July–August 2014, https://hbr.org/2014 /07/how-the-other-fukushima-plant-survived.

29. Mami Onoda, "Fukushima No. 2 Scrambled to Avoid Same Fate as Sister Site Fukushima No. 1," *Japan Times*, September 10, 2014, https://www.japantimes.co.jp/news/2014/09 /10/national/fukushima-2-scrambled-avoid-fate-sister-site-fukushima-1/#.XiM5jy2ZPfY.

30. Onoda, "Fukushima No. 2 Scrambled."

31. Chuck Casto, "Interview with Chuck Casto," Quality World (website), August 9, 2016, https://www.quality.org/knowledge/%E2%80%8Bfukushima-daiichi-and -daini---tale-two-leadership-styles.

Chapter 6

1. Adam Green, "A Pickpocket's Tale," *New Yorker*, December 30, 2012, https:// www.newyorker.com/magazine/2013/01/07/a-pickpockets-tale.

2. Apollo Robbins, phone interview with the author, November 30, 2015.

3. National Geographic, "Apollo Robbins on Focus: Brain Games," YouTube, April 15, 2013, 1:51, https://www.youtube.com/watch?v=d54ydsKUNGw.

4. National Geographic, "Apollo Robbins."

5. Caroline Williams, "How Pickpockets Trick Your Mind," *BBC Future*, November 18, 2014, https://www.bbc.com/future/article/20140629-how-pickpockets-trick -your-mind.

6. George Johnson, "Sleights of Mind," *New York Times*, August 21, 2007, https:// www.nytimes.com/2007/08/21/science/21magic.html.

7. *Focus*, directed and written by Glenn Ficarra and John Requa, starring Will Smith, Margot Robbie, and Rodrigo Santoro (Burbank, CA: Warner Home Video, 2015), DVD. *Focus* film script can be found on Scripts (website), https://www.scripts .com/script-pdf/8369. All film quotes in this section are from this source.

8. Gregory Miller, "How Will Smith Learned to Pickpocket for His New Role," *New York Post*, February 21, 2015, https://nypost.com/2015/02/21/will-smith-learns -how-to-pickpocket-for-focus-role/.

9. Arthur Conan Doyle, "Silver Blaze," The Complete Sherlock Holmes Canon (website), accessed January 27, 2020, https://sherlock-holm.es/stories/pdf/a4/1-sided /silv.pdf.

10. Doyle, "Silver Blaze," 9.

11. Gary Noesner, *Stalling for Time: My Life as an FBI Hostage Negotiator* (New York: Random House, 2010), 74–75.

12. Noesner, *Stalling for Time*, 74–77.

13. Noesner, *Stalling for Time*. 97.

14. Noesner, *Stalling for Time*, 104–105.

15. Noesner, *Stalling for Time*, 110.

16. Kevin Drum, "Lead: America's Real Criminal Element," *Mother Jones*, January–February 2013, https://www.motherjones.com/environment/2016/02/lead-exposure-gasoline-crime-increase-children-health/.

17. George Kelling and James Wilson, "Broken Windows," *Atlantic*, March 1982, https://www.theatlantic.com/magazine/archive/1982/03/broken-windows/304465/.

18. Malcolm Gladwell, *The Tipping Point* (New York: Little Brown, 2002).

19. Clifford Krauss, "New York Crime Rate Plummet to Levels Not Seen in 30 Years," *New York Times*, December 20, 1996, https://www.nytimes.com/1996/12/20/nyregion/new-york-crime-rate-plummets-to-levels-not-seen-in-30-years.html.

20. Drum, "Lead."

21. Drum, "Lead."

22. Steven Levitt and Stephen Dubner, *Freakonomics: A Rogue Economist Explores the Hidden Side of Everything* (New York: Harper Perennial, 2005), introduction.

23. Drum, "Lead."

24. Drum, "Lead."

25. Phil Jackson, *Eleven Rings: The Soul of Success* (New York: Penguin, 2013).

26. Jackson, *Eleven Rings*, 10.

27. Jackson, *Eleven Rings*, 99.

28. Jackson, *Eleven Rings*, 101.

29. Jackson, *Eleven Rings*, 126.

30. Jackson, *Eleven Rings*, 126.

31. Jackson, *Eleven Rings*, 126.

32. Jackson, *Eleven Rings*, 127.

33. Jackson, *Eleven Rings*, 127

Chapter 7

1. David Barno and Nora Bensahel, "Three Things the Army Chief of Staff Wants You to Know," *War on the Rocks*, May 23, 2017, https://warontherocks.com/2017/05/three-things-the-army-chief-of-staff-wants-you-to-know/.

2. Barno and Bensahel, "Three Things the Army Chief of Staff Wants You to Know."

3. Joyce Wadler, "With Promise of Happiness, She Became a Bomber's Pawn," *People Magazine*, October 27, 1986, https://people.com/archive/with-the-promise-of-happiness-she-became-a-bombers-pawn-vol-26-no-17/.

4. "Ann-Marie Murphy and the Hindawi Affair: A 30th Anniversary Review," *Aviation Security International*, April 13, 2016, https://www.asi-mag.com/ann-marie-murphy-hindawi-affair-30th-anniversary-review/.

5. Nelson Schwartz, "Learning from Israel," *Fortune*, January 21, 2002, https://archive.fortune.com/magazines/fortune/fortune_archive/2002/01/21/316588/index.htm.

6. Schwartz, "Learning from Israel."

7. Schwartz, "Learning from Israel."

8. Schwartz, "Learning from Israel."

9. Schwartz, "Learning from Israel."

10. "El Al Deploying Anti-Missile Defense on Civilian Planes," *Defense Industry Daily*, December 16, 2004, https://www.defenseindustrydaily.com/el-al-deploying-antimissile-defense-on-civilian-plane-027/.

11. John Vause, "Missile Defense for El Al Fleet," CNN, May 24, 2004, https://www.cnn.com/2004/WORLD/meast/05/24/air.defense/.

12. Nassim Nicholas Taleb, *Antifragile: Things That Gain from Disorder* (New York: Random House, 2012).

13. Dan Buettner, *Blue Zones: Lessons for Living Longer from the People Who've Lived the Longest* (Washington, DC: National Geographic, 2008).

14. Simon Worall, "Here Are the Secrets to a Long and Healthy Life," *National Geographic*, April 12 2015, https://www.nationalgeographic.com/news/2015/04/150412-longevity-health-blue-zones-obesity-diet-ngbooktalk/#close.

15. Nicholas Christakis and James Fowler, "The Spread of Obesity in a Large Social Network over 32 Years," *New England Journal of Medicine*, July 26, 2007, https://www.nejm.org/doi/full/10.1056/NEJMsa066082.

16. Nicholas Christakis, "The Hidden Influence of Social Networks," *TEDGlobal*, February 2010, 17:59, https://www.ted.com/talks/nicholas_christakis_the_hidden_influence_of_social_networks/transcript.

17. Christakis and Fowler, *Connected: The Surprising Power of Our Social Networks and How They Shape Our Lives* (New York: Little Brown Spark, 2009).

18. Dan Buettner, "The Island Where People Forget to Die," *New York Times Magazine*, October 24, 2012, https://www.nytimes.com/2012/10/28/magazine/the-island-where-people-forget-to-die.html.

19. Buettner, "The Island Where People Forget to Die."

20. David Swensen, "The Mutual Fund Merry-Go-Round," *New York Times*, August 13, 2011, http://www.nytimes.com/2011/08/14/opinion/sunday/the-mutual-fund-merry-go-round.html.

21. Charles D. Ellis, "Murder on the Orient Express: The Mystery of Underperformance," *Financial Analysts Journal* 68, no. 4 (July/August 2012): 13–19.

22. Ellis, "Murder on the Orient Express," 19.

23. Robert Merton (comments at the Boston Finance Forum hosted by the MIT Sloan Alumni Association, Boston, MA, May 16, 2014).

24. Emeley Rodriguez et al., "iGo Green: A Life Cycle Assessment of Apple's iPhone" (working paper presented at iConference 2015, University of Pittsburgh, 2015), https://www.ideals.illinois.edu/bitstream/handle/2142/73760/462_ready.pdf.

25. Kevin Czinger, phone interview with the author, February 10, 2016.

26. Kevin Czinger, "The Future of Car Making: Small Teams and Fewer Materials," *O'Reilly Radar*, June 24, 2015, http://radar.oreilly.com/2015/06/the-future-of-car-making-small-teams-using-fewer-materials.html.

27. Czinger, interview.

28. O'Reilly, "Kevin Czinger: Dematerializing Auto Manufacturing," YouTube, June 25, 2015, 14:19, https://www.youtube.com/watch?v=oKXpFmbEzs4&feature =youtube.

Chapter 8

1. Kenneth Arrow, "Uncertainty and the Welfare Economics of Medical Care," *American Economic Review* 53, no. 5 (December 1963): 951.

2. Arrow, "Uncertainty and the Welfare Economics," 965.

3. Jim Cramer, interview by Jon Stewart, *Daily Show with John Stewart*, Comedy Central, March 12, 2009, http://www.cc.com/video-clips/fttmoj/the-daily-show-with -jon-stewart-exclusive---jim-cramer-extended-interview-pt--1; http://www.cc.com /video-clips/rfag2r/the-daily-show-with-jon-stewart-exclusive---jim-cramer -extended-interview-pt--2; http://www.cc.com/video-clips/qtzxvl/the-daily-show -with-jon-stewart-exclusive---jim-cramer-extended-interview-pt--3. All Cramer/ Stewart quotes in this section are from this interview.

4. Ranjit Dighe, *The Historian's Wizard of Oz: Reading L. Frank Baum's Classic as a Political and Monetary Allegory* (Westport, CT: Praeger, 2002).

5. L. Frank Baum, *The Wonderful Wizard of Oz* (Chicago: George M. Hill, 1899), 184.

6. Baum, *Wonderful Wizard of Oz*, 199.

7. Veronika Kero, "Investor Jack Bogle Founded His Legendary Company Based on His Princeton Senior Thesis," CNBC, January 18, 2019, https://www.cnbc.com/2019 /01/17/investor-jack-bogle-founded-company-based-on-princeton-senior-thesis.html.

8. Justin Fox, "Saint Jack on the Attack," *Fortune*, January 20, 2003, https://archive .fortune.com/magazines/fortune/fortune_archive/2003/01/20/335617/index.htm.

9. John Bogle, "How the Index Fund Was Born," *Wall Street Journal*, September 3, 2011, https://www.wsj.com/articles/SB10001424053111904583204576544681 577401622.

10. Charles D. Ellis, *Winning the Loser's Game* (New York: McGraw Hill, 1998).

11. Jane Wollman Rusoff, "How John Bogle Really Sees ETFs," *ThinkAdvisor*, September 25, 2012, https://www.thinkadvisor.com/2012/09/25/how-john-bogle-really -sees-etfs/.

12. Grant Williams, "Passive Regression," *Things That Make You Go Hmmm*, July 2, 2017, 1.

13. Williams, "Passive Regression."

14. David McLoughlin and Annie Massa, "The Hidden Dangers of the Great Index Fund Takeover," *Bloomberg Businessweek*, January 9, 2020, https://www.bloomberg.com /news/features/2020-01-09/the-hidden-dangers-of-the-great-index-fund-takeover ?sref=1kJVNqnU.

15. *Spymasters: CIA in the Crosshairs*, directed by Gédéon Naudet, written by Chris Whipple, starring John O. Brennan, Robert Gates, and Michael Morell (New York: Showtime Networks, aired November 28, 2015); script available at https://www .springfieldspringfield.co.uk/movie_script.php?movie=spymasters-cia-in-the -crosshairs. All quotations in this section are from the documentary.

16. Duncan Gardham, "Airline Bomb Plot: Investigation 'One of Biggest since WW2,'" *Telegraph*, September 8, 2009, https://www.telegraph.co.uk/news/uknews /terrorism-in-the-uk/6152185/Airline-bomb-plot-investigation-one-of-biggest-since -WW2.html; see also Don van Nata, Elain Sciolino, and Stephen Gray, "Details Emerge in British Terror Case," *New York Times*, August 28, 2006, https://www .nytimes.com/2006/08/28/world/europe/28plot.html.

17. van Nata, Sciolino, and Gray, "Details Emerge in British Terror Case."

18. "Montreal, Toronto Flights Targeted in Alleged British Bomb Plot," Canadian Broadcasting Corporation, April 3, 2008, https://www.cbc.ca/news/world/montreal -toronto-flights-targeted-in-alleged-british-bomb-plot-1.747225.

19. David Swensen, ECON 252: Lecture 9: "Financial Markets" (lecture, Yale University, New Haven, CT, 2008), https://oyc.yale.edu/economics/econ-252-08/lecture-9.

20. David Swensen, *Unconventional Success: A Fundamental Approach to Personal Investment* (New York: Free Press, 2005), 12.

21. Mark Graber, "The Incidence of Diagnostic Error in Medicine," *BMJ Quality and Safety*, 2013, ii21–ii27, https://qualitysafety.bmj.com/content/qhc/22/Suppl_2/ii21 .full.pdf.

Chapter 9

1. *Vantage Point*, directed by Pete Travis, written by Barry L. Levy, starring Dennis Quaid, Forest Whitaker, and Matthew Fox (Culver City, CA: Columbia Pictures, 2008). Movie script available at https://www.scripts.com/script-pdf/22743.

2. James Glanz, Sebastian Rotella, and David Sanger, "In 2008 Mumbai Attacks, Piles of Spy Data, but an Uncompleted Puzzle," *New York Times*, December 21, 2014, https://www.nytimes.com/2014/12/22/world/asia/in-2008-mumbai-attacks-piles-of -spy-data-but-an-uncompleted-puzzle.html.

3. Glanz, Rotella, and Sanger, "In 2008 Mumbai Attacks."

4. Glanz, Rotella, and Sanger, "In 2008 Mumbai Attacks."

5. Glanz, Rotella, and Sanger, "In 2008 Mumbai Attacks."

6. Bob Woodward, "Interview: Bob Woodward Reveals His Doubts about Barack Obama's White House," interview by Alex Spillus, *Telegraph*, October 2, 2010, http:// www.telegraph.co.uk/news/worldnews/8037923/Interview-Bob-Woodward-reveals -his-doubts-about-Barack-Obamas-White-House.html.

7. Bob Woodward, "Bob Woodward," in *What Made Me Who I Am*, ed. Bernie Swain (New York: Post Hill Press, 2016), 193.

8. Woodward, "Interview: Bob Woodward Reveals His Doubts."

9. Personal conversation with Bob Woodward, Washington, DC, December 13, 2016.

10. "Alfred Sloan," *Economist*, June 30, 2009, http://www.economist.com/node /13047099.

11. Peter Drucker, *The Effective Executive* (New York: HarperCollins, 2017), 150.

12. Doris Kearns Goodwin, *Team of Rivals: The Political Genius of Abraham Lincoln* (New York: Simon & Schuster, 2006).

13. Doris Kearns Goodwin, "An Extraordinary President and His Remarkable Cabinet: An Interview with Doris Kearns Goodwin about Lincoln's *Team of Rivals*," in-

terview by Ellen Fried, *Prologue Magazine* (National Archives) 38, no. 1 (Spring 2006), https://www.archives.gov/publications/prologue/2006/spring/interview.html; emphasis added.

14. Deborah Mitchell, Jay Russo, and Nancy Pennington, "Back to the Future: Temporal Perspective in the Explanation of Events," *Journal of Behavioral Decision Making* 2, no. 1 (January/March 1989): 25–38.

15. Gary Klein, "Performing a Project Premortem," *Harvard Business Review*, September 2007, 2.

Chapter 10

1. Amos Tversky and Daniel Kahneman, "Judgement under Uncertainty: Heuristics and Biases," *Science* 185, no. 4157 (September 27, 1974): 1124–1131.

2. David Snowden and Mary Boone, "A Leader's Framework for Decision Making," *Harvard Business Review*, November 2007, https://hbr.org/2007/11/a-leaders-framework -for-decision-making.

3. *Cynefin* (pronounced ku-nev-in) is a Welsh word for habitat, one that Snowden and Boone suggest captures the multiple factors in our environment and our experiences that influence us in complex and interconnected ways.

4. Snowden and Boone, "A Leader's Framework."

5. Joseph Nye, *The Powers To Lead* (New York: Oxford University Press, 2010), 87–96.

6. *Moment by Moment: Averting Disaster on the Hudson*, directed and written by Gary Leva, starring Patrick Harten, Jeffrey Skiles, Chesley Sullenberger (Burbank, CA: Warner Home Video, 2016), DVD.

7. Chesley "Sully" Sullenberger, *Highest Duty* (New York: William Morrow, 2010); *Sully*, directed by Clint Eastwood, written by Todd Komarnicki and Chesley Sullenberger, starring Tom Hanks, Aaron Eckhart, and Laura Linney (Burbank, CA: Warner Brothers, 2016), DVD. *Sully* screenplay available at https://www.scripts.com/script-pdf/19081.

8. Alex Altman, "Chesley B. Sullenberger III," *Time*, January 16, 2009, http://content.time.com/time/nation/article/0,8599,1872247,00.html.

9. "Wife: Sully is a 'Pilot's Pilot,'" CBS News, January 16, 2009, https://www .cbsnews.com/news/wife-sully-is-a-pilots-pilot/.

10. *Sully Sullenberger: The Man behind the Miracle*, directed and written by Gary Leva, starring Tom Hanks, Patrick Harten, and Jeffrey Skiles (Burbank, CA: Warner Home Video, 2016), DVD.

11. *Sully Sullenberger*, directed and written by Gary Leva.

12. *Sully Sullenberger*, directed and written by Gary Leva.

13. *Moment by Moment*, directed and written by Gary Leva.

14. *Moment by Moment*, directed and written by Gary Leva.

15. Sullenberger, *Highest Duty*, 374–375.

16. *Moment by Moment*, directed and written by Gary Leva.

17. *Sully*, directed by Clint Eastwood.

18. William Langewiesche, "The Human Factor," *Vanity Fair*, September 17, 2014, https://www.vanityfair.com/news/business/2014/10/air-france-flight-447-crash.

19. *Moment by Moment*, directed and written by Gary Leva.

20. Sullenberger, *Highest Duty*, 308.

21. Sullenberger, *Highest Duty*, 314–315. See also Vikram Mansharamani, "What Sully Can Teach You about Leadership," *Worth*, September 14, 2016, https://www.worth.com/contributor/what-sully-can-teach-you-about-leadership/.

22. Frank Sesno, *Ask More: The Power of Questions to Open Doors, Uncover Solutions, and Spark Change* (New York: American Management Association, 2017), 21.

23. Noreena Hertz, "How to Use Experts—and When Not To," *TEDSalon London*, November 2010, 18:03, https://www.ted.com/talks/noreena_hertz_how_to_use_experts_and_when_not_to.

24. Hertz, "How to Use Experts."

25. Peter Drucker, *The Practice of Management* (London: William Heinemann, 1955), 353.

26. Jenn Abelson, Jonathan Saltzman, and Liz Kowalczyk, "Clash in the Name of Care," *Boston Globe* Spotlight Team report, accessed January 28, 2020, https://apps.bostonglobe.com/spotlight/clash-in-the-name-of-care/story/.

27. Tony Robbins, *Unshakeable: Your Financial Freedom Playbook* (New York: Simon & Schuster, 2017), 74.

28. Robbins, *Unshakeable*, 75.

29. Robbins, *Unshakeable*, 90.

30. Joseph Nye, "Peering into the Future," *Foreign Affairs*, July/August 1994, https://www.foreignaffairs.com/articles/1994-07-01/peering-future.

31. Nye, "Peering into the Future."

32. Berkshire Hathaway, *Annual Letter to Shareholders of Berkshire Hathaway*, 2014, http://www.berkshirehathaway.com/letters/2014ltr.pdf.

Chapter 11

1. Noreena Hertz, "How to Use Experts—and When Not To," *TEDSalon London*, November 2010, 18:03, https://www.ted.com/talks/noreena_hertz_how_to_use_experts_and_when_not_to.

2. Walter Lord, *A Night to Remember: The Classic Account of the Final Hours of the* Titanic, (New York: St. Martin's Griffin, 1955), xix–xx.

3. Morgen Robertson, *The Wreck of the* Titan *or, Futility* (Rahway, NJ: Rahway, Quinn & Boden Press, 1898), 1–2.

4. *Beyond Belief: Fact or Fiction?* season 2, episode 5, "The Land/Titan/The Diary/Town of Remembrance/The House on Barry Avenue," aired February 27, 1998, on Fox, https://www.dailymotion.com/video/x5vhrlr.

5. Ravi Batra, *The Great Depression of 1990* (New York: Venus, 1985).

6. Kenneth Arrow, "I Know a Hawk from a Handsaw," in *Eminent Economists: Their Life Philosophies*, ed. Michael Szenberg (Cambridge: Cambridge University Press, 1992), 47.

7. Peter Schwartz, *The Art of the Long View* (New York: Currency, 1991), 9.

8. Sir Ken Robinson, "Do Schools Kill Creativity?" *TED2006*, February 2006, 19:13, https://www.ted.com/talks/sir_ken_robinson_do_schools_kill_creativity.

9. National Commission on Terrorist Attacks, *The 9/11 Commission Report: Final Report of the National Commission on Terrorist Attacks upon the United States* (New York: W. W. Norton, 2004), 339.

10. Vikram Mansharamani, "How Avocado Mania Drives Climate Change and Crime," *PBS Newshour*, December 21, 2016, https://www.pbs.org/newshour/economy /column-avocado-boom.

11. Vikram Mansharamani, "Could Hurricane Matthew Turn the Tide in Florida's Voting?" *PBS Newshour*, October 11, 2016, https://www.pbs.org/newshour/economy /column-hurricane-matthew-turn-tide-floridas-voting.

12. Jessamyn West, *To See the Dream* (New York: Harcourt Brace, 1957), 39.

13. Newt Gingrich, foreword to *One Second After* by William Forstchen (New York: Tom Doherty & Associates, 2009), xi.

14. Margaret Atwood, "*The Handmaid's Tale* and *Oryx and Crake* 'in Context,'" *Proceedings of the Modern Language Association* 119, no. 3 (May 2004): 513, http://www.jstor .org/stable/25486066.

15. *Armageddon*, directed by Michael Bay, written by Jonathan Hensleigh and J. J. Abrams, starring Bruce Willis, Billy Bob Thornton, and Ben Affleck (Burbank, CA: Touchstone Pictures, 1998), DVD. Script available at https://www.scripts.com/script -pdf/3094.

16. *Armageddon*, directed by Michael Bay.

17. "If an Asteroid Heads for Earth . . . Taking the Hit," *Economist*, special issue, *The World If*, August 1, 2015, 13–14.

18. "If Donald Trump Was President . . . the World v the Donald," *Economist*, special issue, *The World If*, July 16, 2016, 1–2.

19. "If an Electromagnetic Pulse Took down America's Electricity Grid . . . a Flash in the Sky," *Economist*, special issue, *The World If*, July 15, 2017, 12–13; and "If Donald Trump Won a Second Term . . . Augmented Reality Show," *Economist*, special issue, *The World If*, July 15, 2017, 2–4.

20. Kathryn Schulz, "The Really Big One," *New Yorker*, July 13, 2015, https:// www.newyorker.com/magazine/2015/07/20/the-really-big-one.

21. Mike Berardino, "Mike Tyson Explains One of His Most Famous Quotes," *South Florida Sun-Sentinel*, November 9, 2012, https://www.sun-sentinel.com/sports/fl -xpm-2012-11-09-sfl-mike-tyson-explains-one-of-his-most-famous-quotes-20121109 -story.html.

22. Herman B. Leonard et al., "*Why* Was Boston Strong? Lessons from the Boston Marathon Bombing," Program on Crisis Leadership and Program in Criminal Justice Policy and Management, Harvard Kennedy School, April 3, 2014, https://www.hks .harvard.edu/publications/why-was-boston-strong-lessons-boston-marathon-bombing.

23. Leonard et al., "*Why* Was Boston Strong?"

24. Daniel W. Drezner, "The Challenging Future of Strategic Planning in Foreign Policy," *Avoiding Trivia: The Role of Strategic Planning in American Foreign Policy* (Washington, DC: Brookings, 2009), 4.

25. Dean Acheson, "The Challenging Future of Strategic Planning," in *Avoiding Trivia: The Role of Strategic Planning in American Foreign Policy*, ed. Daniel W. Drezner (Washington, DC: Brookings, 2009), 4.

26. Daniel W. Drezner, ed., *Avoiding Trivia: The Role of Strategic Planning in American Foreign Policy* (Washington, DC: Brookings, 2009), 23.

27. Robert Root-Bernstein et al., "Arts Foster Scientific Success: Avocations of Nobel, National Academy, Royal Society, and Sigma Xi Members," *Journal of Psychology of Science and Technology* 1, no. 2 (October 2008): 51–63.

28. Laura Niemi, "The Arts and Economic Vitality: Relationships between the Arts, Entrepreneurship and Innovation in the Workplace" (Research Report 13-3800-7003), retrieved from https://lauraniemidotcom.files.wordpress.com/2016/07/niemi-research -report-nea-13-3800-7003.pdf.

Chapter 12

1. Ralph Waldo Emerson, *Self-Reliance* (Seattle: The Domino Project, 2011), 1.

2. Stanford, "Steve Jobs' 2005 Stanford Commencement Address," YouTube, June 14, 2005, 15:04, https://www.youtube.com/watch?v=UF8uR6Z6KLc.

3. Isaac Asimov, "Profession," Astounding Science Fiction, July 1957, http:// employees.oneonta.edu/blechmjb/JBpages/m360/Profession%20I%20Asimov.pdf. All quotes in this section, unless otherwise noted, are taken from this short story.

4. "The One Shot Society," *Economist*, December 17, 2011, https://www.economist .com/christmas-specials/2011/12/17/the-one-shot-society.

5. Barack Obama, "Remarks by the President on Opportunity for All and Skills for America's Workers," The White House, President Barack Obama (website), January 30, 2014, https://obamawhitehouse.archives.gov/the-press-office/2014/01/30/remarks -president-opportunity-all-and-skills-americas-workers.

6. Zac Anderson, "Rick Scott Wants to Shift University Funding Away from Some Degrees," *Herald-Tribune*, October 10, 2011, http://politics.heraldtribune.com/2011/10 /10/rick-scott-wants-to-shift-university-funding-away-from-some-majors/.

7. Kelly Holland, "The Case for a Liberal Arts Education," CNBC, November 10, 2014, https://www.cnbc.com/2014/11/07/the-case-for-a-liberal-arts-education.html.

8. Charles Eliot, "The New Education," *Atlantic*, February 1869, https://www .theatlantic.com/magazine/archive/1869/02/the-new-education/309049/.

9. Committee of the Corporation and the Academical Faculty, "Reports on the Course of Instruction in Yale College," Higher Education Resource Hub, accessed January 31, 2020, http://www.higher-ed.org/resources/Yale/1828_curriculum.pdf, 7, 14.

10. Eliot, "The New Education."

11. Fareed Zakaria, *In Defense of Liberal Education* (New York: W. W. Norton, 2015), 67.

12. Zakaria, *In Defense of Liberal Education*, 70.

13. *Yale NUS College: A New Community of Learning*, report of the Inaugural Curriculum Committee of Yale NUS College, April 2013, https://www.yale-nus.edu.sg/wp -content/uploads/2013/09/Yale-NUS-College-Curriculum-Report.pdf; emphasis added.

14. Scott Carlson, "A New Liberal Art," *Chronicle of Higher Education*, September 24, 2017, https://www.chronicle.com/article/A-New-Liberal-Art/241269.

15. Graeme Wood, "The Future of College?" *Atlantic*, September 2014, https:// www.theatlantic.com/magazine/archive/2014/09/the-future-of-college/375071/.

16. "Minerva Schools at KGI," accessed January 31, 2020, https://www.minerva.kgi.edu.

17. Jamie Sullivan, "This Is Water—Full Version—David Foster Wallace Commencement Speech," YouTube, accessed January 31, 2020, 22:43, https://www.youtube.com/watch?v=8CrOL-ydFMI. Later published as a book: David Foster Wallace, *This Is Water: Some Thoughts, Delivered on a Significant Occasion, about Living a Compassionate Life* (New York: Little Brown, 2009). All quotes in this section are from this speech.

18. Wellesley Public Media, "You Are Not Special Commencement Speech from Wellesley High School" (David McCullough Jr.), YouTube, accessed January 31, 2020, 12:45, https://www.youtube.com/watch?v=_lfxYhtf8o4. All quotes in this section are from this source.

19. Mark Twain, as quoted in the *Janesville Daily Gazette*, editorial panorama, May 21, 1947, 6, column 2.

20. Shunryu Suzuki, *Zen Mind, Beginner's Mind: Informal Talks on Zen Meditation and Practice* (Boston: Shambhala, 1987), xiv.

21. Sullivan, "This Is Water—Full Version—David Foster Wallace Commencement Speech."

22. Dalya Alberge, "Nile Shipwreck Discovery Proves Herodotus Right—after 2,469 Years," *Guardian*, March 17, 2019, https://www.theguardian.com/science/2019/mar/17/nile-shipwreck-herodotus-archaeologists-thonis-heraclion.

23. "Frank Goddio Underwater Archaeologist," accessed January 30, 2020, http://www.franckgoddio.org.

24. Bill Weir and Drew Kann, "Egypt: Sunken City of Pharaohs," *The Wonder List with Bill Weir*, October 21, 2017, as aired on CNN.

25. Weir and Kann, "Egypt: Sunken City of Pharaohs."

26. Suzuki, *Zen Mind, Beginner's Mind*, 2.

27. Stanford, "Steve Jobs' 2005 Stanford Commencement Address."

28. Stanford, "Steve Jobs' 2005 Stanford Commencement Address."

29. Nikki R. Haley, prologue to *With All Due Respect: Defending America with Grit and Grace* (New York: St. Martin's Press, 2019), 8.

30. W. F. Strong, "The Airline That Started with a Cocktail Napkin," *Texas Standard*, April 20, 2016, https://www.texasstandard.org/stories/the-airline-that-started-with-a-cocktail-napkin/.

31. James Hagerty, "Southwest Air's Kelleher Created Quirky Style That Produced Reliable Profits," *Wall Street Journal*, January 4, 2019, https://www.wsj.com/articles/southwest-air-co-founder-kelleher-created-quirky-style-that-produced-reliable-profits-11546634503.

32. Jad Mouawad, "Pushing 40, Southwest Is Still Playing the Rebel," *New York Times*, November 20, 2010, https://www.nytimes.com/2010/11/21/business/21south.html.

33. Hector Tobar, *Deep Dark Down: The Untold Stories of the 33 Men Buried in a Chilean Mine and the Miracle That Set Them Free* (New York: Farrar, Straus, & Giroux, 2014).

34. Michael Useem, Rodrigo Jordán, and Matko Koljatic, "How to Lead during a Crisis: Lessons from the Rescue of the Chilean Miners," *MIT Sloan Management Review*, August 18, 2011, https://sloanreview.mit.edu/article/how-to-lead-during-a-crisis-lessons-from-the-rescue-of-the-chilean-miners/.

35. Useem, Jordán, and Koljatic, "How to Lead during a Crisis."

36. Useem, Jordán, and Koljatic, "How to Lead during a Crisis."

37. Tobar, *Deep Dark Down*, 43–55.

38. Hector Tobar, "Sixty Nine Days: The Ordeal of the Chilean Miners," *New Yorker*, June 30, 2014, https://www.newyorker.com/magazine/2014/07/07/sixty-nine -days.

39. Tobar, "Sixty Nine Days."

40. Tobar, "Sixty Nine Days."

41. Laurence Golborne, phone interview with the author, September 28, 2017.

42. Useem, Jordán, and Koljatic, "How to Lead during a Crisis."

43. Laurence Golborne, interview.

44. Gideon Long, "BRAVO: Innovative Leader of the Year—Laurence Golborne, Minister of Public Works, Chile," October 18, 2011, http://latintrade.com/bravo -innovative-leader-of-the-year-laurence-golborne-minister-of-public-works-chile/.

45. Jonathan Franklin, *33 Men: Inside the Miraculous Survival and Dramatic Rescue of the Chilean Miners* (New York: Penguin, 2011), 84.

46. Jack Schwager, *The New Market Wizards: Conversations with America's Top Traders* (New York: HarperBusiness, 1992), 188.

47. Schwager, *New Market Wizards*, 189.

48. Schwager, *New Market Wizards*, 189–190.

49. Schwager, *New Market Wizards,* 190.

50. Schwager, *New Market Wizards,* 193.

51. Stanley Druckenmiller, Comments made to the Lost Tree Club in Palm Beach Florida on January 18, 2015, page 23 of transcript.

52. Sebastian Mallaby, *More Money Than God: Hedge Funds and the Making of a New Elite* (New York: Penguin, 2010), 161.

53. Tess Townsend, "Peter Thiel Tells Graduates 'Don't Squander Your Igno-rance,'" *Inc.*, May 23, 2016, https://www.inc.com/tess-townsend/thiel-commencement -address-hamilton-college-dont-squander-ignorance.html.

54. Matthew Winkler, *The Bloomberg Way: A Guide for Reporters and Editors* (New York: Bloomberg Press, 2014).

55. "Elliott V. Bell Award Winners," New York Financial Writer's Association (website), accessed January 31, 2020, https://web.archive.org/web/20111009140024 /http://www.nyfwa.org/bellwinners.htm.

56. Chris Roush, "*Economist* Editor Mickelthwait replaces Winkler as Bloomberg News Editor in Chief," Talking Biz News, December 9, 2014, https://talkingbiznews .com/they-talk-biz-news/economist-editor-mickelthwait-replaces-winkler-as -bloomberg-news-editor-in-chief/.

57. Matthew Winkler, personal communication with the author, December 13, 2019.

Conclusion

1. Stephan Paternot, *A Very Public Offering: The Story of theGlobe.com and the First In-ternet Revolution* (New York: Actarus Press, 2018), 223.

2. Brian Barth, "The Defector," *New Yorker*, December 2, 2019.

3. Joanna Kavenna, "Shoshana Zuboff: Surveillance Capitalism Is an Assault on Human Autonomy," *Guardian*, October 4, 2019, https://www.theguardian.com/books /2019/oct/04/shoshana-zuboff-surveillance-capitalism-assault-human-automomy -digital-privacy.

4. John Laidler, "High Tech Is Watching You," *Harvard Gazette*, March 4, 2019, https://news.harvard.edu/gazette/story/2019/03/harvard-professor-says-surveillance -capitalism-is-undermining-democracy/.

5. *The Iron Lady*, directed by Phyllida Lloyd, written by Abi Morgan, starring Meryl Streep, Jim Broadbent, and Richard E. Grant (New York: The Weinstein Company, 2011), DVD. Movie script available at https://www.scripts.com/script-pdf/597. Emphasis added.

6. Shellie Karabell, "Leadership and the Art of Orchestra Conducting," *Forbes*, January 10, 2015, https://www.forbes.com/sites/shelliekarabell/2015/01/10/leadership -and-the-art-of-orchestra-conducting/#6063df1371f5.

7. Edward Wilson, *Consilience: The Unity of Knowledge* (New York: Vintage, 1999), 294.

INDEX

ABOUT THE AUTHOR

DR. VIKRAM MANSHARAMANI is a global trend-watcher who shows people how to anticipate the future, manage risk, and spot opportunities. He is an academic, advisor, and author as well as a frequently sought speaker. His ideas and writings led LinkedIn to profile him as one of their Top Voices and *Worth* magazine to list him as one of the 100 most powerful people in global finance. Vikram is currently a lecturer at Harvard University and previously taught at Yale University. He has a PhD and two master's degrees from MIT and a bachelor's degree from Yale University, where he was elected to Phi Beta Kappa.

You can find Vikram at http://twitter.com/mansharamani, http://www.mansharamani.com, https://www.linkedin.com/in/vikramman sharamani/, and https://www.instagram.com/vikram.mansharamani/.